Alexander Alekhine

KOTOV

Translated by Dr. K. P. Neat

B. T. Batsford Limited *London*

First published in 1973 in the USSR
English translation © B. T. Batsford Ltd, 1975

ISBN 0 7134 2963 1

Printed and bound in Great Britain by
William Clowes & Sons, Limited,
London, Beccles and Colchester
for the publishers

B. T. Batsford Limited
4 Fitzhardinge Street, London W1H 0AH

Contents

Abbreviations

+	Check
!	Good move
?	Bad move
!?	Interesting move
?!	Dubious move
!!	Excellent move
1–0	Black resigned
$\frac{1}{2}$–$\frac{1}{2}$	Draw agreed
0–1	White resigned
W or *B*	by the side of a diagram indicates which side is to move

In the text, a number in brackets refers to the corresponding diagram number.

From the Author

Some 25 years ago, with the active help of chess enthusiasts and admirers of the talent of Alexander Alekhine from all parts of the world, I was able to collect more than one thousand five hundred games played by this chess genius. Even now I recall with pleasure the endless hours I spent analysing them. The result of this work was the two-volumed *Shakhmatnoye Naslediye Alyokhina*, in which, of course, only his very best games appear.

Now I have a new task before me – to select from these already selected games only a few dozen, and from the material in them to acquaint the reader with the basic features of Alekhine's creative work. This includes Alekhine the man, his personal qualities, as well as his views on chess. I cannot avoid returning to the events of Alekhine's tragic life, which had a virtually unbroken association with chess, especially since some hitherto unknown documents and facts have appeared.

How should these seventy-five games be annotated? Most of them were annotated by Alekhine himself before being subjected to study by other grandmasters. After much thought I decided to choose the method which, in my opinion, will be the most useful for the reader. We will be interested in the answer to the following question: to what extent are Alekhine's games, played nearly half a century ago, instructive for present-day chess? To what degree have Alekhine's strategic ideas retained their importance to the present time – a time of great development in chess technique and of penetration into the depths of the most complex opening variations?

This was the path I took when sorting through the peerless Alekhine combinations and deep strategic plans. In the book, emphasis is also made of Alekhine's mastery in the endgame – an amazing combination of unblemished accuracy with inexhaustible fantasy.

While playing through the games, the reader may involuntarily ask himself about the role of Alexander Alekhine in chess, about his place among the great masters. Nowadays it has become fashionable to ask the world's leading players who, in their opinion, has been the greatest player in the whole history of chess. What surprises one comes across in their replies! Some do not even include Alekhine among the five, and sometimes even ten, strongest players of all time.

How should one assess the greatness of a chess player? It seems to me that the importance of a grandmaster should be determined by the degree to which he surpasses others in the following ways:

1. Sporting achievements – results in tournaments and matches. Here, of course, one should take into account how he came to the chess throne, how many years he 'ruled', and what were his results during his 'ruling' years.

2. Creative achievements: quality of games played, combinative mastery, depth of strategic thought.

3. Contributions to opening theory. History remembers the names of players who did not win the world championship, but who nevertheless devised a number of opening systems which have long outlived the players themselves. Among these are Nimzowitsch, Reti, Grünfeld and Rauzer. A player's contribution to the theory of openings is not an insignificant factor.

4. Breadth of philosophical approach to chess, ability to discern deeply hidden truths, and to understand the subtlety of chess psychology. A candidate for chess greatness also has to be a deep thinker.

If we examine Alekhine according to the factors listed above, we soon come to the conclusion that 'in total' he easily eclipses his most dangerous rivals. His sporting achievements surpass those of all other world champions, except, perhaps, Emanuel Lasker. He also overshadows them all in the field of creative achievements. Hundreds of first-class games by Alekhine are studied by all chess players in this century, and will no doubt be studied in centuries to come. Players of the future will doubtless be delighted by the Alekhine combinations, surprised by his plans, and entranced by the wonderful combination of excellent technique and little combinations in the endgame. Also great is the contribution of Alekhine to the psychology of chess: his advice and instruction are well known. In this book the reader will also find a number of unusual views by Alekhine, published in various newspaper articles.

In 1956, during the chess Olympiad in Moscow, the author approached a number of leading grandmasters and chess theorists, and asked them for their opinions on Alexander Alekhine. While greatly admiring Alekhine as a chess player, many at the same time were concerned about the question of his human qualities. Since it is impossible to acquaint the reader with the whole collection of these opinions, I decided nevertheless to insert in the book a number of extracts, which will give a clear impression of the way of life, character, strength of will, stubbornness and persistence of the man who in his own lifetime was called 'the genius of chess combination'.

From the Editor (R. G. Wade)

Alexander Kotov, on pp. 197–8 and 200, severely criticizes English and American players, but this cannot be based on a full knowledge of the circumstances.

There is no evidence that the acute financial difficulties of the world champion were realized.

There were charges, never substantiated, that Dr. Alekhine had been a Nazi collaborator. The average chess player did not know what to think, but hoped that the charges were unfounded.

In 1941, the *Pariser Zeitung* published a series of articles, allegedly written by Alekhine. He admitted that this was based on two subjects by him, one about reconstruction of the International Chess Federation, the second a critical appreciation, written before 1939, of the theories of Steinitz and Lasker. Material, added by the editors, to convey a marked anti-Jewish, pro-Nazi slant, caused world-wide offense.

The general attitude of British and American chess players is not fully represented by the author's criticisms. For instance, the *British Chess Magazine* (Jan. 1946) quoted a remark to reflect their feelings: 'One expects a chess master to play chess well and Dr. Alekhine does play good chess. It is not for chess players to set up as judges. . . .' On 28th January 1946, the president of the U.S.A. Chess Federation, Elbert A. Wagner Jnr., wrote to *The New York Times* as follows: I advised . . . that the Federation could not approve the holding of a tournament which would deprive Dr. Alekhine of his title of World Champion and, at the same time, deny him an opportunity to defend it.'

On 23rd March 1946, the British Chess Federation, probably grateful to sidestep embarrassing problems, welcomed the initiative taken by the U.S.S.R. chess authorities in allowing Mr. M. Botvinnik to challenge Dr. Alekhine to a match for his world title, and agreed to act as stake-holder and organizer. Alekhine died next day of angina pectoris.

In his Native Country

IMPETUOUS ENTHUSIASM

Outstanding players, the strongest masters of their time, have entered our beloved world of chess in various ways. Some have had phenomenal success even in early childhood – these are the infant prodigies. Little José Capablanca, at the age of four, was able to beat his father and his father's friends, and within a few years became a really strong player. Even more astonishing was the development of Samuel Reshevsky. At the age of eight he toured Europe and America, giving large simultaneous displays against grown-ups.

In the other extreme, players have learned chess relatively late in life. Thus Mikhail Chigorin was fairly grown-up (more than twenty) when he first played chess, while the Austrian grandmaster Rudolph Spielmann was even older. This did not prevent them from covering, in a very short time, the 'distance' necessary for the mastering of that intrinsic interaction of the pieces and of the rules of chess harmony, which players who learn chess in childhood seem to receive 'from their mother's milk'.

Alexander Alekhine belongs to those players who approached chess in the usual, 'normal' way. He was not an infant prodigy, but learned and fell in love with chess at an early age. His development as a chess player was at the same rate as his general development as a youth. He received a good education, and entered life as a sufficiently knowledgeable person, although from his childhood years until his final breath it was chess that constantly occupied his thoughts. He devoted to chess alone his spare time, and the ardour of his stormy temperament. It is worth remembering, that most leading chess players take up the game in just this way. Such players as Emanuel Lasker, Mikhail Botvinnik, Max Euwe, Vasily Smyslov, Tigran Petrosian, Mikhail Tal and Robert Fischer all developed in late childhood and adolescence.

Alekhine was born into a rich family, but his childhood could in no way be described as happy. His father, a governing Marshal of Nobility, was rarely with his family, while his mother also led her own particular life. She was Agnessa Prokhorova, a merchant woman who held shares in a textile mill in Krasnaya Pryesna. Many are surprised that the son of such rich parents should choose for his profession chess – an occupation not greatly respected by business people at that time. This fact can be attributed to many causes, among them purely his family situation, which drove the young Alekhine into the world of abstract truths.

Alexander Alekhine was born on 1st November 1892 in Moscow. In those days chess was ever more surely spreading across the world. Europe had taken to the ancient game, had long since held its first international tournament, and was organizing, in fairly serious fashion, chess competitions of the most diverse forms. Many gambit tournaments were played at that time, while town championships were held in the capital cities and in local clubs, all producing their own domestic champions. Finally, Wilhelm Steinitz was declared world champion in 1886, which still further stimulated interest in chess.

Chess became extremely popular in distant America. The amazing rise of Paul Morphy, who conquered both continents – America and Europe – stirred the national pride of the inhabitants of the New World, and they readily donated money for various tournaments. The capital of the small island of Cuba became the venue for a number of fascinating battles, which aroused interest in many countries.

There were constant reports in the press on the battles between the ageing chess hero Wilhelm Steinitz and the youthful Emanuel Lasker. Harry Nelson Pillsbury – a player of rare talent – crossed the chess horizon like a meteor, but, alas, he thoughtlessly dissipated himself, and died while still young.

When Alekhine was only 9 years old, he witnessed a blindfold simultaneous display by Pillsbury over 22 boards at the Moscow chess club. This performance caught the imagination of Alekhine and left a deep impression on him. Without doubt, Alekhine followed with interest the appearances of Mikhail Chigorin, from whose hand he was soon to take the banner of the Russian chess school.

Young Alekhine's chess development was also influenced by the fact that often were to be found at his home such interesting players as Nenarokov, Blumenfeld, Duz-Hotimirsky and others. Fyodor Ivanovich Duz-Hotimirsky many years later told me that some time at the turn of the century he had given young Alekhine lessons at home, for which he was paid fifteen roubles. With his characteristic humour, Fyodor Ivanovich said that in all probability it was these lessons that explained those short-comings in Alekhine's play which appeared later.

A considerable influence on the development of the talent of the future chess king was Alekhine's elder brother Aleksey, a player of first category rating. As often happens between brothers, at first Aleksey, being by four years the elder, was able to beat his younger brother easily, but then the latter left him well behind.

According to the rules which then existed, boys were not allowed to attend chess clubs, and so the brothers displayed all their energy and love for chess in playing by correspondence. In the period from 1902 to 1904 they played a large number of postal games, and these battles with strong opponents undoubtedly helped to develop their talent.

Some time in the 1950s the discovery was made of two of the young Alekhine brothers' notebooks, with recordings of games, analyses, and commentaries. The thoughts expressed about chess were as yet simple and naive, while the games themselves were not distinguished by their depth or accuracy. At the same time, even in Alekhine's short notes, one feels his great love for chess, which naturally lead to the subsequent perfecting of his outstanding natural talent.

We should be grateful to those unseen, and to a large extent, unknown chess enthusiasts, who day after day sit at their chess boards searching for the best move in battles with opponents who may live thousands of miles away, often in another country, or on another continent. Correspondence games played an enormous role in the development of Alexander Alekhine. It is worth mentioning that in the lives of other grandmasters, for example Paul Keres, postal play has helped a many-sided chess talent to develop.

In order to understand the eventful, and, in many ways, tragic, life of Alexander Alekhine, we must dwell on one more factor. In various books about the life of Alekhine published abroad (i.e. outside the Soviet Union), there is repeated information from somewhere or other to the effect that, before the First World War, Alekhine's father lost a million roubles in a Monte-Carlo casino, and later Alekhine was taken under guardianship. It is further stated that Alekhine's mother died in 1913 in Basle, the loss of her mental faculties having been caused by a condition of chronic intoxication. In all the years in which I have been collecting material about the life and creative work of Alexander Alekhine, I have not once come across confirmation of this information. It is quite possible that it results from the typically fervent imagination of certain authors.

But one thing is certain: the Alekhine children inherited from their parents a terrible failing – a pathological addiction to alcohol, which they had not the strength of mind to break.

To return to Alekhine's childhood – it can be said with certainty that the children were not spoiled by the attention of their parents. Much of the time they spent under the care of their grandmother. It was perhaps for this reason that young Alekhine had such a great urge to escape into the distracting world of chess, into the endless analysis of games, into that many-sided world which is open to he who passionately devotes himself to the secrets of chess.

The information which has reached us about this period in Alekhine's life is only too scant. The chess set – a present from his grandmother, careless notes in the margins of huge exercise books, an unrestrained passion for chess. The adults were unable to separate the child from his board and make him go to sleep; he used to hide a set under his pillow and at night would secretly analyse chess positions by the light of an icon-lamp. . . .

'I DEVELOPED MY CHARACTER'

'I have been playing chess since I was seven years old, but only began playing seriously at the age of twelve,' – wrote Alekhine himself. Even so, in 1905 we do not yet see his name in the Moscow club tournaments, and only by 1907 had Alekhine's chess talent matured to the extent that he was rightfully able to take on the strongest players.

In one of Alekhine's chess notebooks, which has been preserved to this day, are recorded 17 games played by him in 1907 in the so-called 'Spring tournament of the Moscow society of chess enthusiasts'. The notes to these games are as yet naive, the future chess giant was only testing his strength.

Alekhine's play in those years was not so strong that he could achieve victories in serious tournaments. Thus the autumn tournament of the same Moscow society brought him a place in the lower half of the table. All this speaks for the fact that it would be wrong to assert that Alekhine's native talent alone was sufficient for his tournament triumphs. Also needed were hard work, painstaking analysis, and strict self-criticism for a talented youngster to rise into that colossus, who was to remain in the history of chess as the unsurpassed genius of combination.

It was Alekhine's ability to expose the short-comings in his own play, ruthlessly criticize them, and then decisively eradicate them, his ability to scrupulously perfect his technique, that enabled him to cover the path from beginner to grandmaster. It was a most laborious path, demanding that he give his all to his beloved art of chess.

'What made me become a master was, firstly, the search for truth and secondly, the urge for a fight' wrote Alekhine about himself. 'While still a young boy I sensed this talent for chess within me, and already then I felt this inner urging and unbounded passion for the game. By means of chess I developed my character. Chess teaches one first of all to be objective. In chess one can become a great master only by recognizing one's own mistakes and short-comings. It is exactly the same in life'.

A little later we will be examining the first game played by Alekhine in a tournament. The reader will not be confronted by that Alekhine which he is used to seeing. In the play of 15-year-old Alexander, there was not the solidity in the formulation and solution of strategic problems which was usual for his later games; prevalent was the urge to solve the problems of the position by tactical means.

It is also noticeable that, from his first few steps in chess, Alekhine worked incessantly to master the game, and steadily moved forward. This is best illustrated by his tournament performances. While in the autumn of 1907 he was unsuccessful in the Moscow Amateur Tournament, in the following year he came first. Between these tournaments he made his international debut – at the Dusseldorf tournament of 1908 he shared fourth and fifth places, which for a youth was a respectable result.

The fifteen-year-old Alekhine was eager for any chess confrontation. After the Dusseldorf tournament he played a series of matches abroad and at home. Everyone was astonished by the severe defeat $(4\frac{1}{2}-\frac{1}{2})$ which he inflicted on the master Bardeleben; the result of this three-game match against Fahrni was satisfactory – $1\frac{1}{2}-1\frac{1}{2}$. On the eve of his sixteenth birthday, Alekhine crushed Blumenfeld – at that time already a well-known master – by the score of $4\frac{1}{2}-\frac{1}{2}$. All this spoke for the fact that into the chess world had emerged a talent which was to bring fame to the chess movement of his native country.

The chess reviewer R. Falk, in one of the articles of this period devoted to Moscow players, mentions: 'the Alekhine brothers, of whom the younger, who has just reached his sixteenth birthday, is unusually gifted'.

We have talked about how Alekhine succeeded Mikhail Ivanovich Chigorin as leader of the Russian chess school. In connection with this,

I would like to include an extract from the memoirs of that Honoured Master, Pyotr Arsenevich Romanovsky, which were written during the 1956 chess Olympiad in Moscow. It is well known that in 1914 Romanovsky was together with Alekhine in Germany. The outbreak of the First World War found them at the international tournament in Mannheim, where they were both interned.

'On one occasion we were discussing the masters of the past – Pillsbury, Zukertort, Chigorin,' – writes Romanovsky. 'I especially remember the conversation about Chigorin.'

'In a way he stands above the other masters of the last century,' said Alekhine 'he was a special figure. Chigorin had enormous talent, perhaps he was even a genius. The depth of his conceptions was sometimes incomprehensible to mere mortals. Whether I shall reach the height of Chigorin's thought, I don't know, but in any case I will try to organize my life differently. I will not allow superficial hindrances to affect the class of my play, as very often happened with Chigorin.'

'And, fortunately for the chess world, Alekhine was able to fulfil this promise'.

His success in the Moscow tournament of 1908 gave Alekhine the right to take part in the All-Russian Amateur Tournament in the following year. This competition was also a stepping-stone; the up till then merely promising youngster became a recognized chess master – one of the strongest players in Russia.

The All-Russian Amateur Tournament in St. Petersburg in 1909 had a strong entry, and so the sixteen-year-old Alekhine's victory made a great impression. Before this they had written about his talent, and had predicted a great future; now this future had become the present. The high-up people of Russia had long dreamed about the world championship being held by one of their countrymen, and had been dejected by Chigorin's failures in his matches with Steinitz. Then Rubinstein had become Russia's chess favourite. Now many placed their hopes on the realization of this dream with the young Alekhine.

Of his sixteen games in the St. Petersburg tournament, Alekhine won twelve and drew two, which gave him a significant lead over his nearest rivals. The quality of the young victor's games was also high, although, at the same time, the tournament revealed many of his shortcomings. But the main features which distinguished the rising chess star were strength of character, persistence and resolution.

'I first met Alekhine during the St. Petersburg tournament of 1909, and already then, as a competitor and the victor in the All-Russian

Tournament, he exhibited that will to win, that purposefulness, which was to characterize his whole life, and which should not be confused with mere ambition.' Thus wrote grandmaster Savily Tartakower in 1956 in his review on Alekhine, one of those of which I spoke earlier.

Chess was the main interest in Alekhine's life, although he accurately carried out everything that was demanded of a youth, and then a young man, of his social group. In the private school where he studied, Alekhine carefully did his work, and obtained fairly high marks, although, according to the boy with whom he shared a desk, he more often than not was simply present at lessons, and spent them continually drawing chess diagrams with pieces in his notebooks.

'I remember one algebra class', writes Korsakov, his class-mate. 'Alekhine suddenly stood up and with a beaming face looked round the class, at the same time, in his usual manner, twisting with his left hand a lock of hair which had fallen down onto his forehead.'

'Well, have you solved it?' asked his teacher Bachinsky.

'Yes. I sacrifice the knight, the bishop moves . . . and White wins.'

'The class burst into laughter. Even the usually proper and reserved Bachinsky chuckled into his long whiskers. . . .'

After finishing school, Alekhine entered a college of law. Korsakov relates how he there also used to meet Alekhine in the company of common acquaintances. 'Then I heard how the student lawyers made fun of Alekhine's unusual "professor-like" absent-mindedness, his "civilian" soul, his lack of a dignified bearing, and especially of his inability to drink wine, which, according to the lawyers' unwritten code of honour, was most reprehensible'.

Inability to drink wine. . . . It is a great pity that this 'short-coming' in the young Alekhine's make-up was not maintained for his whole life !

GRANDMASTER AT 21

Obtaining the title of master gave Alekhine the right to compete in international events, and during the next few years he played in several tournaments: Hamburg in 1910, Karlsbad in 1911 and Stockholm in 1912. The path of Alekhine's chess progress in its early states, unlike for instance Capablanca's, was not a bed of roses. Only in Stockholm did he take first place, while in the other tournaments he had to be satisfied with places towards the bottom of the first ten.

All the efforts of young Alekhine were directed towards the battle ⁊gainst the short-comings in his chess mastery. Although nature had endowed him with rare gifts, his many-sided talent needed polishing. This is why the work on chess done by Alekhine in his younger years was so significant, and it was thanks to this tiring work that his chess mastery took a big step forward.

'What is the secret of Alekhine's achievements?' – writes Tartakower in his review on Alekhine's creative work. – 'Which psychological and other factors contributed to the abundant flowering of his talent?

1. First of all, a whole-hearted love of chess, which was for Alekhine a real art.

2. A powerful intellect and an all-round education.

3. An inexhaustible supply of ideas.

4. Continual work towards self-perfection (but not by the compilation of variations, as was done by Grünfeld or Dr. Euwe, but by the creative working-out of schemes, plans and combinations).

5. Maxim: set the opponent problems on almost every move.

6. Be steadfast, not only in the face of failure, but also when successful, regarding each achievement only as a step along the path to the next higher one. Alekhine thought of his whole chess career in the form of such steps.

And from these noble elements arose that series of deep and brilliant games, to play through which gives each of us enormous aesthetic satisfaction'.

An expressive characterization!

1909 was the year of the first step in Alekhine's chess life. The second, and even more important, was 1914. The participation of Alekhine in a very strong international tournament aroused enormous interest. A sharp struggle was going on at the time for the right to a match with Emanuel Lasker, the world champion. There were two generally recognized competitors: Capablanca and Rubinstein. It was expected that the battle for the first places would be between these two, since a good result would give hope for a match with Lasker.

But most unexpectedly the young Russian Master Alekhine joined in the struggle for the prizes. The tournament was conducted rather unusually: at first there was a preliminary stage of eleven players, the top five of whom then played a final stage of two games against each other. The points scored in each stage were added. After the preliminary stage Alekhine was in fourth place with three wins and one defeat, and went on to the final. Here he had only average success, scoring fifty percent of the possible points, but in the end he finished higher than such famous names as Marshall, Rubinstein and Tarrasch. Third prize behind only Lasker and Capablanca was a splendid achievement. Alekhine became a grandmaster and moved up into the ranks of the strongest players in the world.

'Alekhine has an amazing wealth of ideas, and many fine achievements can be expected from him', wrote Spielmann in that year.

The author Shishko writes that as early as 1911 Alekhine began thinking about the struggle for the world championship. But 19 years – isn't that the sort of age at which one allows oneself to dream a little? It is more likely that Alekhine began to seriously prepare himself for the battle for the chess throne only after his success in St. Petersburg.

It is interesting that Alekhine never intended to play a match with Lasker, since he realized that the world title would soon be won by Capablanca.

Pyotr Arsenevich Romanovsky remembered about this from one conversation with Alekhine. As early as 1914 Alekhine told him that he was intending to prepare for a match with the Cuban.

But Lasker is the world champion! – exclaimed the astonished Romanovsky.

It will soon be Capablanca – stated Alekhine confidently.

In those pre-war years, when Capablanca visited Russia, Alekhine became friendly with him. The two men, who within a few years would not be able to endure the presence of each other, and who would walk out of a room if the other came in, in these days shared both their leisure and their work.

Russian chess players triumphed in 1914: one more step was made towards the cherished goal – to win the world championship. Alekhine went to a new tournament, in Mannheim, and was winning game after game. A new success seemed imminent, but . . . the peaceful life of people was shattered by the volleys of guns: the First World War had begun. And the time has come for us to leave for the moment Alekhine the chess player, and talk about Alekhine the man.

A STRONG MAN WITH MANY WEAKNESSES

At the outbreak of war Alekhine found himself in a foreign country, and was interned, but did everything possible to return to his homeland, and was eventually successful.

After returning to Russia, Alekhine volunteered for the front, where he served in the medical corps.

In Tarnopole Alekhine had to go into hospital with shell-shock;

here a group of chess players visited him, and he played his famous blindfold game against Feldt. After regaining his health, Alekhine did not return to the front, and the events of 1917 found him in Moscow.

We have almost no information about the life and affairs of Alekhine during the stormy days of the revolution. According to an eye-witness (the Moscow chess player Iglitsky told me about this), Alekhine was in Odessa in 1917, from where, it was said, he was intending to go abroad. Then he changed his mind, and once again was to be seen in Moscow. In any case, among his surviving games there are some played at this time against Moscow chess players.

In the first years of the revolution Alekhine worked energetically in his capacity as a lawyer. Recently one of the executives of the Moscow Criminal Investigation Department interested me with some new information. Among some archives was found an order, dated 1920, enlisting Alexander Alekhine as an investigator (at a salary of 4800 roubles). Information has been preserved indicating that Alekhine did not carry through his investigation work to a conclusion, and his duties were only to keep a careful watch on the localities and affairs of criminals. In the Museum of Criminology in Moscow, a special place is to be set aside to demonstrate the work of Alexander Alekhine as an employee of the Criminal Investigation Department in 1920.

I did not manage to find out for how long Alekhine worked in this department; it is known only that from there he went to work as an interpreter for the Comintern (Communist International), and that besides this he had ambitions to become a film actor – he had studied in Gardin's studio. From childhood Alekhine had known both French and German. Working among foreigners, he met a Swiss woman journalist, Anna Roog,* who was an active public figure, and married her. In 1921, together with his wife, Alekhine travelled via Riga to Berlin, and then on to Paris. In my archive is kept a photocopy of the passport issued to Alekhine for his exit abroad.

 '*The Peoples' Commissariat for Foreign Affairs raises no objections to the passage into Latvia through Sobyezh of citizen Alekhine Alexander Alexandrovich, as witnessed by the signature below.*
 Deputy Peoples' Commissar – Karakhan.
 No. 01139–231V–21.'

This document suppresses any arguments to the effect that Alekhine secretly escaped from Soviet Russia.

* On 16th November 1920, Anna Roog was the guest of Lenin.

And so, Alekhine left his native country. To explain (but not of course to justify) this and many of his other actions, we must take into account his origin and position in old Russia. A member of the nobility, a man of wealth (he inherited a significant percentage of the textile mill shares), Alekhine, just like the majority of the representatives of his class, did not immediately accept the October Revolution. At the same time he loved his country, and did not straight away decide to leave it. His sister Varvara and brother Aleksey were still in Russia, in Moscow he had spent his childhood. . . . But his soul was torn by the ambitious desire, by the dream which he had cherished since childhood – to become champion of the world.

However, Alekhine considered that in Russia this would be impossible. In a period of great social upheaval there would be no place for chess . . . and so he left.

I would like to mention that after leaving his native country, Alekhine did not speak out against Soviet power, as did many other emigrants. It is true that certain of his views in the booklet *Chess in Soviet Russia*, published in Germany in 1922, have been sharply criticized; however, the sharpness of this criticism can be explained by the lack of objectivity shown by the critics. Alekhine wrote in his book that Russia is overshadowed by hunger and cold, that 'the bourgeois melt down chess pieces, and chess kings break up in the fire'. Well, wasn't it in fact just like that? It should not be forgotten that, together with these lines, we also see a series of excellent articles, in which Alekhine admires the enthusiasm of Soviet chess players, popularizing the game among the people.

At this time there occurred in the chess world an important event, which had been foreseen by Alekhine a long time previously. Capablanca won his match against Lasker and became world champion. According to Alekhine's 'life plan' the time was approaching for him to challenge Capablanca to a match. . . . And he began searching for patrons.

GRANDMASTER OF RUSSIA

One often hears the ridiculous assertion that as soon as Alekhine went to the West he became a grandmaster of the highest class, able to defeat Capablanca and ascend to the chess throne. It is not difficult to refute such absurd arguments.

Alekhine grew up and developed into a grandmaster in Moscow, together with the best players in Russia. His development was influenced by masters such as Blumenfeld, Duz-Hotimirsky, and Nenarokov. Later these were joined by Levenfish and Romanovsky. These talented representatives of the Russian chess school went side by side with Alekhine for many years, enriching his creativity with interesting ideas.

Another factor which played an important role in Alekhine's progress was the bitter rivalry which existed in the pre-war years in Russia between him and that other outstanding theorist and strong player – Aron Nimzowitsch. For many years they went 'neck and neck' in the race of tournaments and matches. Even after they had both left Russia, their rivalry remained an excellent stimulus for self-perfection.

Alekhine's third prize at the St. Petersburg tournament of 1914 was a result of grandmaster class. At that time he was already one of the strongest players in the world. It should not be forgotten also that, after going abroad, Alekhine immediately began taking the first prize in practically all the tournaments in which he took part. This means that the class of his play was already extremely high, and in the immediate post-war years he was one of the main challengers for the world championship.

Several curious facts are known, which speak of the efforts which Alekhine made in those difficult years to maintain his form for the coming battles with Capablanca. As early as 1918, Alekhine and his colleagues did everything to make it possible to play chess with each other. They found a simple, though original solution. They played tournaments with 'sliding' rounds – held in each of the competitors' flats in turn. They played by the light of a hand-lamp – one would hold it while the other was thinking – they played hungry, knocking their feet together under the table in unsuccessful attempts to keep warm.

The widow of the master Nikolai Mikhailovich Zubaryev told me that the honourable, but in those days difficult, duty of receiving the visitors fell on her shoulders. On arrival, saccharin cakes made from flour of dubious quality were handed round. 'I was surprised that when Alekhine came to play he always took out of his pocket some old piece of confectionary, unwrapped it, and drank with it unsweetened tea.' – Vera Konstantinovna related. 'It was an attempt to keep his brain intact – the most important organ for his coming chess battles. A brain without sugar is not a brain!'

Together with his colleagues, Alekhine played splendidly in the first Olympiad in 1920, and scored a confident victory. Although he was the one grandmaster who was significantly stronger than all the other competitors, Alekhine patiently endured all the discomforts. Even on the list of competitors, who at one difficult moment demanded 'an immediate issue of cheese and tobacco' (about which they wrote a special declaration to the tournament committee), Alekhine's name does not appear. He passionately gave himself to his chess games, all the time helping himself to improve.

The results of the Olympiad make it possible to draw the conclusion: Alekhine left Moscow, already a grandmaster of extra class.

FOLLOWING CHIGORIN

Alekhine's inseparable link with the Russian chess school is indicated by his chess stamp, those principles which he propagated through his creativity. At the beginning of the 1920s a bitter battle was fought against the teachings of Tarrasch, who would have restricted chess once and for all to a series of prescribed rules and precepts. Young players, led by Reti and Nimzowitsch, rebelled against these canonized laws, and proposed their own chess philosophy, which they called by the then fashionable term 'hypermodernism'.

Alekhine, with his striking creative individuality, from the very start of his career held special views on the principles of chess, views which he had adopted from Chigorin and other Russian masters. They did not reject rules, but at the same time did not raise them up to be the absolute truth. A concrete appraisal of the position, determination of the peculiarities inherent in the given situation, with the given alignment of the forces – for them this was the basic law.

While in the advice of some acknowledged theorists can be seen a desire to provide a prescription for all events in life, Alekhine, together with his predecessors, and then with his followers – Soviet chess players – considered the most important principle to be a concrete tactical analysis of the position. At the present time this principle has been accepted by all chess players in the world.

All this gives a basis for asserting that Alekhine was the direct successor to Chigorin – the founder of the Russian chess school. As a chess player and creator, Alekhine, over a period of almost four decades, gave to the world wonderful examples of strategic and tactical mastery, and created games, full of bold ideas, originality, and a wide degree of fantasy. It was for just these qualities that his creative predecessors were distinguished.

During his developing years, Alekhine followed the inspiring example of Chigorin, his ideas as a master and artist; he remained true to these ideas during the whole of his chess career.

Alekhine left his native country at the age of 29. Although in his play, as in the play of any chess master, however great, there were short-comings, he had by this time not only become a grandmaster of extra class, but was also a very erudite theorist and thinker, bringing new ideas into the understanding of chess. In order to better understand the Alekhine of those years, we will examine the creative views and principles, which had been cultivated by the Russian champion at that time. These principles were formulated by him in annotations to games and in special articles, and concern all aspects of chess, both creative and practical (Alekhine would never separate one from the other). As the reader will see, the creation of a highly artistic work – this was the main objective which Alekhine saw in chess.

CHESS – HIS FAVOURITE ART

'Chess for me is not a game, but an art', wrote Alekhine. 'Yes, and I take upon myself all those responsibilities which an art imposes on its adherents'.

Always and everywhere, throughout his fruitful chess career, Alekhine put forward this view of chess. 'The aim of chess I see as scientific and artistic achievements, which places the game alongside other forms of art'.

Alekhine, of course, came out against those views on chess which belittle its importance, and reduce it to the level of a mere table game. He sharply criticized those grandmasters for whom victory was the sole aim of the game, and predicted that such an attitude would lead inevitably to the degeneration of chess.

Alekhine also severely criticized certain outstanding players who proposed that the game of chess be reformed and made more complicated. As the reader is probably aware, both Lasker and Capablanca made such suggestions when they each lost the world championship title. Their predictions of the imminent 'death of chess due to drawing' were decisively refuted by Alekhine.

'The "Reformists" maintain that theoretical progress will lead to a deadening of the game of chess, and propose to revive it by changing the rules', wrote Alekhine. 'But what does this assertion signify? First and foremost, a scornful attitude towards intuition, to fantasy, to all the elements which raise chess onto a level with the arts'.

It was with just these qualities of creative personality – the ability to perceive the unusual by intuition and fantasy – that Alekhine was liberally talented. Among his contemporaries there was no one to equal him in this. Alekhine complained that his opponents hindered him from creating those works of art which he wished to create. In some cases the opponent would not find the strongest reply, when the combination would have been more beautiful and interesting, in others the whole concept was spoiled simply because the opponent resigned. 'I would be happy to create all alone', said Alekhine, 'without the necessity, as occurs in a game, of considering my own plan together with my opponent's, in order to produce something of value. Oh, that opponent, that partner who is linked to you! Each time his idea of beauty diverges from yours, and the means (forces, imagination, technique) so often are insufficient to actively assist with your intentions. How much disillusionment does he bring to the true chess artist, striving not just for victory, but for the creation of a work of art, which has some real value. How one suffers (and this is unknown in any other field of art or science) to feel that one's ideas and fantasy are inevitably stifled, due to the very nature of things, by the ideas and fantasy of someone else, which are all too often mediocre, and which always differ deeply from one's own!'

This love for creativity in chess was preserved by Alekhine during his whole life. The reader will see later how boundless was Alekhine's love for chess, even at an age when many grow tired of it, and others give it up altogether. From his childhood analyses by the light of an icon-lamp, to his last dying breath by a chess board, Alekhine maintained a profound love for chess, which became for him the meaning of life itself.

THE PRACTICAL ASPECT OF THE CHESS PLAYER

It may appear paradoxical, but it was just Alekhine's desire to create, which explains his attention to the practical aspect of chess, his urge to achieve in it, if not perfection, then at least a sufficiently high standard.

The play of a grandmaster is valued for the depth of its conceptions, for the brilliance of its combinations – but only by experts. His play is also appreciated for his ability to crown his ideas with victory – this is what interests masses of amateurs, since literally millions of people are familiar with the number of points he scores in competitions. Which is more important? There is a long history of arguments on this question. Alekhine's conception was that a player's practical qualities are important not for themselves, but to help him to produce perfect works of chess. A combination is worthless if, due to the noise in the hall, the grandmaster at the decisive moment suddenly leaves a piece en prise. Therefore you must train your nerves, discipline yourself to endure noise, and the tenseness of the situation, and the mannerisms of your opponent.

We have already recalled the conversation of Alekhine with Romanovsky, when the young grandmaster spoke of the practical shortcomings in Chigorin's character, and promised to follow a different path. The Russian champion formulated his practical creed in a few short phrases, which, I am sure, help many young players to form themselves into stubborn, imperturbable tournament fighters.

'There is one feature which, along with others, determines the strength of a chess player; this is the undivided attention, which must absolutely isolate the player from all the outside world'.

Absolutely isolate the player from the outside world! Let the hall become noisy, your opponent become excited, your neighbour be tormenting himself – it has nothing to do with you at all. It is your duty to create, and creativity demands passion, aloofness. And you must cut yourself off from everything away from the board. During his best years, Alekhine played with just such passion.

In one of his articles Alekhine writes: 'During a chess competition a chess master should be a combination of a beast of prey and a monk'. How strikingly precise: a beast of prey and a monk! As far as your attitude to your opponent goes, you are a beast of prey, tear him to pieces! But regarding your conduct during the tournament, never forget – you must be a monk. No over-indulgences, which can interfere with your routine; it is your duty to conserve your strength, otherwise you may not stand the strain of a difficult tournament.

Alas, Alekhine himself was not always a monk. . . .

One more most important quality is the ability to endure a defeat. There is no chess player who is not delighted by a win, who is not spurred on by one. On the other hand, there is also no player, even among the most staunch, who is not upset by a defeat. What we are talking about here is how to be self-controlled during misfortunes, and how to be in good form for the next game.

'In a long tournament, one should not be afraid of a defeat, but of the psychological depression that goes with it'. Alekhine himself not only resisted this depression after a loss, but, on the contrary, played even more strongly. Many of his games which received brilliancy prizes were played when he had suffered a defeat the day before.

A player must be able to solve psychological problems of a purely chess nature. Alekhine considered it important to be able to discover the strong and weak points, not only in the opponent's play, but also in one's own. But how they dislike this, those who are accustomed only to praise and encouragement! With rare self-criticism, Alekhine set about appraising his own positive and negative qualities, and this enabled him to overcome serious misfortunes.

CREATIVITY FROM THE VERY FIRST MOVE

Right from the start of his chess career Alekhine's style of play in the opening was distinguished by the following characteristics.

1. **Universality.** It is difficult to think of another world champion who was so universal in the choice of his openings. As White the Russian Champion played both 1 P–K4 and 1 P–Q4, and sometimes even 1 N–KB3, and was, of course, prepared for any reply by the opponent. As Black he employed almost all the recognized defences against both 1 P–K4 and 1 P–Q4. In his repertoire were the Sicilian Defence, French Defence and Alekhine's Defence. On occasions he even adopted the Caro-Kann Defence. But of course his main reply to 1 P–K4 was the Ruy Lopez, and he was naturally very familiar with all the Open Games.

2. **With Black – counter-attack.** About the time of the start of this century a player with Black would set himself a limited goal: to equalize the game. Alekhine revived Chigorin's principle, that the main aim of the opening is to set up counter-play, and successfully adopted it in the most important encounters. This aim was served by Alekhine's Defence, Nimzowitsch's Defence to 1 P–Q4, and the Grünfeld Defence, all of which found their way unfailingly into Alekhine's opening arsenal.

3. **The concrete solution of opening problems.** Although Alekhine always followed the general rules and precepts which had developed from the practice and experience of chess battles of the past, he always associated them closely with the specific situation on the board. Following his intuition and concrete analysis he would then find exceptions to these generalities.

A striking example of Alekhine's concrete thinking in the opening are the concepts he introduced of 'the concrete-tactical opening' and 'the disruption of equilibrium at the start of the game'.

Alekhine's concrete approach to the position began from the very first moves. Even in the very opening Alekhine used to discover hidden tactical possibilities. This is why many of Alekhine's games were decided already in the opening (the question is not of an opening advantage, but of the opponent's position being destroyed). Alekhine was able to provoke sharp tactical complications, in which his opponent was not always able to find his way.

The majority of Alekhine's sudden attacks are irreproachably correct, but in certain cases analysts in later years have found refutations. In my opinion this in no way detracts from the beauty of Alekhine's concepts. Their practical justification is irrefutable – Alekhine's opponents could not find their way through the jungle of variations, and the attacks were successful. At present a similar picture can be seen, for example, in the games of Tal.

Alekhine-Böök, Margate 1938

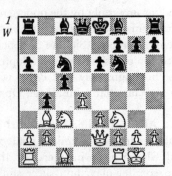

1
W

This position arose after the moves
1 P–Q4 P–Q4   2 P–QB4 P×P
3 N–KB3 N–KB3   4 P–K3 P–K3
5 B×P P–B4 6 0–0 N–B3 7 Q–K2
P–QR3 8 N–B3 P–QN4 9 B–N3
P–N5 (*1*)

There can be no doubt that very few players would have taken the path chosen by the chess magician with his unlimited inventiveness.

10 P–Q5!	**N–QR4**
11 B–R4+	**B–Q2**
12 P×P	**P×P**
13 R–Q1!	**P×N**
14 R×B! (*2*)	

This sacrifice is the point of the combination. Alekhine provokes boundless complications.

2
B

14 ...	**N×R**
15 N–K5	**R–R2**
16 P×P	**K–K2**

Alekhine considers the following possible defences:

a) 16 ... P–N3   17 Q–B3 (also good is *17 Q–Q3 K–K2 18 P–K4*

N–KB3 19 Q–B3) 17 . . . Q–K2 (or
*17 . . . K–K2 18 P–K4 N × N 19
B–KN5+* and *20 Q–Q1+*) 18 B–R3!,
and Black has no defence to the
threats of 19 R–Q1 and in some cases
B × P;

   b) 16 . . . Q–N1 17 N × N R × N
18 Q × P Q–B2 19 Q × P+ K–Q1
20 P–K4! and there is no defence to
the threats of 21 B–B4 and 21
B–KN5+;

   c) 16 . . . B–Q3 or 16 . . . B–K2
(the best defence) 17 Q–R5+ P–N3
18 N × P P × N 19 Q × R+ B–B1
20 P–K4, and White, with two pawns
for a knight, maintains his attack.

   And yet, as was discovered later,
16 . . . Q–N1 would have won for
Black: 17 N × N R × N 18 Q × P
Q–Q3! or 17 Q–R5+ P–N3 18
N × P P × N 19 Q × R K–B2!

   17 P–K4!   **N–KB3**
   18 B–KN5   **Q–B2**
   19 B–B4   **Q–N3**

Alekhine complains that his opponent 'spoiled' the combination, losing
in simple fashion when he could have
lost beautifully. The world champion
expected 19 . . . Q–N2, after which he
had the following win prepared:
20 Q–K3 K–Q1 21 Q–Q3+ K–B1
22 R–N1 Q × P 23 N–B7!! (*3*), and
there is no defence to the mates on
Q8 or QN8.

   In the game there followed:

   20 R–Q1   **P–N3**
   21 B–KN5!   **B–N2**
   22 N–Q7   **R × N**
   23 R × R+   **K–B1**
   24 B × N   **B × B**
   25 P–K5!   **1–0**

It is difficult to reproach the master
Böök for failing to find the best defence. Similarly Alekhine can hardly
be reproached for deciding to try out
such an interesting and unexpected
form of attack.

   A refutation has been found. Well,

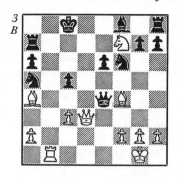

so what. . . . Many more defences will
be found to attacks which at the time
seemed irresistible. Chess is inexhaustible, and for this reason we love it.

   Among Alekhine's games there are
some in which the opponent plays the
opening stage too flippantly, disregarding all the accepted rules, thus
unlawfully disturbing the equilibrium,
and impairing his own position. In
such cases Alekhine considered it his
duty to mete out immediate punishment to the opponent.

Alekhine–Rosanoff, Moscow 1908

   The following position arose after
the moves 1 P–K4 P–QN3 2 P–Q4
B–N2 3 N–QB3 P–K3 4 N–B3 P–Q4
5 B–QN5+ P–QB3 6 B–Q3 N–B3
7 P–K5 N3–Q2 (*4*)

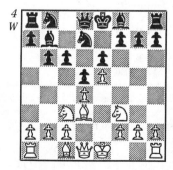

   One can hardly fail to notice that
Black has freely disregarded the
principles of development, for which

he must be punished. Alekhine's retribution is swift.

8 N–KN5 !   **B–K2**

White was threatening to win immediately by 9 N × KP! and 10 Q–R5 + .

9 Q–N4 !   **N–B1**

9 . . . B × N was stronger. The move of the knight is just one more liberty.

10 N × RP !

A sacrifice of two pieces for a rook, accurately calculated by Alekhine.

10 . . .   **R × N**
11 B × R   **N × B**
12 Q × NP   **N–B1** (5)

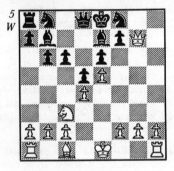

13 P–KR4 !

And here it is, the punishment. The pawn threatens to march through to the eighth rank, and so Black is forced to capture it.

13 . . .   **B × P**
14 R × B !   **Q × R**
15 B–N5   **Q–R8 +**
16 K–Q2   **Q × P**
17 Q–B6 (6)

And now mate can be averted only by giving up the queen for the bishop. Black did this, and although he resisted for several more moves, it was a hopeless struggle.

17 . . . Q × B+   18 Q × Q N–N3 19 P–B4 N–K2 20 R–R1 N–Q2 21 N–Q1 N–KB1 22 N–K3 B–B1 23 N–N4 B–Q2 24 R–R8 N2–N3 25 N–B6+ K–Q1 26 Q × N 1–0.

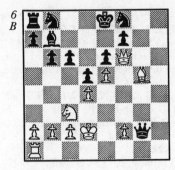

In the games which follow we will see examples of the concrete-tactical opening, and of punishment for disturbing the equilibrium. I would just like the reader to once more observe the difference between these concepts: in the concrete-tactical opening there is no suggestion of an error on the opponent's part, in the other case he alone is at fault.

GAMES FROM THE YEARS 1907–1921

In the biography of a great person, the reader is always interested in the moment when his career begins: when did an author write his first novel, or an artist paint his first picture; when did an actor first appear on the stage, or a general direct his first battle? When did Alekhine play his first game of chess?

As we have already said, he learned the game at the age of seven, but at first played only at home with his older brother Aleksey. They conducted correspondence games together, and there are a number of interesting games among these, but we have no right to talk about the individual authorship of one of the brothers.

History has preserved for us the first tournament game played by Alexander Alekhine, and with it we will begin.

1) Alekhine-Rosanoff, Moscow 1907
Scotch Game

1 P–K4	P–K4
2 N–KB3	N–QB3
3 P–Q4	

At that time the Scotch Game was one of the regularly played openings – it fully satisfied the needs of the chess masters. The prevailing principles were those of Tarrasch, who persistently repeated: 'occupy the centre with pawns', while still alive were the traditions of open battles in the style of Morphy, Anderssen and Chigorin. The new attitude towards the centre was only just beginning to develop: Reti, Alekhine and Nimzowitsch were still preparing the principle, which was only later accurately formulated, of pressure on a pawn centre by pieces. Tournament players at the start of the century aimed to open the centre as soon as they could, and, if possible, to occupy it with pawns, so as to rapidly develop the pieces and get down to the main thing – the attack on the enemy king. The Scotch Game fully corresponded to these aims, and this is why the opening frequently occurs in Alekhine's early games.

3 ...	P × P
4 N × P	N–B3
5 N × N	

In important tournament games the future world champion usually chose this exchange of knights, although on occasions he adopted other, sharper continuations. His short draw with Lasker (Moscow 1914) became famous: after 5 N–QB3 B–N5 6 N × N NP × N 7 B–Q3 P–Q4 8 P × P P × P 9 0–0 0–0 10 B–KN5 B–K3 11 Q–B3 B–K2 12 QR–K1 P–KR3 Alekhine, playing White, sacrificed first a bishop and then the exchange to give perpetual check: 13 B × P P × B 14 R × B! P × R 15 Q–N3+ K–R1 16 Q–N6 ½–½.

5 ...	NP × N
6 B–Q3	P–Q4
7 P × P	P × P
8 0–0	B–K2
9 N–B3	0–0
10 B–KN5	P–B3
11 Q–B3 (7)	

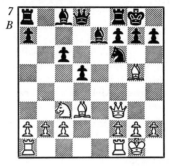

One of the controversial positions in the Scotch Game. White's play in this old variation contains something of the modern understanding of the centre: White has completely rid himself of his central pawns, so as to exert piece pressure on the opposing pawn centre. Both sides have completed their development, and have begun to carry out their respective plans.

It is quite natural that White will aim for an attack on the K-side, and to increase the pressure along the open files and diagonals. Against this, Black will try to exploit the open QN-file, and also the strength of his pawn centre.

11 ...   **B–KN5**

So as to transfer, as quickly as possible, this bishop via ... KR4 to ... KN3 where it will neutralize the action of White's dangerous KB. Another possibility, considered Black's best, is 11 ... R–N1. Yet another move – 11 ... N–N5 ? was made in the game Alekhine-Manko, played by correspondence between 1906–1907. This short encounter ended in complete triumph for the young Alekhine:

12 B×B Q×B 13 QR–K1 Q–Q3
14 Q–N3! Q–B3 15 P–KR3 N–R3
16 R–K5! P–N3 17 N–K2 B–B4
18 P–KB4 KR–K1 19 Q–K3 R×R
20 P×R Q–R5 21 N–Q4 B×B 22
R–B4! Q–K2 23 P×B R–QB1 24
R–B6 P–B4 25 N–B6 Q–K1 26
P–K6!! N–B4 27 P×P+ Q×P
28 R×N! 1–0.

12 Q–N3   B–R4
13 Q–K5

There are no chess players without
faults, however richly gifted they may
be. Although he had a rare talent for
combination, Alekhine was markedly
weaker in positional manoeuvring and
in strategy. As a result, as the reader
will see, he had to work at this a
great deal.

In the given position White should,
first of all, have outlined the aim of
his next few moves. It is not difficult
to decide upon it: he should set up
pressure along the open K-file, and
combine this with combinative threats
against the enemy king position. The
solution to these problems is provided
by the natural continuation 13
KR–K1!, so as after 13 . . . B–N3
14 B×B RP×B to play 15 Q–R4!
with the terrible threats of R–K3–R3.

Instead of this, the 15-year-old
Alekhine is carried away by a tactical
possibility: 14 B×N B×B 15 Q×B/
R5 is threatened. It is no wonder that,
playing without a plan, his position
soon becomes difficult.

13 . . .   B–N3
14 B×B   RP×B
15 QR–Q1

Once again his uncertainty in
strategic manoeuvring is seen. Correct
was 15 KR–K1! with a good game
for White. It is interesting to follow
how Black successfully exploits his
initiative, and, with a few clever
moves, faces his opponent with difficult problems.

15 . . .   B–Q3
16 Q–Q4   Q–B2
17 Q–KR4

White already has to think about
defence. Bad was 17 B×N P×B 18
Q×BP in view of 18 . . . B×P+
19 K–R1 B–K4!, and Black's pieces
take up strong central positions.

17 . . .   N–R2
18 B–K3   P–KB4
19 P–B4   K–B2!

An excellent move. Since it is
obviously impossible to take the
knight – 20 Q×N?? R–R1 – Black
seizes the open KR-file for active
operations.

20 B–Q4   R–R1
21 R/Q1–K1? *(8)*

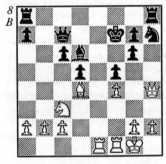

A player aiming to learn the strategy and tactics of chess, to understand
its principles, should carefully analyse
the subsequent events in this game.

Let us make a detailed analysis of
this position. White's pieces appear
to be threateningly placed, but this is
only apparent – Black's solid pawn
centre restricts the action of all White's
army. One cannot help regretting the
time wasted on the aimless 13th and
15th moves. Black has energetically
exploited his opponent's slackness –
his rook, bishop and queen have taken
up dangerous attacking positions,
while his knight is ready to move
with tempo via KB3 to one of two

excellent squares for the coming attack – K5 or KN5. An experienced player with White would try to find a way of neutralizing the pressure, to somehow simplify the position. Most probably he would decide to exchange bishops, so as to remove Black's threats along the KR2–QN8 diagonal, and at the same time expose the black king.

This aim could be realized by the following defensive plan: 21 Q–B2! N–B3 22 P–KR3. If Black then plays 22 ... N–K5, then 23 N × N QP × N 24 B × NP! K × B 25 Q–Q4+ or 23 ... BP × N 24 P–B5! P–N4 25 B–K3! followed by P–B4 leaves White with a marked advantage.

22 ... N–R4 leads to a sharp struggle. Now the defensive 23 B–K3 gives Black the advantage after 23 ... P–N4!, but the simple 23 B–B5! liquidates all threats, and Black's king may unexpectedly find itself in a dangerous position. The following variations illustrate the possibilities for both sides in the sharp position arising after 23 B–B5.

a) 23 ... B × B 24 Q × B N × P 25 N × P! N × N 26 R × N with advantage to White.

b) 23 ... N × P 24 B × B N × RP+ 25 P × N Q × B, and White should win.

c) 23 ... B × P 24 P–KN4! B–N6 25 Q–N2! N–B3 (or *25 ... N–B5 26 Q × B N × P+ 27 K–N2*, and Black has insufficient compensation for the piece) 26 P × P P–N4 27 R–Q3! B–B5 28 N–K2!, and White stands better.

The variations given indicate that, in answer to 23 B–B5!, it is unfavourable for Black to capture the KBP, and he must therefore agree to the exchange of bishops, which leads to a quiet positional struggle with roughly equal chances.

Such a plan would have been chosen by the 'adult' Alekhine, but then he was only 15, and had seen the possibility of striking an unexpected and spectacular blow ...

21 ... **N–B3**
22 Q–N5

He has to continue to walk the tightrope, since, on other retreats by the queen, Black can win a pawn by a knight fork on ... KR4 or ...KN5.

22 ... **N–N5?** (*9*)

Intending to trap the queen by 23 ... R–R4, but overlooking White's brilliant reply. Had Black played 22 ... R–R4, or even 22 ... N–K5, he would have remained with an excellent position.

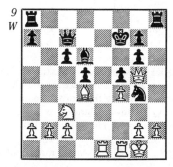

23 R–K6!!

This instantly changes the course of the game. Now White's pieces become very active, and co-operate to attack the black king.

23 ... **K × R**

No better is 23 ... R–R3, since after 24 R1–K1 there is no defence against the threat of 25 P–KR3. If Black continues 24 ... B × P, then 25 R–K7+ K–N1 26 R × Q B × Q 27 R × NP+ K–B1 28 P–KR3 B–B3 (bad are 28 ... N–B3 29 R1–K7, or 28 ... P–B4 29 R × RP! R × R 30 B × P+ R–K2 31 P × N) 29 B × B N × B 30 R1–K7, and White has an indisputable advantage.

24 Q × NP+ **K–Q2**

25 Q × BP+	K–Q1
26 Q × N	

The struggle is effectively at an end. White has two pawns for the exchange, plus a very strong attack. Rosanoff attempts to hide his king on the Q-side, but there as well the rampant white forces track him down.

26 ...	B–B1
27 R–K1	Q–Q2
28 Q–N5+	K–B2
29 R–K3!	

Preparing to transfer the rook to QN3, while at the same time avoiding the trap: 29 B × NP? B–B4+! 30 K–R1 QR–KN1! 31 B–K5+ K–N2 32 Q–B6 R × P+! 33 K × R Q–R2+ and mates.

29 ...	K–N2
30 N–R4	R–K1
31 R–QN3+	K–R1
32 Q–N3	

Alekhine conducts the attack with great mastery. The place for the white queen is among the storm stroops, on the QR6 square, and it is to there that the young player directs her.

32 ...	R–R3

32 ... R–QN1 was a more stubborn defence.

33 Q–Q3	R3–K3
34 B–K5!	

Now Black has to reckon with 35 Q–R6.

34 ...	P–B4
35 R–N5	R–B1?

This loses immediately. The only move to continue the resistance was 35 ... Q–B3! with the threat of ... P–B5. Now Black's position collapses.

36 P–B4!	

This forces the opponent to reconcile himself to new losses, since entirely bad is 36 ... P–Q5 37 N × P B × N 38 Q–KB3+ R3–QB3 39 R × B.

36 ...	P–R3
37 N–N6+	R × N
38 R × R	K–R2

39 Q–N6	Q–R5
40 R–N3!	Q–B3
41 Q–B7+	K–R1
42 P × P	1–0

We have analysed Alekhine's first tournament game in such detail, so as to once more convince the reader of the correctness of that well-known truth: grandmasters are not born, highest mastery is achieved only by an enormous amount of work.

Although he had the ability to foresee unexpected combinational blows (such as 23 R–K6!!), the young Alekhine was virtually helpless when it came to solving complex strategic problems. One can find many defects in his positional play in simple positions. Through the years he was to overcome these, with tournament experience, after large numbers of notebooks had been filled with analyses of his virtues and his shortcomings. It will be interesting for us to see how, for practically his whole life, this outstanding player never ceased to sharply criticize himself, and how by passionate, selfless work, all aspects of chess mastery were painstakingly acquired.

But Alekhine used his great combinational talent from the very start of his tournament career. Here is an example of how, by combinational means, he elegantly and confidently decides the outcome of a game in which his opponent's king has lingered in the centre.

2) Alekhine–Levenfish, St. Petersburg 1912
Benoni Defence

1 P–Q4	P–QB4

At the present time this move initiates a complicated strategic struggle for the centre, in which subsequently skirmishes can also break out on the flanks. At the time when the game was played, the advance of the black pawn was not associated with any deep conceptions – Black merely hoped to confuse his opponent. It is not surprising that often, as for instance in the present game, it is Black himself who first becomes confused.

2 P–Q5	**N–KB3**
3 N–QB3	**P–Q3**
4 P–K4	**P–KN3**

Modern theory recommends either 4 . . . P–K4, blocking the centre and leading to a slow struggle, or else 4 . . . P–K3, followed by exchanging on White's Q5. Which path should be chosen is a matter of taste. Levenfish chooses a third path, and soon is faced with insuperable difficulties, though it is true that to demonstrate this, Alekhine has to play directly and very energetically.

5 P–B4!	**QN–Q2**
6 N–B3	**P–QR3**

Black is not in a position to prevent the central breakthrough P–K5–K6, so he at least removes the possibility of a very dangerous check by the white bishop on QN5.

7 P–K5	**P × P**
8 P × P	**N–N5**
9 P–K6!	**N/2–K4**
10 B–KB4	**N × N+**

Black hopes to hold the position after 11 Q × N P × P! 12 Q × N P–K4!, but he has overlooked White's clever reply.

11 P × N!

Winning an important tempo. Now Black should have retreated his knight to R3, so as to transfer it to B4.

11 . . .	**N–B3**
12 B–B4	**P × P**
13 P × P	**Q–N3**

After the exchange of queens, White's pawn on K6 deprives Black of any hope of saving the difficult ending.

14 Q–K2   **Q × NP** (*10*)

Black allows Alekhine to conclude the game with a brilliant combination involving the sacrifice of two rooks. However, had he allowed White to castle Q-side, then his position would all the same have remained hopeless.

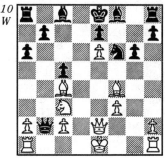

15 N–N5!

Giving Black the choice of either one knight or two rooks. After 15 . . . P × N 16 B × P+ K–Q1 17 R–Q1+ B–Q2 18 B–K5! Q–N5+ 19 P–B3 Black's king would soon be mated.

15 . . .	**Q × R+**
16 K–B2	**Q × R**
17 N–B7+	**K–Q1**
18 Q–Q2+	**B–Q2**
19 P × B	**1–0**

After the best defence 19 . . . P–K4 (*19 . . . N × P   20 B–K6*) then the simple 20 B × KP mates most quickly, though it is possible also to give mate with checks: 20 N–K6+ K–K2 21 P–Q8=Q+ R × Q 22 Q × R+ K–B2 23 N × B+ K–N2 24 Q–K7 mate.

The following game illustrates the young Alekhine's ability to see the most well-hidden combinative blows, and not only to set, but also to discover, the most cunning traps. It is the achievement of a chess master.

3) Nimzowitsch-Alekhine, Vilna 1912
Queen's Pawn Game

1 P–Q4	**P–Q4**
2 N–KB3	**P–QB4**

3 B–B4	N–QB3
4 P–K3	N–B3
5 N–B3	

A dubious move. The natural harmonious development of White's pieces – 5 QN–Q2, 6 P–QB3, 7 B–Q3 etc. – suggests itself.

5 . . .	B–N5
6 B–QN5	P–K3
7 P–KR3	B–R4

This allows White a dangerous initiative by attacking the pinned knight on QB3. The simple exchange of bishop for knight was indicated.

8 P–KN4	B–N3
9 N–K5	Q–N3

9 . . . R–B1? loses to 10 N×N P×N 11 B–QR6 R–R1 12 B–N7.

10 P–QR4!	P–QR4
11 P–R4!	P–R4
12 N×B	P×N
13 NP×P	NP×P
14 Q–K2	0–0–0 (*11*)

11
W

15 0–0–0

The ingenious Nimzowitsch sets a cunning trap. It appears that Black could now have captured White's QP without fear – 15 . . . P×P 16 P×P N×P. Now the pin 17 Q–K3 is not dangerous for Black in view of 17 . . . B–B4, while the thrust 17 Q–K5 leads to an unclear position after 17 . . . N×B 18 N×N N–N5 19 N–R7+ K–Q2 20 R×P+ P×R 21 Q×QP+ K–K1 22 R–K1+ B–K2 23 Q–K4 Q–N5 !

Why then did Alekhine not capture the QP? Was he afraid of the attack in the variation which we have just analysed? Nothing of the sort ! In that case Nimzowitsch would have announced a dramatic mate by 17 R×N ! Q×R 18 Q×KP+ N–Q2 19 Q–QB6+ ! P×Q 20 B–QR6 mate.

Such a trap could have been thought up only by a player of unusual fantasy, and discovered only by one with subtle combination intuition.

15 . . .	B–Q3
16 B×B	R×B
17 B–Q3	

This is a serious mistake. Firstly the bishop ends up on a bad square, and finally perishes in the heart of the enemy position. Secondly, Black obtains a dangerous attack on the king, since his heavy pieces can quickly be doubled on the QN file.

17 . . .	P–B5!
18 B–N6	N–K2
19 KR–N1	Q–N5
20 K–Q2 (*12*)	

12
B

20 . . .   R–N3!

An answering trap, no less cunning than the one set by White five moves ago. The reader's attention is drawn to the fact that both experts set their traps not by chance, they do not play only for traps. Their subtleties flow naturally from the demands of the position, and help them to carry out their basic strategic plans.

21 P–B3!

Nimzowitsch is also on the ball. Had he made some other passive move, the game could have concluded brilliantly: 21 ... N × B! 22 R × N Q × NP! 23 R–QN1 Q × N + !! 24 K × Q N–K5 mate.

21 ...   R–KR3!

But now White's bishop becomes trapped among the tangle of black pieces.

22 B–B7   N–B4
23 Q–R2   Q–K2

The bishop is lost. Nimzowitsch launches a despairing attack, but only succeeds in ensnaring his own queen as well.

24 N–N5   Q × B
25 N–R7+   K–Q2
26 Q–N8

Black easily parries this desperate sally: 26 ... N–Q3   27 R–N5 N/B3–K1   28 R1–KN1 R–KB3   29 P–B4 P–N3 30 K–B1 Q–R2 31 P–B3 Q–B2 32 K–N1 Q–K2 33 K–R2 R–B1 34 N–N5 N × N 35 P × N N–B2 36 Q–R7 Q–Q3 0–1. The queen is trapped; (*37 R × NP N × P 38 R–N7+ K–B3 39 Q × RP R–R3*).

The following two games are examples of Alekhine's fantastic 'super-combinations'.

4) Alekhine–NN, Moscow 1915
French Defence

1 P–K4   P–K3
2 P–Q4   P–Q4
3 N–QB3   N–KB3
4 B–KN5   B–N5

The so-called McCutcheon Variation of the French Defence. This sharp opening was frequently adopted at the start of the century.

5 P–K5   P–KR3
6 P × N

Theory asserts that this capture

allows Black to equalize without trouble, and recommends instead the retreat of the bishop to Q2.

6 ...   P × B
7 P × P   R–N1
8 P–KR4   P × P
9 Q–N4   B–K2

An inaccuracy. After 9 ... Q–B3! Black experiences no difficulties.

10 P–KN3   P–QB4
11 NP × P   P × P

This allows the KRP, helped by a series of sacrifices, to reach the 8th rank. It was not yet too late to eliminate the menacing white KNP by 11 ... B–B3.

12 P–R5!   P × N
13 P–R6   P × P
14 R–N1   Q–R4+

Black is forced to accept the challenge, since otherwise he has no means of combating White's K-side pawns.

15 K–K2   Q × P
16 P–R7   Q × R
17 P × R = Q +   K–Q2
18 Q × BP   Q × P +
19 K–B3   N–B3

Only in this way can Black hope to fight White's considerable forces. The opportune knight move allows him to simultaneously defend both the bishops.

20 Q/N4 × P +   K–B2
21 Q–B4+   K–N3
22 Q/K6–K3+   B–QB4

Other moves lose immediately. For example, 22 ... P–Q5 23 B–Q3! or 22 ... K–R4 23 Q–Q2+ Q × Q 24 Q × Q +.

23 P–N8 = Q   P–N8 = Q *(13)*

In the case of 23 ... B × Q 24 Q/B4 × B+ hopeless for Black are both 24 .., P–Q5 25 Q/K3–N3+ and 24 ... K–B2 (*24 ... K–R4 25 Q × QP +*) 25 Q–KN3+!, and the two white queens mate without difficulty.

'In this crazy position White wins

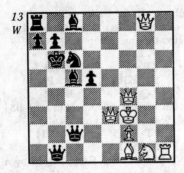

13
W

by the quiet move 24 R–R6!! (with the threat of *25 Q–Q 8* mate, while if *24 ... Q × B* then *25 Q–Q N4+ Q–N4 26 Q–Q 8+* and *27 Q/K3–R3+* with mate in two moves).

The position reached after Black's 23rd move is probably unique in the history of chess !' (Alekhine).

Some seventy years later this game still delights chess enthusiasts, while its mysterious history adds further to the interest. Where, and in which tournament was it played? And who was the unidentified NN?

In 1916 in the journal *Shakhmatny Vyestnik* there appeared a game Grigoriev-Alekhine. In his notes to White's 11th move Alekhine wrote: 'On 11 NP × P I intended to play 11 ... B–B3, since 11 ... P × P would lead to very difficult complications. Here, for instance, is one of the fantastic variations possible from this position'. Following this, Alekhine gives all the moves of the game with NN, indicating that 24 R–R6 !! leads to victory.

In his book *My best games*, which appeared many years later, Alekhine writes differently: 'One of my games (Moscow 1915) continued in the following way' – and gives exactly the same moves, but now as if they were played in a game with an unknown opponent.

Was this game actually played, or

is it the fruit of Alekhine's invention; did it evolve in the imagination of this ingenious and fervent artist during home analysis? It is doubtful whether the question can be decided. But even if the game was not in fact played, it is nevertheless so interesting and fantastic, and so characteristic of the young Alekhine's style, that here it is not out of place to rephrase a well-known proverb: 'If the game had not been played, it would have had to have been invented !' It is just unbelievable that a player not possessing such a fervent imagination would be able to think up such a game, and also discover the unexpected quiet move of the rook.

In any case, this improbable game is destined, for many years to come, to astound connoisseurs of chess combinations.

And so:

24 R–R6!!   1–0

The rook move forces Black to immediately resign the game. Can he defend against the threat of Q–Q8 mate? The capture 24 ... B × Q leads to mate after 25 Q–Q8+ K–B4 26 Q × P+ K × Q 27 Q–Q6 (two of the queens perish, but the third mates). The attempt to escape with the king to QR2 is also unsuccessful: 24 ... P–R3 25 R × N+ ! P × R 26 Q–Q8+ K–R2 27 Q/Q8–K7+ ! and wins. It will doubtless be interesting for the reader to work his way through all the unusual stratagems of this unique game.

The following finish occurred in a game against a well-known opponent – the strong amateur Gofmeister. In this game also, Alekhine's unrestrained fantasy is apparent. When one plays over the moves of this phenomenal combination, one is amazed at the sheer energy with which the white pieces seem to be endowed.

5) Alekhine-Gofmeister, Petrograd 1917

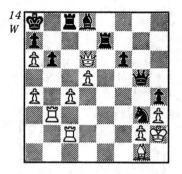

It is White to move *(14)*. At first glance it is difficult to perceive any mating threats to the black king. One even gains the impression that he is out of danger in the far corner, while the same can certainly not be said about the white king. The prospect of perpetual check by the knight on the squares ...B8 and ...N6 seems to be the logical development from the position, and forces us to suppose that a draw is the natural outcome. This assumes that White, on his first move, can meet the threat of 1...N-K5! followed by check with the bishop on ...QB2.

The young Alekhine exploits, with rare ingenuity, the latent possibilities of the position, and makes a move which at first sight seems absurd.

1 P-B5

White by combinational means defends against the threat to force perpetual check. Now on 1... N-B8+ 2 K-R1 N-N6+ there follows 3 R×N! Q×R 4 P×P!, generously offering either a rook or a queen. But which one to take? It turns out that neither can be taken. 4...R×R is answered by 5 Q×B+ Q-QN1 6 Q×R P×P 7 Q×P and White has a strong attack plus material advantage. In the case of 4...Q×Q

5 R×R+ Q-N1 6 P-N7+ R×P 7 P×R+ K×P 8 R×Q+ K×R 9 B-B2, White's extra pawn must bring him victory. It remains to be said that attempts by Black to cover the QB-file are unsuccessful: 4... R2-QB2 5 R×R, or 4...R-N1 5 P-N7+, and in each case White wins.

Does this mean that 1 P-B5 wins the game? No, in fact Black had at his disposal a subtle defence, which he failed to exploit. By playing 1... R-K7! with the threat of 2... N-B8+ and 3...Q×NP mate, he would have forced the exchange of rooks – 2 R×R N×R with considerable advantage, since the threat of 3...B-B2 is irresistible. It would have been possible to have considered Alekhine's combination beginning with this second move, (2 P×P), but we will not deviate from the generally accepted, since in all books about Alekhine, the position given is just the one in the diagram.

1... **P-N4**

But now after this move White's combinative threats become irresistible.

2 P×P **N-K5**

All other moves lose by force. For example, 2...R-K7 3 R×R N×R 4 P-N6!, removing the threat of 4...B-B2. Checks by the knight similarly do not help: 2...N-B8+ 3 K-R1 N-N6+ 4 R×N Q×R 5 P-N6! A picturesque position has arisen, in which even Black's extra rook cannot avert the pawn check on N7. See how beautifully attempts by Black to set up a defence are refuted.

a) 5...P×P 6 P×P Q×Q 7 R×R+ Q-N1 8 P-N7+ R×P 9 P×R+ K×P 10 R×Q+ K×R, and with his extra pawn White easily wins the endgame;

b) 5...Q×Q 6 P×Q R×R 7 P×R B×KP 8 P-N7+ K-N1 9

B–R2+ R–B2. At first sight it appears that White has not achieved anything, but a series of subtle manoeuvres allows him to demonstrate the advantages of his position. 10 B–B4 B–B4 (the black bishop endeavours to occupy its K4 square) 11 P–N3 P×P 12 P–R4 B–Q5 13 B×R+ K×B 14 P–Q6+ K–N1 15 P–Q7 B–N3 16 P–R5, and White's passed pawns are unstoppable.

3 P–N6!

Queens and rooks don't matter! The issue is decided by the white pawns.

3 . . .   **N×Q**

4 P×N (*15*)

White is a whole queen down, and yet his pawns are so strong that his opponent's superior forces are unable to stop them.

Here are some possible variations:

a) 4 . . . R×R 5 P–N7+ R×P 6 P×R+ K–N1 7 B×P+ and mate in two moves;

b) 4 . . . R–N1 5 P–N7+ with mate in three moves.

c) 4 . . . P×P 5 R×R+ K–R2 6 P×R Q–B5+ 7 K–R1 B×P 8 B×P+ K×P 9 R–QR8+ K–N2 10 B–K3+ ;

d) 4 . . . B–B2! 5 P–N7+ K–N1 6 P×B+! R/K2×P (*6 . . . R/B1×P loses to 7 B×P+*) 7 R×R! Q–K4+ 8 K–R1, and Black can resign, since if the rook is captured by king or queen

then 9 B–R2 decides, while 8 . . . R×R still loses to 9 B×P+.

There remains but one chance to save the game, which is what Black tried.

4 . . .   **R2–QB2**

5 P–N7+   **K–N1**

6 P–Q7!!   **Q–N6+**

7 K–R1 (*16*)

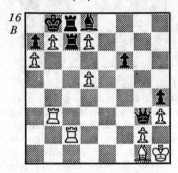

A fantastic position. It represents the ultimate triumph of mind over matter – the two white pawns on N7 and Q7 have conquered the whole black army, even with the extra queen in its ranks.

The author was all set to send off the manuscript to the editor, when some chess players from the German Democratic Republic drew his attention to an interesting possibility.

After 1 P–B5 P–N4 2 P×P N–K5 3 P–N6, the following most unexpected defence is possible: 3 . . . P×P 4 P×P Q×NP+!!

Since the king cannot capture the queen, White must play 5 R×Q N×Q. After this, by continuing 6 P–N7+ N×P 7 P×N+ R×P 8 R–R2+ K–N1 9 B–R7+ K–R1 (*9 . . . K–B2 10 R–QB2+ K–Q3 11 R2×R R×R 12 R×B+*) 10 R3–R3!, he can still reach a winning position.

It is more difficult for White to win after an analogous sacrifice in the variation 1 P–B5 N–K5 2 P×P

Q×NP+!! Here he has to agree to the variation 3 R×Q N×Q 4 P–N7+ N×P 5 P×N+ R×P 6 R×R K×R 7 R–N7+ R–B2 8 R–N4! P–B4 9 R–N4+ K–R1 10 R–KB4 with only a better endgame.

If you take into account that players all over the world have been analysing this combination of Alekhine for over half a century, you can't help being amazed at the unlimited possibilities in chess!

The games given so far demonstrate the breadth of Alekhine's imagination, his rare ability to discover combinations. While still young, Alekhine was noted for his unusual combinative vision. But, as is well known, by itself the ability to make combinations is insufficient – one must also be able to think strategically, and build up the correct plan. Although Alekhine was recognized for his mastery of positional play only in later years, a number of games of the young Alekhine show him to be an outstanding strategist.

6) **Alekhine–Tarrasch,** Mannheim 1914
Gioco Piano

1 P–K4	P–K4
2 N–KB3	N–QB3
3 B–B4	B–B4
4 P–B3	Q–K2
5 P–Q4	B–N3
6 0–0	P–Q3

An ancient variation of the Gioco Piano, which has nowadays completely disappeared from important tournaments. This opening does not set the players great strategic problems, and therefore does not satisfy modern masters, who have become accustomed to complicated set-ups and subtle strategic schemes.

7 P–QR4	P–QR3
8 B–K3	B–N5

Tarrasch considered it favourable to pin the opposing pieces, and never let slip the opportunity to limit the mobility of the enemy forces. However here it was better to refrain from the impulsive bishop move, and play the elastic 8 . . . N–B3.

9 P–Q5	N–N1
10 P–R5!	

'Weaker would be 10 B×B P×B, as Black's counter-chances along the open QB-file would compensate for the weakness of his Q-side pawns. The move in the game forces Black either to retreat the bishop to R2, which leaves the rook on a poor square after 11 B×B R×B, or else open the KB-file for White, leaving him with the initiative on both flanks' (Alekhine).

10 . . .	B×B
11 P×B	N–KB3
12 QN–Q2	QN–Q2
13 Q–K1	N–B4
14 Q–N1	B–B1

For some unknown reason Tarrasch decides to safeguard his bishop, and loses precious time. After the indicated 14 . . . B×N or else the transfer of the bishop via R4 to N3, Black would have every reason to face the future with confidence.

15 P–QN4	N4–Q2 (17)

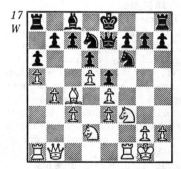

17
W

White can be satisfied with the results of his opening campaign:

besides his advantage in development he has seized a large part of the board. He holds the open KB-file, and has excellent chances of opening further files on the Q-side. Even so it is early to talk about a decisive advantage, which would allow White to launch an immediate attack: there are no noticeable weaknesses in Black's position, and he only needs two or three moves to make up his lack in development.

What plan should White adopt? Young Alekhine finds the best possibility, closely associated with the peculiarities of the position. A side which does not have a noticeable advantage, especially in the absence of weaknesses in the opponent's position, must limit itself to positional manoeuvring, so as to lure the opposing pieces out of hiding, and create weak points in the enemy camp. This is just what positional manoeuvring in chess consists of – it is one of the most difficult techniques of the game.

The reader should follow how skilfully Alekhine manoeuvres, gradually provoking weaknesses in Black's defensive set-up. Each of his moves is a probe to disquiet the opponent, and at the same time a telling blow against his solid armour.

16 N–R4!

It is easy to foresee that Black will not allow the white knight a threatening outpost on KB5, but this can be prevented only by advancing the KNP. After this the knight on R4 will be inactive, and will have to move back. So it was a waste of time? Not at all! The weakening of the K-side by . . . P–KN3 is so important that it is worth sacrificing two tempi to provoke it.

| **16 . . .** | **P–KN3** |
| **17 Q–K1** | **P–B3!** |

Tarrasch was never one to defend

passively. Now he intends to seize control of his important central square K4.

| **18 N4–B3** | **P × P** |
| **19 P × P** | **P–K5** (*18*) |

Where should the white knight move to? The majority of masters would reply: 'of course, to Q4'. But this would be a routine solution to the strategic problems, and Alekhine was always anything but routine. The course of his reasoning, which made him make the following original thrust with his knight, was roughly the following:

'The formation with a white knight on Q4, and a black one on his K4, leads to a status quo in the centre, and White has no objects to attack. My task is to weaken as much as possible Black's position in the centre and on both flanks. To this end the black KP must be kept under fire for as long as possible, besides which Black's K-side pawns must be forced into further advances. When I come to carry out the important breakthrough P–QN5, the opponent will have gaping weaknesses on all parts of the board'.

20 N–N5!

The start of a beautiful manoeuvre: from KB3 the knight is aiming for the important square . . . Q4! In choosing this path, Alekhine provokes the advance of the enemy infantry, which as usual leads to a weakening of his camp.

20 ...   **P–R3**

Immediately driving back the knight. Black would have a very poor position after 20 ... N–K4 21 B–N3! B–B4 22 B–R4+ K–B1 23 B–B2.

21 N–R3

Note that 21 Q–R4? loses to 21 ... N–R2.

21 ...   **Q–K4**

'Black over-estimates his counter-chances. He should still have played 21 ... N–K4, after which would follow 22 N–B4 B–B4 23 P–R3 P–R4 24 B–N3 R–QB1 25 P–B4 and then N–K2–Q4 with the better position for White' (Alekhine).

22 R–B1   **N–N5?**

But this is already a serious mistake. Also poor was 22 ... N × P, since there follows 23 B × N Q × B 24 N–KB4 Q–B3 25 P–B4!, and Black's position is cheerless. It was best to castle.

23 N–B4   **P–KN4**
24 P–R3   **N5–B3**

Or 24 ... P × N 25 P × P!, and White's attack becomes irresistible.

25 N–K2   **N × P**
26 B × N   **Q × B**
27 N–Q4! *(19)*

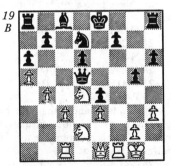

The triumph of Alekhine's strategic conception. After many wanderings, the knight has found its way all the same to Q4, but now in most favour-able circumstances. Black's K-side is seriously weakened, and the white pieces are threatening to break through on the KR5 and KB5 squares. Thus the deeply thought-out ma-noeuvre N/B3–N5–R3–B4–K2–Q4 in-stead of the immediate N–Q4 has enabled White to obtain a decisive positional advantage.

27 ...   **Q–K4**

It turns out that the black queen is almost encircled – there is a terrible threat of 28 R–B5 N–K4 29 P–B4! If after 28 R–B5 the queen attempts to escape on ... QR7, then it falls into another trap – 28 ... Q–R7 29 R–R1 Q–N7 30 N–B4!

This is why the queen tries to escape via K4. Against 27 ... N–B1 Alekhine intended 28 Q–K2! threat-ening N–B4–N6, and on 28 ... B–K3 29 P–B4 Q–K4 30 P–B5 P–Q4 31 P–B6 P × P 32 R × QBP followed by 33 R × RP, winning Black's Q-side pawns.

28 N–B4   **Q–Q4**
29 N–B5!

The fruitful manoeuvre by White's knight has conclusively weakened Black's position, and now the white cavalry enjoys mastery of the enemy camp. Black's position is beyond hope.

29 ...   **K–B1**
30 N/B5 × QP   **R–KR2**
31 R–Q1   **Q–B3**
32 R–Q4   **P–N4**
33 P × Pep   **B–N2**
34 N–R5   **1–0**

Subtle positional manoeuvres also enabled young Alekhine to win the following interesting game.

7) **Levenfish-Alekhine,** Vilna 1912
Ruy Lopez

1 P–K4	**P–K4**
2 N–KB3	**N–QB3**
3 B–N5	**P–QR3**

4 B–R4	N–B3
5 Q–K2	B–K2
6 P–B3	P–Q3
7 P–KR3	B–Q2
8 P–Q3	0–0
9 B–B2	

White has played a variation of the Ruy Lopez without any great pretensions. The slowness and indecisiveness of his opponent allows the young Alekhine to begin, immediately after the opening moves, energetic operations on the K-side. Strategically his actions are well-founded, and are closely linked with the peculiarities of the position, as is demonstrated by the further course of the game.

9 . . .	**K–R1**

'The restrained character of White's play allowed me to immediately begin preparations for an attack' (Alekhine)

10 0–0	N–KN1
11 R–K1	Q–K1
12 P–Q4	P–B3

'Following the principle that an advance of flank pawns is possible only when the centre has been strengthened' (Alekhine).

13 QN–Q2	**P–KN4!**

Exploiting the fact that White has lost time, and in effect handed over to Black the advantage of the first move, Alekhine seizes the initiative with both hands. How accurate was his understanding of basic chess strategy, how deep his calculation of the smallest details of a specific position! His correct strategy soon enables Alekhine to achieve a decisive advantage.

14 P–Q5	N–Q1
15 P–KN4	P–KR4
16 N–R2	N–R3
17 N/Q2–B1	P–B3
18 N–N3	BP × P
19 KP × P	Q–B2!

With this move Black not only attacks the white QP, but also plans to open the KB-file by . . . P–B4, and

begin an intrusion along it. Levenfish takes all possible measures to avoid the opening up of the position.

20 N–B5	N × N
21 B × N	B × B
22 P × B	Q–R2! (*20*)

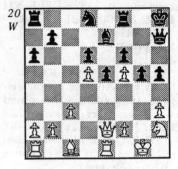

20
W

Alekhine unerringly exploits the weakness of White's K-side pawns – he now threatens by 23 . . . Q × P 24 Q × RP+ K–N2 followed by . . . R–R1 to decide the game using the open KR-file.

Can White hold the game? It all depends on whether he can prevent the position being opened up. As soon as Black's pieces are able to break out, their threats against White's weakened K-side will become irresistible. This is why Levenfish does all he can to contain the black pieces inside their own camp.

23 Q–K4	N–B2
24 N–B1	N–R3
25 N–K3	R–KN1
26 K–N2	B–Q1
27 P–QR4	P–R4!
28 P–N4!	

White understands that further delay is equivalent to capitulation, and so he hastens to provoke a lively battle on the Q-side.

28 . . .	P × P
29 P × P	B–N3
30 N–B4!	

The attack on the QP, together

with the open QB-file – it is on these that White is pinning his hopes. So as to obtain some counter-play, Levenfish sacrifices two minor pieces for a rook.

30 ...	**B–Q5**
31 B–N2	**QR–QB1**
32 QR–B1	**R × N**
33 R × R	**B × B**
34 Q–B2! (*21*)	

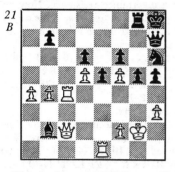

21
B

This is the point of the sacrifice. White plans to answer 34 ... B–Q5 by 35 R–B7 R–N2 36 R × R Q × R 37 Q–B8+ K–R2 38 R–QB1, and the threat of the rook's intrusion on QB7 is most unpleasant. So what does this mean – Alekhine's strategy was correct, but the results far from convincing? Nothing of the kind! After devising a deep strategic plan, and accurately carrying it out, he has not 'forgotten' to also foresee tactical possibilities. Giving back a piece, he initiates the long-planned attack on the king.

34 ...	**N × P!**

An excellent tactical resource! If White now captures the bishop, the intrusion of the black queen quickly decides the game – 35 Q × B N–R5+ 36 K–R2 N–B6+, or 36 K–R1 Q–Q6! 37 R–B3 Q × QP+ 38 P–B3 N × P, and Black wins.

35 R–B7	**Q–N3**
36 R–B8	

Here 36 Q × B is answered by 36 ... P–N5!, decisively breaking open the K-side.

36 ...	**P–N5!**
37 R × R+	**K × R**
38 Q × B	**P × P++**
39 K × P	**0–1**

After 39 K–B1 Q–N7+ 40 K–K2 Q–K5+ 41 K–B1 Q × R+! 42 K × Q P–R7 a new black queen would immediately appear on the board.

Having made his 39th move, White resigned, since Black has a forced mate: 39 ... Q–N5+ 40 K–R2 N–R5 41 P–B4 N–B6+ 42 K–R1 Q–R6+.

The mastery of a chess player and the universality of his talent are determined by several qualities. Besides combinational vision, tactical ingenuity, the ability to think strategically and to give an overall assessment of a position, there is also the distinctive art of endgame play. There even exists an unwritten rule – a player can become world champion only after completely mastering endgame technique. Alekhine, especially during his preparations for the match with Capablanca, had to devote a great deal of attention to the study of the concluding phase of the game, so as to even 'surpass the Cuban in endgame technique'. For the match with him in 1927, Alekhine arrived with a brilliant command of technique, although it should be said that, even during the early stages of his chess career, his mastery of endgame play was outstanding.

We will examine three more games from tournaments in the first period of Alexander Alekhine's chess life. The first of these illustrates his art in the playing of simple positions – when the queens have disappeared from the board. The reader will see how even then Alekhine was able to combine accuracy of technique with sudden bursts of fantasy – qualities which were soon to place him among the strongest grandmasters in the world. The two other games show the young Alekhine's mastery of analysis even in the endgame.

8) **Verlinsky-Alekhine,** St. Petersburg 1909
Ruy Lopez

1 P–K4	P–K4
2 N–KB3	N–QB3
3 B–N5	P–QR3
4 B × N	QP × B
5 P–Q4	P × P
6 Q × P	Q × Q
7 N × Q	

An ancient variation of the Ruy Lopez, which is rarely met in present-day tournaments. Only seven moves have been made, and already the queens and one minor piece each have disappeared from the board. Why has this happened? White hopes to exploit his pawn majority on the K-side, and for this the queens are not needed. Black's hopes are associated with his active bishops, which fully compensate for any positional defects

7 ...	P–QB4
8 N–K2	B–Q2
9 P–QN3	

This method of development was suggested by Emanuel Lasker 'himself'. However, the following pawn sacrifice caused it to disappear from tournament practice.

9 ...	P–B5!

Black seizes the initiative.

10 P × P	B–R5
11 P–QB3	0–0–0
12 N–Q2	B–B7
13 P–B3	B–B4!

See how active Black's pieces are, while White's, all bunched together, have a sad role to play. Besides,

White's king feels uncomfortable in the centre of the board. And all this for the price of a pawn !

14 P–QR4	N–B3
15 B–R3	...

Greater chances of saving the game were offered by the complex endgame with opposite-coloured bishops resulting from 15 N–Q4 B × N 16 P × B R × P 17 B–N2, and White can put up a determined resistance. Now his king is destined to perish in the centre of the board under fire from all the enemy pieces.

15 ...	B–K6!
16 N–KB1	B–R2
17 P–R5	R–Q6
18 P–B5	R1–Q1
19 K–B2	

A further inaccuracy, and this time the final one. A little hope was offered by 19 B–N4 R–Q8+ 20 R × R R × R+ 21 K–B2 N–Q2 22 N1–N3 R × R 23 N × R N × P 24 B × N B × B+ 25 N–Q4 P–QN3 26 P × P P × P, although even then great demands would not be made on Black's technique to realize his advantage.

19 ...	N–Q2
20 N–K3 (*22*)	

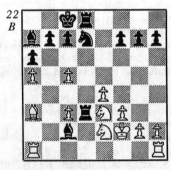

22
B

20 ...	N × P!

Precisely calculated ! After 21 N × B Black gives mate in five moves: 21 ... N × P + + 22 K–K1 (*22 K–B1*

R–Q*8*+ *23 R × R R × R+ 24 N–K1
N–Q7* mate) 22 . . . R–Q8+ 23
R × R B–B7+ 24 K–B1 R × R+
25 N–K1 R × N mate.

21 N–Q4   **B–N6**

After the combination comes a
quiet but convincing move. White
cannot defend his QBP, since he must
still not allow the check on his Q2.

22 K–K2   **R × P**
23 B–N2

This loses by force, although White
already had no satisfactory defence.

23 . . .   **R6 × N+ !**
24 K × R   **N–K3**
25 R–R3

No salvation is offered by 25
QR–Q1 B × R 26 R × B N × N, since
after the general exchange of pieces
the resulting king and pawn ending is
easily won for Black.

25 . . .   **N × N**
26 K–B4   **B–B4**
27 R1–R1   **N–K7+**
28 K–N4   **B–K3+**
0–1

9) Alekhine-Marshall, St. Petersburg 1914
Petroff's Defence

1 P–K4   **P–K4**
2 N–KB3   **N–KB3**
3 N × P   **P–Q3**
4 N–KB3   **N × P**
5 P–Q4   **P–Q4**
6 B–Q3   **B–Q3**
7 P–B4   **B–QN5+**
8 QN–Q2   **N × N**

White has played the opening
without challenging for the initiative,
and has allowed Black the chance to
fully equalize by 8 . . . 0–0 9 0–0
B × N ! 10 B × B B–N5 ! Instead of
this the American grandmaster strives
for exchanges, but loses several tempi
and gets into a bad endgame.

9 B × N   **Q–K2+**

It was still not too late to keep the

queens on, by playing 9 . . . B × B+
10 Q × B 0–0.

10 Q–K2   **Q × Q+**
11 K × Q   **B × B**
12 K × B   **B–K3**

Black is already hampered by his
lack of development. Since his QP
must be defended he does not succeed
in castling.

13 P × P   **B × P**
14 KR–K1+   **K–Q1**

Although both kings have stayed
in the centre, their fates are by no
means identical. The white monarch,
surrounded by his active pieces, is
excellently placed, while the black
king will feel uncomfortable for some
time to come.

15 B–K4 !   **B × B**
16 R × B   **R–K1**
17 R1–K1   **R × R**
18 R × R   **N–B3** (*23*)

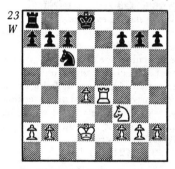

23
W

Although the sides are level on
material, the position can in no way
be called equal. With a series of
energetic blows on the K-side Alekhine obtains a decisive material
advantage.

19 R–N4   **P–KN3**
20 R–R4   **K–K2**

He is forced to give up a pawn.
After 20 . . . P–KR4 21 P–KN4
K–K2 22 P × P P × P 23 R × P White
would also have an extra pawn on
KR2, but it would be passed, and

Black would have very little chance of saving the game. But now outstanding technique is demanded from Alekhine in order to realize his extra pawn.

21 R × P	R–Q1
22 R–R4	R–Q4
23 R–K4+!	

This is the accurate move order. Before bringing up his own king, Alekhine wishes to determine the position of the black monarch. Since it is unfavourable to advance it in view of the possible intrusion by the white rook on K8, and since he does not wish to leave the KBP undefended, Black is forced to retreat to the back rank.

23 ...	K–B1
24 K–B3	R–KB4
25 R–K2	P–R3
26 P–QR3	N–K2
27 R–K5!	R–B3
28 K–Q3	P–N3

White has an extra pawn, but how is it to be realized? The ability to discover hidden possibilities of strengthening one's position is what is meant by endgame technique. It seems that Alekhine thought for a long time on this position, in seeking a way to win. The way in which he gains a winning advantage is both original and instructive.

29 R–K2! (*24*)

24
B

The rook is transferred to the QB-file in order to attack the QBP, which at one time the black king was forced to abandon. Besides, the position of the rook on the 2nd rank allows White to advance his king and knight.

| 29 ... | N–Q4 |
| 30 K–K4 | N–B5 |

Or 30 ... R–K3+ 31 N–K5 N–B3+ 32 K–B3.

| 31 R–B2 | N × P |
| 32 N–K5! | |

The threatened knight fork on Q7 leaves Black no time to defend his QBP.

32 ...	K–K1
33 R × P	R × P
34 N–B4!	

By returning his extra pawn, Alekhine has formed his small, but active forces into an efficient unit, which he soon throws at the enemy, easily overcoming resistance. Endgame techniques in chess are characterized by such transformations of material advantage into piece activity and vice versa.

34 ...	P–QN4
35 N–Q6+	K–B1
36 P–Q5	P–B3
37 N–N7!	

This provides a safe passage to the queening square for White's mobile QP, which Black's pieces are unable to stop.

37 ...	N–B5
38 P–N4	P–N4
39 P–Q6	N–K3
40 K–Q5! (*25*)	

A simple, but effective stroke. If Black takes the rook then the QP queens. However, Black will be forced to give up his rook for this pawn in any case.

40 ...	N–B5+
41 K–B6	R × P
42 N–B5!	

A whole rook – that will be the price for the QP.

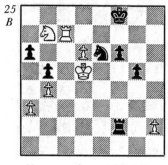

25
B

42 ...	R–Q7
43 R–B8+	K–B2
44 P–Q7	N–K3
45 N × N	K × N
46 P–Q8 = Q	R × Q
47 R × R	P–N5

At times one is surprised that strong players should continue resistance in positions where the win for the opponent is elementary. Evidently the champion of the United States could not reconcile himself to defeat.

48 R–K8+ K–B2 49 R–K2 P–B4 50 K–Q5 K–B3 51 K–Q4 P–B5 52 K–K4 K–N4 53 R–QB2 P–B6 54 R–Q2 K–R5 55 K–B4 1–0.

The following fascinating game was played in the first official championship of the Soviet Union.

10) Ilyin-Zhenevsky-Alekhine,
Moscow 1920
Ruy Lopez

1 P–K4	P–K4
2 N–KB3	N–QB3
3 B–N5	P–QR3
4 B–R4	N–B3
5 P–Q3	

The master Ilyin-Zhenevsky used to play this modest variation of the Ruy Lopez very well, and in the present encounter he obtains an excellent position from the opening. In this system of development White for the time being refrains from advancing the pawn to Q4, reserving

this possibility for a later stage of the game. In a number of games Ilyin-Zhenevsky obtained a decisive advantage namely by the opportune advancement of the pawn from Q3 to Q4. Nevertheless, modern theory recommends that the pawn should be moved two squares forward, after the preparatory P–QB3.

5 ...	P–Q3
6 P–B3	P–KN3
7 0–0	B–N2
8 R–K1	0–0
9 B–KN5	P–R3
10 B–R4	B–Q2
11 QN–Q2	Q–K1 (*26*)

26
W

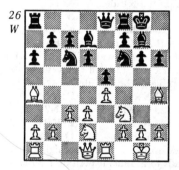

With the unambiguous threat of ... N–Q5, which White should have parried by retreating the bishop to B2. But for some reason Ilyin-Zhenevsky ignores the threat, and thereby significantly facilitates the solution of Alekhine's strategic problems.

12 N–B1	N–Q5
13 B × B	N × N+
14 Q × N	N × B
15 N–K3	P–QB3

The white knight now has no squares on which to invade, and the position must be considered roughly equal. At the same time the energetic advance ... P–KB4 could in some cases give Black a dangerous K-side initiative.

16 QR–Q1   **Q–K3**
17 P–KN4!

Bold and resolute. The pawn on QR2 does not matter; what is important is to prevent . . . P–KB4.

17 . . .   **B–B3!**

Alekhine was not in the habit of capturing doubtful pawns. He refuses the offer, and by the exchange of bishops strives to weaken the black squares on White's K-side.

18 B × B   **Q × B**
19 Q–N3!

White is seeking a sharp conflict, and plans the active P–KB4, which would immediately improve his chances on the K-side.

19 . . .   **N–B4**
20 N–N2   **N–K3**
21 R–KB1   **N–B5**

Effectively 'sealing' the . . . KB5 square, and radically preventing the opening of the KB-file.

22 N × N   **P × N**
23 Q–B3   **K–N2**
24 K–N2   **P–KR4!**
25 P–KR3   **Q–N4?**

A mistake, which straight away leads to a difficult position for Black. By continuing 25 . . . R–R1 followed by the transfer of the QR to K4 via K1, Black would have maintained a sound position.

26 R–KR1   **P–KB4**
27 KP × P   **NP × P**
28 R/Q1–KN1! (*27*)

White is conducting this part of the game excellently. He has accurately calculated the possible variations, and has taken into account all the tactical subtleties. If Black should now capture twice on . . . KN5 – 28 . . . BP × P 29 P × P P × P (taking with the queen loses to *30 K–B1!*), then White plays all the same 30 K–B1!, after which both 30 . . . P × Q 31 R × Q+ K–B3 32 R–N4! and 30 . . . P–N6 31 R–R5 Q–N3 32

27
B

R–R4! are bad for Black.

28 . . .   **BP × P**
29 P × P   **P–R5**

Alekhine must have been reluctant to make this move. Now his king is insecurely placed, while White's is covered by the black KB and KR pawns. Besides, hanging over Black's position is the terrible threat of exchanging all the pieces, after which White's king will capture the presumptuous pawns. Alekhine's mistake on his 25th move has caused him much difficulty, and he now has to demonstrate ingenuity and resourcefulness in order to save the game.

30 R–K1   **QR–K1**
31 K–R3   **K–N3**

This sets a cunning trap: after 32 P–Q4 Q–Q4 33 Q–Q3+ K–N4 34 P–B4 R–K6+!!   35 Q × R Q × R+! Black wins.

32 R–K2   **R × R**
33 Q × R   **Q–K4**
34 R–K1   **R–K1**
35 Q–K4+   **Q × Q**

Black sees the opponent's idea just in time. After 35 . . . K–N4? 36 Q–R7! Q × R 37 Q–N7 is mate.

36 R × Q   **R × R!!**

'I am proud that at the board I was able to work out with complete accuracy the following king and pawn ending' (Alekhine).

37 P × R   **K–N4**
38 P–B3 (*28*)

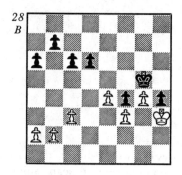

28
B

The chess journals of the time report that at this point the game was adjourned, and the players left for a meal. (In those days one didn't miss the chance of a bowl of soup and a piece of black bread.) Witnesses claim that on the resumption of play, before making a move on the board, Alekhine handed Ilyin-Zhenevsky a notebook crammed with the possible variations from the position in the diagram. The reliable and detailed

analysis came to the conclusion – draw!

38 ...   P–R4!!

Only this move leads to a draw. 38 ... P–Q4 loses immediately to 39 P × P P × P 40 P–N4 P–N3 41 P–R4. Also bad is 38 ... P–B4 39 P–R4 P–N4 40 P × P P × P 41 P–N3! or 38 ... P–N4 39 P–N4 P–B4 40 P–K5! BP × P 41 KP × P. In all these variations White puts his opponent into zugzwang, and forces the black king to abandon the KRP.

But after the problem-like move 38 ... P–R4!! the draw becomes clear after just two more moves.

39 P–B4

It was even not too late to lose – 39 P–N4? P × P 40 P × P P–N4, and now it is Black who wins. Nothing is achieved by 39 P–R4 P–N4 40 P–N3 P × P 41 P × P P–Q4! with a draw.

39 ...   P–N4
40 P × P   P × P
          ½–½

2 The Dream Comes True

By 1921 the wounds suffered by the western world during the First World War had to some extent healed, and in many European capitals chess once more came to life. International tournaments were held, the match for the world championship between Lasker and Capablanca took place, and there was no shortage of tours and simultaneous displays.

After travelling from Moscow to Riga, and then on to Berlin and Paris, Alekhine avidly set about playing chess. Just think, seven years wasted in war, hunger and devastation! While some grandmasters, in particular Capablanca, had not lost time, and had already played in several tournaments. This omission had to be made up for right away! So Alekhine played and played. . . . During his first six months abroad he took part in no less than three international tournaments, while also playing matches against grandmasters Teichmann and Sämisch.

During this first stage of his struggle for the world championship, the fervent Russian champion set himself two goals. Firstly, he had to straight away re-establish his position in the chess world, which had been somewhat undermined by his seven-year absence; he had to demonstrate that he, Alekhine, and no one else, was the immediate pretender to the chess throne. And there was also the purely every-day aim – he had to somehow provide for himself materially.

But life had to build literally out of nothing. This is why, for the whole of 1921, Alekhine roamed from one country to another, from one international tournament to another. At first Triberg, then Budapest, and finally The Hague. Three tournaments. But the Russian wanderer's journeying was not in vain – in all three tournaments he won first prize!

This set the chess world thinking. Here, it seemed, was the one to challenge the new world champion! Neither the 53-year-old Lasker, nor Rubinstein, who had declined since the war, were a danger to José-Raul, while the challenge offered by the chess originals – Reti and Nimzowitsch – could hardly be considered serious. Their desire to demonstrate the correctness of their views on chess theory seemed to prevail over practicality. But now Alekhine! He had both considerable theoretical knowledge, and great practical strength.

New triumphs began to be expected of Alekhine, while he too believed in his own prowess. Should he challenge Capablanca to a match or not? – This was the question he was faced with from his very first day abroad. It is true that he sent a challenge to the world champion, but this was merely a reconnaissance manoeuvre. How would José-Raul respond? Since he was almost certain of a refusal, he was not distressed when the refusal arrived: perhaps it was for the better. What was the hurry? He had first to become stronger, and establish himself firmly in the chess world. Also he should wait for the international tournament in London – the first appearance of the world champion after winning his title. He would come ahead of Capablanca in the London tournament, and then. . . .

Alas, fortune had prepared a blow against him. At the London international tournament Capablanca was in splendid form. The 34-year-old champion was at the height of his powers, and at the zenith of his successes. Surrounded by his halo of fame, contented, and not long married, José-Raul was the very messenger of 'chess heaven': every gesture, every move, displayed his confidence in victory; it seemed that all the secrets of chess had been opened to him.

How could anyone compete in those days with the brilliant envoy from Cuba? The world champion won game after game in London, drawing further and further away from his rivals. When the tournament was still far from finished, it became clear to everyone that it was to be an unprecedented triumph for the world champion. But for Alekhine, things did not turn out as well as he would have liked. It is true that, in this tournament as well, he was able to leave the other challengers behind, but neither on results, nor in quality of play, could he compare himself with the world champion.

And then came an unpleasant surprise. Capablanca circulated among the tournament contestants a new set of conditions, drawn up by him, for the conducting of world championship matches. There were a number of points, but one in particular was especially ominous for the challengers. 'If you wish to play a match with me,' – Capablanca's conditions read – 'by all means, but first you must provide a prize fund of ten thousand dollars'.

Ten thousand dollars! And besides that, about a further five thousand for the cost of organizing the match. It was a colossal sum! How could a challenger possibly accumulate it? Grandmasters were crestfallen, even the usually self-confident Alekhine was dejected. After commencing the London tournament fully hopeful of success, Alekhine finished it in a state of confusion. His attempts to overtake the Cuban had been unsuccessful, while the new conditions (which were designated the 'London conditions'), in effect deprived him of any possibility of a match.

On top of this he was depressed by the unsettled state of his personal life. His wife, who was wrapped up in her social affairs, could not devote much attention to her husband. In any case, she categorically refused to accompany him on any of his tournament travels. And Alekhine had no sort of home comfort, so necessary both for relaxation after tiring appearances, and for the great amount of work before him.

Evidently this moral depression and temporary loss of energy explains Alekhine's comparative failure in tournaments in 1923. He only managed to share fourth to sixth places at Vienna – it was the worst setback in the whole of Alekhine's chess career as a grandmaster. At the tournament in Margate he shared second to fourth places. It was absolutely clear that an immediate revision was needed, a review of the position, a strict self-critical examination. Alekhine said on a number of occasions: a chess player must know the strong and weak points of his opponent, but what is most important is to have a clear impression of one's own positive and negative qualities. The time had come to examine his 'chess mechanism' and to carry out extensive repairs.

And so Alekhine set about the examination of his chess arsenal. How he did this, unfortunately, remains a secret. But one of his methods of work is well known – he analysed in detail all the games he had played up to that point. This was best done while working on a book of his collected games. So just at this time he published a large and interesting volume *My Best Games of Chess* in which he makes detailed comments on his encounters with grandmasters and masters during the period 1908–1923.

There is no doubt that Alekhine took the opportunity to try out in practice ideas which occurred to him while working, and it is most probable that his poor results can be accounted for by this experimentation. The same reason explains, to a great extent, his refusal to take part in tournaments during 1924; in this year he took part in only one event – the New York tournament. Even here he did not let slip the opportunity to analyse in detail the sharp battles of this outstanding event, and published a collection of all the hundred and ten games of the tournament. Alekhine's comments were so profound, his analysis so deep and accurate, that after the book's appearance the chess press unanimously conferred on Alekhine the title of 'Best Chess Annotator'.

'Rarely has anyone been able to put across in a few simple words the essence of each position, as does Alekhine. A brilliant master of combination, he gives a profusion of convincing variations, which before him no one had been able to find; in those phases of the game which do not lend themselves to exhaustive analysis, he gives a general appraisal with a careful formulation of the basic plans dictated by the position for both sides.

'The main value of Alekhine's annotations is that in each game he discovers the turning points of the struggle – those critical moments, when a position from being better, almost unnoticeably becomes equal, from being equal – worse etc.'.

This was N. D. Grigoriev's appraisal of Alekhine's annotations.

Gradually his personal life also settled down to a more steady routine. At a ball in Paris he met the widow of General Vasilyev, Nadyezhda Semyenovna (née Fabritskaya), and after divorcing his first wife, soon made a new marriage. Nadyezhda Semyenovna was older than Alekhine, had a placid temperament, was highly cultured, and was able to provide him with everything necessary for a quiet life and for work.

While working on the novel *Byeliye i Chorniye*, which is devoted to the tragic life of Alekhine, and also after its appearance, the author carried out a lengthy correspondence with the daughter of Nadezhda Semyenovna by her first marriage – Gvendolina. She wrote about the life which the couple used to lead, and about the touching care with which Alekhine's wife used to regard his endless work and analysis.

Alekhine's time was not wholly devoted to chess. Since according to French law, the education he had received at the St. Petersburg Law College was not formally recognized in France, Alekhine decided to sit the necessary exams externally. Among my archives there is a letter sent by Alekhine to his Moscow friend Nikolai Dmitrievich Grigoriev. In it Alekhine asks Grigoriev to arrange things so that he is not invited to the Moscow international tournament (1925), since he does not want to have to refuse. And further on Alekhine explains why: 'Until the beginning of next year I do not intend to take part in any chess events, since I am utterly engrossed in preparations for my Doctor of

Law examinations, which I will sit this year at the end of November. This work demands a great deal of time – the main difficulty is becoming accustomed to French juridicial terminology'.

For almost seven years after leaving Moscow, Alekhine did not for one minute break his connections with Soviet chess players. The journal *Shakhmaty* regularly published his articles and analyses, while his numerous friends – chess masters, received letters from him with advice on various aspects of the game. Our journals and newspapers featured articles in which it was wondered whether, or even the hope was simply expressed that, 'Alekhine will soon return, he only has to beat Capablanca and then he will return'. There is no doubt that his associations with his native chess environment helped Alekhine in his striving to win the world title.

1924 was a fruitful and regular 'working' year in Alekhine's chess career, since immediately following his period of home study, he threw himself once more into the very heart of chess battles. During the first months of 1925 he played in three tournaments: in Paris, in Berne, and in Baden-Baden. Once again three tournaments and three first prizes.

And what first prizes! At Baden-Baden there were twenty-one contestants, but not one of them was able to force the uncompromising Russian to say the words 'I resign'. In all, only eight draws out of twenty games; twelve wins, including nine in a row. Alekhine's main rival in discussions about a match with Capablanca – Akiba Rubinstein – was one and a half points behind, the rest a further point or more.

In terms of points scored, it was a brilliant victory, but the creative aspect was even more striking.

His victories over Tarrasch, Nimzowitsch, and Marshall are part of the golden treasury of chess, while his win with Black against Reti is considered by many to be the most beautiful game ever played.

'We are witnessing a wonderful mystery: the hopes of the great Chigorin are beginning at last to be fulfilled' – wrote Tartakower after the tournament in Baden-Baden. 'And if Morphy was the poet of chess, Steinitz – the fighter, Lasker – the philosopher, Capablanca – the wonder-machine, then Alekhine, in keeping with the eternally restless and self-torturing Russian spirit, is showing himself to be the seeker of chess truth. . . .

'. . . We think that the chess world (and all of a generally cultural-sportive nature), eagerly following this wonderful flight to the height of chess fame, will find the inevitable comparison of Alekhine with the two world champions made easier by the following formulation:

'Capablanca has the title, Lasker has the results, but only Alekhine has the style of a real world champion'.

At this time Alekhine was 33 years old. Age is a critical factor in chess, and many maintain that a player reaches the height of his powers at 35. He had to hurry and challenge Capablanca to a match, otherwise it might be too late, and he might lose the chance to fulfill his whole life's dream. But how was it to be done? Alekhine had already made a number of attempts to raise money for a match in the United States, but, alas, as also earlier in Europe, without success. In reply to his requests, patrons simply lowered their eyes. 'What a crank, requesting money for an absolutely hopeless venture. Who can possibly defeat the invincible Capablanca? He is a man-machine, a chess computer! Faultless, impassive. No, let someone else take the risk'.

But he wasn't to be deflected from his intended goal! And Alekhine once again resorted to the method which he had practised in the past. By what means could he get through to these thick-skinned patrons, and force them to open their purses? There was only one way – to convince them, to force them to believe in the strength of the challenger, in the strength of himself, Alekhine.

And Alekhine began to surprise the chess world. This was one of his aims in writing the book *My Best Games*. It says: look at these games of mine, see how full they are of depth, brilliance, unexpected turns, and far-sighted combinations. What will you not find in this book; there are even combinations, calculated twenty moves deep, even a game with five queens! We are even introduced to a mysterious opponent – NN. By whom and when was Alekhine seen sitting at the board opposite this enigmatic NN?

As had happened previously, journals featured Alekhine's best games from the tournaments in 1925, especially those from Baden-Baden.

The brilliance of Alekhine's sparkling games – it was this that made a breach in the imperturbability of the patrons. And in addition there were his amazingly imaginative simultaneous displays, especially blindfold. Alekhine had despaired of finding the money in Europe, and was no more successful in the United States, so after receiving his Doctorate in Law, he set off to South America. There followed a series of triumphant successes in spectacular blindfold simultaneous displays on several dozen boards, in which head-spinning combinations occurred. And the result of all this was an announcement by telegraph from Buenos-Aires: 'The Argentinian government has provided the necessary sum of money for the meeting of Capablanca and Alekhine, between whom a match for the World Chess Championship will be held in Buenos Aires'.

The chess world was astonished: why should the Argentinians suddenly come up with the money? Some thought that it was simply the desire to demonstrate a new triumph for a representative of the Latin race – Capablanca. There was some truth in this, but it was not the whole truth. This was concealed elsewhere.

Since becoming world champion, Capablanca had only once gratified the admirers of his talent with a convincing tournament victory – in London in 1922. Year after year passed, but the long-awaited repetition of this triumph never occurred. At New York in 1924 he was second (after Lasker), and at Moscow in the following year only third.

So this is, in all probability, what the Argentinians thought: why not give our José the possibility of ridding himself in one blow of this tiresome Russian? Where could you find more congenial surroundings for Capablanca than in Buenos Aires? The support of the excitable inhabitants of the Argentinian capital could not fail to help him. Alekhine will be crushed – that's just what he needs. Let him see what it means to lift a hand against our José-Raul.

As far as Alekhine was concerned, the question was: now or never! It was the chance of a lifetime, and, of course, wouldn't happen again: who would put up money for a return match, were he to lose to Capablanca? It was his one chance, and therefore he had to be fully armed, and in his very best form. He had to prepare, and once again prepare!

EVERYTHING TO THE ACHIEVEMENT OF HIS GOAL!

One can imagine what an enormous amount of work Alekhine put into his preparations for the match with Capablanca, how many notebooks were filled, how many games analysed! Alekhine worked according to the principle which is already known to us – a chess player must know his own weak points. He had 'gained an understanding' of them following his failure at London in 1922, and also during the scrupulous analysis of his hundred best games for the book. Now he had to determine accurately the opponent's strong and weak points. The notes and conclusions made by Alekhine while studying Capablanca's games did not reach the chess world, but they were briefly formulated in his deep and philosophical foreword to the book *The New York International Chess Tournament of 1927*.

Above all else, a general conclusion was demanded – an appraisal of Capablanca's play at that time. At first glance this should have been enough to send Alekhine into despair: articles in newspapers and journals, written by prominent chess players, were full of headlines, such as: 'Is it possible to beat Capablanca?, 'Can a chess machine be beaten?' and so on. The easiness and elegance of the Cuban's play had everyone entranced, and it is understandable that no one noticed the patches on this radiant sun.

Courage and boldness were needed to come to an independent opinion, and challenge the opinions already established in chess circles. The machine was by no means faultless! In his games there occurred such inaccuracies, miscalculations and oversights, that he was in no way distinguished from the remaining 'sinners of this world'.

On arriving at such a conclusion, Alekhine makes the reservation: 'However I must emphasize that this criticism is only directed at the semi-mythical "super-player" title of Capablanca. For if you take the trouble to separate from his chess-playing ability his overwhelming legend, then you will come to the conclusion that he is a first-class master, whose strength lies more in intuition than in critical thinking'.

Later in the afore-mentioned article, Alekhine analyses all aspects of Capablanca the chess player. '1925 brought Capablanca the greatest disappointment' – writes Alekhine – 'that he was to experience in the whole of his international tournament career: at the Moscow tournament he took only third place, at the cost of enormous effort, and he lost two games . . . Already at that time certain voices from the press began to point out various disquietening symptoms . . . The reason for this lies in the distinct tendency over the last few years towards simplification, towards the possibility of settling the game by pure technique, which has killed in him that "spirit of life", which so clearly manifests itself in his games from the tournaments at San-Sebastian in 1911, and at St. Petersburg in 1914'.

Having given a general assessment of the imminent decline of his future opponent's striking natural talent, Alekhine destroys the myth of Capablanca's invincibility, his faultlessness. 'A chess machine? The champion of all time?' What absurd assertions about a player, in the overwhelming majority of whose games there is, if not a direct mistake, then two or three slips which either put the win in doubt, or even let it slip altogether. In some cases the correct reply by the opponent would even leave his (Capablanca's) position severely compromised . . .'

The conclusion is that there is no machine, but a mere chess player. Strong, versatile, and possessing a rare intuition, but nevertheless just a person, not a machine. And it is in man's nature to make mistakes, and it is perfectly possible for one man to beat another. This means that, having established the strength of the opponent, it is sensible to examine the details of his play, to determine how he plays the different stages of the game, what he likes and what is not to his taste.

After making an exceptionally detailed analysis of Capablanca's chess qualities, Alekhine came to some highly interesting conclusions, which were unexpected for many people at that time. Alekhine observed that Capablanca had a limited opening repertoire, but he did not draw the conclusion that he should use a variety of openings in the forthcoming match. Just the opposite! He also decided to play a small number of openings. But why? This was because of the instinct of self-preservation, which had been developed to a high degree by the Cuban. 'The instinct of self-preservation, by which he has nullified so many beautiful, enticing ideas, because of which he has placed so many rooks on open files in order to exchange them!' This instinct, to which at the present time his subtle intuition is almost wholly devoted, means that any attempt to obtain an advantage against Capablanca by an unexpected move in the opening is doomed to failure'.

And so this unparalleled defensive technique of Capablanca, based on simplification, forced Alekhine to choose special tactics in the match: not to prevent the opponent from seeking a solution to his opening problems by simplifying the position, but to meet him halfway, and to discover in these very simplifications small inaccuracies, insignificant weakenings of the position, and to exploit these for an energetic offensive.

Alekhine further determined two most important qualities of the world champion, which manifested themselves in the middlegame: extreme rapidity in the appraisal of a position, and very subtle, almost faultless intuition. Although these gifts of nature and of an early acquaintance with chess appeared to be great advantages, it was Alekhine's opinion that they served Capablanca badly. It had drawn him to the conclusion that 'the art of chess is very close to its end, it will soon be almost exhausted'. But how can you give your whole soul to a dying art?

This also explains the rapidity with which Capablanca was able to find the very best moves, which under closer examination turned out to be simply good moves. 'As a result of his not being "punished" for not making the best moves, he has become unaccustomed to that concentration of thought, which alone gives a guarantee against possible elementary oversights . . .' While Capablanca's self-confidence had grown without limit, and had practically reached self-adoration. . . .

Alekhine draws for himself an important conclusion from this scrupulous and deep study of his opponent: 'In the middlegame one should not simply trust him, rather every tactical possibility should be checked most accurately, since miscalculations on his part can by no means be ruled out'.

Along with the study of Capablanca's play in the opening and middlegame, his endgame technique was also examined. And here the conclusion reached was also unexpected: it turned out that the chess machine 'is not an exceptional master of the endgame, that . . . other masters in certain types of endgame surpass or used to surpass him (for example, Rubinstein in rook and pawn endings)'.

To sum up, the overall conclusion was: in the opening Capablanca is a powerful force only as a defender; the middlegame is his forte: in some cases he plays actively; in the endgame no first-class master need be afraid of him, 'here only in exceptional cases does he manage to rise above the ordinary. . . .'

Of course, in many of these words, which were written after the match, when relations between Alekhine and Capablanca had become strained, there is a great deal of subjective comment, but nevertheless we can boldly state: such a deep analysis of the virtues and shortcomings of an opponent had not been made before this, and perhaps has not been made since. This selfless work enabled Alekhine to detect deeply hidden defects in the play of his formidable opponent, and to draw up the most correct, and possibly the only, plan to defeat him.

'I cannot imagine that I will be able to win six games against Capablanca,' said Alekhine when he set off for Buenos Aires, (the victor was the first to win six games), 'but I also cannot imagine how Capablanca can win six games against me . . .'.

A TITANIC MATCH

The autumn of 1927 was drawing to a close, everything had been discussed, all details of the regulations had been settled. And suddenly . . . everything was almost blown sky-high! Not long before the start of the match, Capablanca's supporters decided to hold a large international tournament in New York. 'For safety's sake' Lasker was not invited – he might once again 'play a trick' and come ahead of their favourite! Other opponents dangerous to the world champion were similarly not invited.

This was nothing serious, but at the last minute the organizers included in the programme a cunning item: 'the winner of the tournament, or the second prize winner if the winner should be Capablanca, will receive the right to a match with the world champion'. This was a fine thing – once again they wanted to put to the test Alekhine's right, and perhaps ruin the Argentinian arrangements, all the preparations! The Argentinians had given the money to Alekhine, but they wouldn't give it to anyone else! That meant one player might not have the right, while another might not have the money? And Alekhine sent off a categorical protest, threatening not to come to New York. The organizers were forced to withdraw this 'trappy' suggestion.

And so we find Alekhine with his wife in Buenos Aires. Here everything 'breathed' of Capablanca. The Alekhines were greeted patronizingly, and in the looks of the Argentinians just one thought could be read: 'Never mind, you will, of course, lose and will understand that it wasn't worth even trying to dethrone our José-Raul. Play a dozen games or so, and then . . . go home. After that no one will try again to lay a hand on our chess hero'.

This is why Alekhine's win in the first game of the match was such a bombshell. Capablanca was surprised and despondent. What affected him most was not the fact of the defeat, but the character of it. This Russian played very exactly, he refuted a most cunning attempt to obtain a draw! Capablanca took a day off, and went away with friends to rest. A draw in the second game, and a win in the third. Both Capablanca's supporters, and Capablanca himself, breathed more easily. Everything now would go in the usual direction, everything would be in order. And it seemed that that was just what happened.

A win in the seventh game, and almost a win in the ninth. Although many would try to explain Alekhine's defeat as being due to some dental trouble (he had to have six teeth extracted) – even so the Cuban's horizon appeared cloudless. And suddenly – two terrible blows: a splendid counter-attack in the eleventh game, ending in mate with four queens on the board, and yet another, already the third, defeat for the world champion in the following, twelfth, game. And here the defeat was symptomatic – as the result of a blunder. One recalls that Capablanca was always somewhat demoralized after a defeat, and this fully explains why he lost a rook for a bishop in a comparatively simple position in the twelfth game. The chess throne was beginning to shake, the chess king began to get nervous. Capablanca even suggested to Alekhine that the match should be stopped, and a new one begun the following year. The intractable Russian did not agree.

At this most difficult moment Capablanca's natural fighting qualities came to the fore. By mobilizing all his determination, the world champion was able to draw the next eight games in a row. The spectators left bored and unhappy after these short, often uninteresting games. But everyone understood: Capablanca was playing for time in which to pull himself together.

Alas, he wasn't quite able to. Alekhine conducted the twenty-first game in masterly fashion. One more win for him – and the score stood at 4–2. Just two more wins separated Alekhine from his cherished goal. . . .

And the world waited excitedly, eagerly snatching at each announcement from Buenos Aires. Reports on the match were printed in Paris, London, Berlin, and of course Moscow. Letters were written to Alekhine from there, while Capablanca sent to Moscow reports and annotations of the games – he had agreed with the newspaper *Izvestiya* to do this during his stay in the Soviet capital in 1925. The dream that the chess throne would belong to a Russian was about to be fulfilled. But how difficult was the finish of this titanic encounter !

It seemed that the Cuban was morally depressed, but this was far from the truth ! Summoning all his will power, and helped by his outstanding instinct for self-preservation, Capablanca made tremendous efforts in each game. The twenty-second game looked hopeless for him. But no, by skilfully slipping out of the net in a most difficult position, the condemned chess king was able to put off the final blow. In the twenty-seventh game only a bad mistake by White allowed Alekhine to save himself by perpetual check, and then the twenty-ninth game was won by Capablanca. And once again the Cuban's supporters were heartened: 4–3 – he had almost saved the match ! Strictly speaking, it was almost equivalent to the score being equal, since, according to the conditions of the match, a score of 5–5 would terminate the match and leave Capablanca as the world champion.

Only the most knowledgeable chess players understood that this resistance of Capablanca was equivalent to the desperate blows of a boxer, who has lost both confidence and strength. The final collapse could be expected at any day. Alekhine's onslaught in the thirty-second game, and then some amazing play in all the stages of the thirty-fourth.

A second adjournment – and the news goes out by telegraph: 'Alekhine is on the eve of winning the title of World Champion'. There was only one more night to wait.

And then the following day. Oh, that wonderful following day! Alekhine arrives at the tournament hall with his wife. The judge starts the clock, but Capablanca is not there. The organizers become agitated, and keep looking at the door. But there is no sign of José-Raul. He is in no hurry to part with the chess crown. After all, who wishes to have his impressive title prefixed by 'ex'! But now a messenger rushes into the hall, and hands Alekhine a note. 'I resign the game and wish you success as World Champion. My congratulations to your wife'.

(Afterwards American newspapers for some reason preferred to describe an apparently friendly announcement by the opponents. But this was pure fiction, as I have specially checked through eye-witnesses).

There followed scenes of great enthusiasm. At that very moment Alekhine became lost in a great crowd of Argentinians, who had by now gone over to his side. The ecstatic throng carried him through the streets of the capital to his hotel.

All this happened ten thousand miles from Moscow. . . .

Tempestuous Buenos Aires saluted a new world champion.

The dream of Alekhine's Russian supporters had come true.

GAMES FROM THE YEARS
1921–1927

11) Treybal-Alekhine, Pistyan 1922
Ruy Lopez

1 P–K4	P–K4
2 N–KB3	N–QB3
3 B–N5	P–QR3
4 B–R4	N–B3
5 N–B3	

Treybal adopts a method of development which Alekhine himself chose on a number of occasions as White.

5 ...	B–K2
6 0–0	P–QN4
7 B–N3	P–Q3
8 P–QR4	R–QN1
9 P×P	P×P
10 P–R3	0–0
11 Q–K2	B–Q2
12 P–Q3	

It is bad to capture the QNP: 12 N×NP N×P 13 N×BP N×QP, and Black stands very well.

12 ...	Q–B1
13 K–R2	N–Q5
14 N×N	P×N
15 N–Q5	N×N
16 B×N	P–QB3
17 B–N3	B–K3!
18 P–KB4	

After 18 B×B P×B 19 P–KB4 B–B3 and then ... P–K4 Black would have an excellent position, but even so this is how White should have

played. White's impetuous pawn advances lead only to a worsening of his position, and in particular his QB remains inactive to the very end.

18...	B × B
19 P × B	R–R1
20 R × R	Q × R
21 P–B5	P–B3
22 P–KN4	P–B4
23 P–R4	P–Q4! (29)

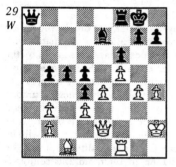

29
W

A counter-blow in the centre is the best way to meet a flank attack. The correctness of this very important law of chess strategy is confirmed in the present game.

24 P–N5

The alternative is 24 P × P B–Q3 + 25 B–B4 R–K1 26 Q–N2 B × B + 27 R × B Q–N1 28 Q–B3 Q–K4, with advantage to Black. No better for White is 24 P–K5 Q–N1! 25 B–B4 P × P 26 B × P B–Q3.

24...	QP × P
25 QP × P	

Now the black pieces take up threatening positions. It was better to seek chances in the endgame after 25 Q × P Q × Q 26 P × Q followed by bringing the king to the centre.

25...	Q–B3
26 K–R3	P–B5
27 P–K5	P–Q6
28 Q–K1!	

Alekhine's ability to calculate combinations is illustrated by the following variation, which was pointed out by him: 28 Q–K3 P × KNP 29 RP × P R × P! 30 R × R Q–K3 31 Q–K4 P–N3 32 K–N4 P × R + 33 Q × KBP Q × Q + 34 K × Q B–R6!!, and there is no defence against 35 ... B × P or 35 ... P–B6.

28...	P × KP
29 Q × P	B–N5!
30 P × P	P × P
31 Q–Q4!	

Treybal conducts a difficult defence with admirable mastery. While preventing the further advance of the QP, he simultaneously threatens to break up the black pawns by 32 P–N3.

31...   **Q–N4!**

Alekhine answers White's resourceful move with one no less resourceful. The black queen 'secretly' threatens White's rook 'through' the two black pawns: there threatens 32 ... P–Q7 33 B × P P–B6!

32 P–B6	P–Q7!
33 Q–B4! (30)	

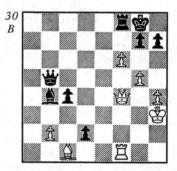

30
B

The best defence. Now 33 ... P × B = Q 34 R × Q R–B1 35 Q–N4 would give White chances of a draw. However the queen move allows Alekhine to carry out a combination of rare depth and of record length.

33...   **Q–Q2 +!**

'Black achieves a won pawn ending by the following combination, the longest I have ever made' (Alekhine).

34 K–N2	P–Q8=Q!
35 R × Q	Q × R
36 Q × P+	R–B2
37 Q × B	Q × B
38 Q–N8+	R–B1
39 P–B7+	K × P

In this position White played 40 Q–QN3+ ?, and after the reply 40 . . . K–N3 !, immediately resigned. The main variation of the combination, in which Alekhine calculated 20 moves ahead, would result after the subtle check by the white pawn on N6. Although this did not in fact occur, we have every right to consider this variation to be the logical conclusion of this interesting game, and therefore for the reader's convenience we give it as the main line.

40 P–N6+ !
The aim of this is to deny the black king the use of his KN3 square.

40 . . .   K × P!
This is the only way to win. It is bad to retreat the king to N1 in view of 41 P × P+, while after 40 . . . P × P the white queen gives perpetual check on QN3, QN8, QR3 and KB3, in this way always keeping the black rook under attack.

41 Q × R	Q × P+
42 K–R3!	

Bad is 42 K–B3 Q–B3+ 43 Q × Q+ P × Q!, and Black wins the pawn ending without trouble. White's task is to avoid the exchange of queens, but, as Alekhine has accurately calculated, he is not able to do this.

42 . . .	Q–B6+
43 K–N2	Q–Q7+
44 K–N3	Q–K6+
45 K–N2	Q–K5+
46 K–N3	

He cannot go to R3 – 46 K–R3 Q–B4+.

46 . . .	Q–K4+
47 K–N2	K–R4!

A 'quiet' move, which quickly decides the game.

48 Q–B3+
Other moves also lose quickly.

48 . . .	K × P
49 Q–KR3+	K–N4
50 Q × P	Q–K7+
51 K–N3	Q–N5+!

And after 52 K–B2 Q–B4+ or 52 K–R2 Q–R4+ the queens are exchanged.

The following game, which was played by Alekhine during the period of his preparation for the match with Capablanca, has passed into the golden treasury of chess as an example of accurate calculation, a model of inexhaustible inventiveness, a unique display of tactical-combinational blows. The reader who is playing over this game for the first time will be amazed at the ability displayed by Alekhine to maintain the combinative tension. Those, who have already had the pleasure of playing through the game, can once more, with excitement and delight, follow the many stages of this complex and astonishing chess battle.

12) Reti-Alekhine, Baden-Baden 1925
Reti Opening
1 P–KN3
Some time in the future a chess researcher may make a detailed study of changing tastes in chess, and explain why a particular move is considered good during one period, and denounced during another. The move 1 P–KN3 by White was for a long time condemned by theory, until the chess thinker Richard Reti came along and forced the theorists to change their views on the immediate flank development of the bishop. The years passed, and once again the move 1 P–KN3 fell into disfavour,

and was rarely adopted, but, as if to make up for it ... in every modern tournament you will find a number of games in which a similar advance of the black pawn 1 ... P–KN3 on the first move is regularly made.

1 ...	P–K4
2 N–KB3	P–K5
3 N–Q4	P–Q4
4 P–Q3	P × P
5 Q × P	N–KB3
6 B–N2	B–QN5+

The idea behind this apparently pointless check is simple: White intends to play P–K4, but now, after the plausible 7 P–QB3, the advance of the KP will leave the Q3 square seriously weakened. Therefore Reti finds a different way to defend against the check.

7 B–Q2	B × B+
8 N × B	0–0
9 P–QB4	

Reti usually used to link the first moves of his opening with deep, far-sighted plans: refraining from occupying the centre with pawns, he would postpone the struggle for the central squares until later, when the enemy pawns established in the centre would come under fire from the mobilised white forces. In the present game the advance of the pawn to QB4 forces the exchange of the opponent's central pawn, and there begins a complicated struggle for the centre, in which the chances are roughly equal.

9 ...	N–R3
10 P × P	N–QN5
11 Q–B4	N5 × QP
12 N2–N3	P–B3
13 0–0	R–K1
14 KR–Q1	B–N5
15 R–Q2	Q–B1
16 N–B5	B–R6!
17 B–B3	

Reti refuses the offered pawn

sacrifice, since after 17 B × B Q × B 18 N × NP N–KN5 19 N–B3 N4–K6! 20 P × N N × KP 21 Q × KBP+ K–R1 22 N–R4 R–KB1 White loses immediately.

17 ...	B–N5
18 B–N2	B–R6
19 B–B3	B–N5
20 B–R1	

On what trifles sometimes depends the creation of a work of art in chess, which is destined for glory and long life! A moment's caprice can prevent it from ever happening.

Were Reti to have played here 20 B–B3, then goodbye to the great combination, which for over half a century has delighted chess enthusiasts from all corners of the globe! A draw would have been agreed due to the position having been repeated three times. The caprice of fortune rules in the art of chess, though is this true only of chess?

20 ...	P–KR4!

From here and until the end of the game, Alekhine carries out an ingenious attack on the enemy king position. The point of the KR pawn's advance is clear: by exchanging pawns Black wants to weaken the important KN3 square.

21 P–QN4	P–R3
22 R–QB1	P–R5
23 P–R4	P × P
24 RP × P	Q–B2
25 P–N5	RP × P
26 P × P (*31*)	R–K6!

The next step in the storming of White's king position. The rook places itself en prise, and for six whole moves the sword of Damocles will hang over it. It is clear that the rook cannot be taken, as mate quickly follows: 27 P × R? Q × P+ 28 B–N2 N × P, while the rook itself threatens to capture on KN6.

27 N–B3	

31
B

Alekhine considered that this move is inaccurate, and after the game he said that 27 K–R2 was stronger, defending the KNP, and forcing the black rook to declare its intentions. But several years later analysts discovered that in this case 27 ... R1–R6 ! maintains Black's attack.

27 ...	**P × P**
28 Q × P	**N–B6 !**

Another important move in Black's combinational attack. If the queen retreats to B4, then 29 ... P–QN4 forces it all the same to give up the defence of the KP. So White decides to give up this pawn immediately.

29 Q × P	**Q × Q**
30 N × Q	**N × P +**
31 K–R2	

On 31 K–B1 Alekhine gives the variation 31 ... N × P + 32 P × N B × N 33 B × B R × B + 34 K–N2 R1–R6 35 R–Q8 + K–R2 36 R–KR1 + K–N3 37 R–R3 R/B6–N6, and Black wins.

31 ...	**N–K5 !**

Alekhine conducts the combinational attack in splendid style. Despite the absence of queens, the sharpness of the struggle is growing with every move. The knight move is associated with a multitude of complex variations, and is a preparation for the final multi-move combination.

32 R–B4 !	**...**

Reti finds the best defence. Worse would be 32 P × R N5 × R and White loses material.

32 ...	**N × BP**

At last Black's rook is rid of the troublesome KBP. Alekhine's move is once again the strongest; weaker would be 32 ... N × R 33 N × N ! R–Q6 34 N–B5 ! R × N 35 B × R or 32 ... B × N 33 R4 × N R × R 34 B × B.

33 B–N2 (*32*)

32
B

33 ...	**B–K3 !**

It is not at all easy to find one's way through the tangle of pieces. Alekhine finds a forced path to victory, and brings his attack to a dramatic conclusion.

34 R4–B2

The rook has no other retreat: on any other move 34 ... N–N5 + 35 K–R1 R–R8 + is decisive. However, even now this threat allows Alekhine to obtain a decisive advantage.

34 ...	**N–N5 +**
35 K–R3	**N–K4 +**
36 K–R2	

After 36 K–R4 the QR enters the game: 36 ... R–R5 + with a quick mate.

36 ...	**R × N !**
37 R × N	**N–N5 +**
38 K–R3	**N–K6 +**
39 K–R2	**N × R**

40 B × R	N–Q5! (*33*)
0–1	

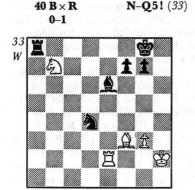

The final blow. After 41 R–KB2 N × B+ 42 R × N B–Q4! the stray knight on QN7 is lost. White therefore resigned. The final stage of Black's attack – the combination beginning with 33 . . . B–K3! – was calculated ten moves deep.

Alekhine had to calculate many variations before deciding to sacrifice his queen in the following game. On the other hand, it is an exceptional example of a positional queen sacrifice at such an early stage of the game.

13) Alekhine-Sämisch, Berlin 1923
Sicilian Defence

1 P–K4	P–QB4
2 N–KB3	N–QB3
3 B–K2	P–K3
4 0–0	P–Q3
5 P–Q4	P × P
6 N × P	N–B3
7 B–B3	

The modern theorist would smile on seeing this move, which blocks the advance of the KBP, and places the bishop on a poor square. Also the theorist would immediately find the best reply – 7 . . . P–K4! with an excellent position for Black. Evidently, 50 years ago the move . . . P–K4 was regarded as anti-positional, and even

such an important theorist as grandmaster Sämisch does not make it.

All this casts doubt on the relative value of the fashionable variations and systems which are adopted nowadays. At some time in the future the most ingenious set-ups in today's games will appear to the future critic to be no less inappropriate, or even absurd, than Alekhine's move.

7 . . . **N–K4**

'Played in order to obtain the two bishops, which constitute an illusory advantage in this position' – writes Alekhine. This is an instructive appraisal of the position, and a categorical solution to the notorious question of the advantage of two bishops over any other pair of minor pieces. Everything depends on the peculiarities of the position – this is the most reliable criterion to follow when exchanging minor pieces. Sometimes knights are stronger than bishops, in other positions the bishops are irrepressibly active – this was Alekhine's view on the problem of the two bishops, and it fully corresponds to the concrete approach to chess, which is generally accepted in the theoretical views of the Soviet chess school.

8 P–B4! **N × B+**

Rather than hurry with this exchange, it would have been better to first complete the development of his K-side pieces.

9 Q × N	B–K2
10 N–B3	0–0
11 P–QN3	N–Q2
12 B–N2	B–B3
13 QR–Q1	P–QR3
14 Q–N3	

The KBP is to take part in the action – with a swift advance it will strike a serious blow against Black's K-side.

14 . . . **Q–B2**

15 K–R1

Yet another 'atavism'; nowadays such prophylactic king moves are rarely made, since they lose an important tempo, and instead every possibility of the opponent obtaining counter-play along the KN1–QR7 diagonal is concretely calculated.

15 ...   R–Q1
16 P–B4   P–QN3

A mistake, which loses the game. But can Sämisch be reproached for this move? – after all, White wins by a combination which could have only been foreseen by a player possessing exceptional combinational flair.

17 P–KB5   B–K4 (*34*)

Sämisch hopes, after the queen moves, to consolidate his position by transferring the knight to KB3. Other replies also leave Black with an indifferent position, e.g. 17 ... P–K4 18 N–Q5 Q–N2 19 N–K6!, and White wins. Relatively best was the stubborn 17 ... R–K1.

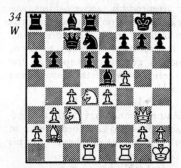

34
W

18 P×P!

This queen sacrifice brings White a speedy victory. Before deciding on the sacrifice, Alekhine had to calculate a large number of complicated variations to demonstrate its correctness.

18 ...   B×Q
19 P×P+   K–R1
20 N–Q5!!   1–0

The effect of this simple move on

Sämisch was so strong, that he immediately resigned the game. The following variations, calculated beforehand by Alekhine, show that Black has no defence.

a) 20 ... Q–N1 21 N–QB6 B–K4 (*21 ... Q–N2 22 N×R*) 22 B×B P×B 23 N×Q R×N 24 N–B7! (threatening *25 N–K8*) 24 ... R–B1 25 N–K6 P–N3 26 N×R N×N 27 R–Q8 K–N2 28 R1–Q1 R–R1 29 R1–Q6 B–N2 30 R×R B×R 31 R×QNP B×P 32 R×RP, and White's three Q-side pawns must win.

On his 21st move Black can make a different retreat with his bishop, but then after 21 ... B–R5 22 N×Q R×N 23 P–N3 B–N4 24 P–KR4 B–R3 (*24 ... B–B3 25 N×B P×N 26 R×BP!*) 25 P–KN4 White wins back his piece and remains with a decisive advantage.

b) 20 ... Q–R2 21 N–QB6 B–K4 22 B×B P×B 23 N×Q R×N 24 N×P R–B1 25 N×B R×N 26 R×N and 27 P–B8 = Q+.

c) 20 ... Q–N2 21 N–K6 B–K4 (mate on KN7 was threatened) 22 N×R.

d) 20 ... Q–B4 21 N–K6 B–K4 22 B×B P×B 23 N×Q P×N 24 N–B7 R–QN1 25 N–K8!, and Black can resign.

Although in the first of these variations Black could have continued the resistance, it is nevertheless not difficult to understand why grandmaster Sämisch decided to give up the struggle immediately.

The battle in the following game is based on a continuous stream of concrete variations. Alekhine's mastery in a tactical struggle is matched by his opponent's outstanding inventiveness and ingenuity, and this all adds to the value of this unusual game.

14) Alekhine-Reti, Vienna 1922
Ruy Lopez

1 P–K4	P–K4
2 N–KB3	N–QB3
3 B–N5	P–QR3
4 B–R4	N–B3
5 N–B3	

This is one more noticeable influence of the time: Alekhine used to
like this move, and often used it in
his most important games. It has
completely disappeared from the
repertoire of present-day masters.

5 ...	P–QN4
6 B–N3	B–B4

This move initiates a most interesting tactical skirmish, in which both
grandmasters demonstrate outstanding mastery.

7 N × KP!	N × N
8 P–Q4	B–Q3
9 P × N	B × P
10 P–B4!	B × N+
11 P × B	0–0
12 P–K5 (35)	

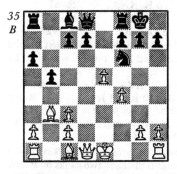

35
B

At first sight White appears to have
an undisputed advantage: the black
knight will be forced onto a bad
square – K1, and then the white
bishops will seize important diagonals.
But Reti has prepared an interesting
surprise.

12 ...	P–B4!

This is one of those cases when a
tactical blow also enables a strategic

problem to be solved. The threat of
... P–B5 means that the knight may
not have to retreat, while the advance
of the QBP has allowed the black
queen access to QR4.

The pawn thrust sets Alekhine
difficult problems, with which he deals
brilliantly.

13 B–R3!!

A move which sharpens the struggle
still further. Before making it, Alekhine worked out a number of variations, the most important of which we
give below.

a) 13 P × N R–K1+   14 K–B1,
but then after 14 ... P–B5 Black has
an excellent game;

b) 13 P–B4 P–Q4!   14 P × N
R–K1+   15 K–B1 Q × P followed by
16 ... QP × P;

c) 13 0-0 P–B5   14 P × N Q × P
15 Q–Q5 Q–QN3+ and 16 ...
B–N2;

d) 13 B–Q5 N × B   14 Q × N
Q–N3! 15 B–K3 B–N2 16 Q × QBP
Q–N3! once more with excellent play
for Black.

Alekhine's ingenious idea is met by
Reti with no less ingenuity!

13 ...	Q–R4
14 0–0!	Q × B
15 P × N	P–B5

It seems that White's bishop is
trapped, but in fact White has good
chances thanks to the mobility of his
queen and the threatening position
of his pawn on B6.

16 Q–Q5   ...

Not only threatening the rook, but
also mate by 17 Q–N5 P–N3 18
Q–R6. But Reti has foreseen all this,
and straight away parries both
threats.

16 ...	Q–R4!

Accurately played! If now 17
Q–N5, then Black gives check with
the queen on N3, and then captures
the KBP. While if 17 Q × R, then

Black plans to trap the queen by 17 ... Q–N3+ 18 K–R1 B–N2. It appears that it is White who is now in difficulties, but Alekhine has a long-planned saving possibility.

17 P × P !   Q–N3+
18 K–R1   K × P (*36*)

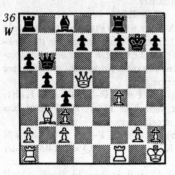

36
W

19 B × P !

With the help of a tactical trick the bishop breaks out of captivity. Now on 19 ... P × B   20 Q × R B–N2 21 QR–N1 ! Q × R   22 Q × R+ K × Q 23 R × Q it is White who wins. For this reason Reti decides to settle for a slightly worse endgame.

19 ...   B–N2 !
20 Q–K5+   Q–KB3
21 B–Q3   KR–K1 !

Subtly played. Now after 22 Q × Q+ K × Q 23 B × RP R–K7 ! the activity of Black's pieces fully compensates for his material deficit.

22 Q–R5   P–R3
23 Q–N4+   K–R1
24 Q × P   R–K2
25 Q–Q4   Q × Q
26 P × Q   R–Q1 !

Reti has temporarily sacrificed a second pawn, but is bound to win one back, and the excellent positions of his pieces give him every justification for counting on a draw.

27 P–B5 !

Worse is 27 P–B3 P–N5 ! 28 P × P

R × P, and the black pieces are very threatening.

27 ...   P–B3 !

Reti is careful to the very end. Hurriedly capturing the QP would allow Alekhine to weave a mating net around the black king by 28 P–B6 !

28 QR–K1

The variation 28 R–B4 R–N2 29 B–B1 R–QB1 ! 30 R–B2 R–B6 demonstrates best of all the strength of the active black rooks. In this case White would have no way of holding on to his extra pawns.

28 ...   R–N2 !
29 B–K4   R × QP
30 B × B   R × B
31 R–K6   K–N2
32 R × RP   R–QB5
33 R–B3

Alekhine also strives to activate his pieces. After 33 R–B2 R2–QB2 the QBP is lost.

33 ...   R × P
34 P–KR3   K–B2
35 R–KN3   R–B7
36 R–KN6   R × BP
37 R × RP   K–N2

There is little material left on the board, and little hope of realizing the extra pawn.

38 R–KR4 P–N5   39 R–N4+ K–B2 40 R–N3 R4–QN4 41 R–N3 K–N3 42 K–R2 R–QB4 43 R–R4 R4–QN4 44 P–R4 R4–N3 45 K–R3 R–N1 46 P–N3 P–B4.

So as to avoid the black king being forced to the back two ranks by P–N4.

47 R–R5 R–QB1   48 R–KB3 R–KB3 49 K–N2 R–B6 50 R–R8 R × R 51 K × R R–B3 52 R–QN8 R–B5 53 R–N6+ K–N2 54 P–R5 R–Q5 55 R–QB6 R–K5 56 R–KN6 + K–B2 57 P–N4.

This allows Black to transpose into a clearly drawn ending. But even with the rooks on the position was drawn.

57 ... R×P! 58 R×R P×R+
59 K×P K–N2 ½–½.

During the period of his preparation for the match with Capablanca, Alekhine played a number of most interesting combinative games, which amazed the world by their unprecedented flights of fantasy and depth of concept. Among them were games full of combinations, where a far-seeing calculation was decisive; there were others where the outcome was settled by one single move. But this move was always a surprise to the opponent, stunning him by its originality and unexpectedness.

At this time Alekhine was already being called a genius of chess combination. He himself did all he could to maintain this reputation, portraying certain games with ostentatious commentaries, trying to present chess in such a way that there was no doubt about the exceptional chess talent of Alekhine – the challenger for the world championship. Only in this way could he hope to collect the necessary fifteen thousand dollars.

Among Alekhine's combinational achievements a special place is held by his game against Bogoljubow from the Hastings tournament of 1922. In it Alekhine carries out an ingenious sacrificial combination, in which three black queens, one after another, take part!

15) Bogoljubow-Alekhine, Hastings 1922
Dutch Defence
1 P–Q4   P–KB4
'A risky defence, which I adopt only in exceptional circumstances', – writes Alekhine. This opinion is not fully shared by modern theory and practice. A number of convincing victories have been won by Mikhail Botvinnik using this opening. And

nowadays many masters happily allow the sharp Staunton Gambit – 2 P–K4 P×P 3 N–QB3 N–KB3.

2 P–QB4	N–KB3
3 P–KN3	P–K3
4 B–N2	B–N5+
5 B–Q2	B×B+

Every player has his own way of using this early-developed bishop: one will exchange it, another will retreat it to K2. There are also those who defend the bishop by 5 ... Q–K2 or 5 ... P–QR4. It is difficult to say which is best – the decision is a matter of taste.

6 N×B	N–B3
7 KN–B3	0–0
8 0–0	P–Q3
9 Q–N3	

The basic question, which determines who is successful in such positions, is: can White carry out the central advance P–K4, or can Black forestall him by himself playing ... P–K4? It is not difficult to see that Black is significantly ahead of his opponent in the solving of this very important strategic problem.

| 9 ... | K–R1 |
| 10 Q–B3 | P–K4! |

Exploiting the fact that White cannot capture three times on K5 due to the undefended knight on Q2.

| 11 P–K3 | P–QR4! |

Not only preventing P–QN4, but also initiating a combinative offensive on the flanks and in the centre.

| 12 P–N3 | Q–K1! |
| 13 P–QR3 (*37*) | Q–R4! |

Along with his combinative mastery Alekhine demonstrates his deep understanding of strategy. The queen move gives the signal for active operations on the K-side, the object of which is to provoke a serious weakening of the pawns covering the white king.

After carrying out this important operation on the K-side, Alekhine,

37
B

convinced that a direct storm is unfeasible, begins encircling man-oeuvres, so as to approach the white king from the Q-side.

14 P–KR4

It is clear that once again White could not capture three times on K5; after Black's ... N–KN5 he would lose his queen. On the other hand, the unpleasant 14 ... P–K5, forcing the knight onto the back rank, was threatened.

Bogoljubow forestalls all his oppo-nent's threats, but in doing so seriously weakens his K-side, which is just what Alekhine wanted.

14 ...   N–KN5

Here the black knight occupies a menacing post, and White considers it necessary to drive it away. But this leads to a further weakening of his K-side.

15 N–N5   B–Q2
16 P–B3

The attempt, instead of this, to win the KP by 16 B × N B × B 17 P–B3 does not succeed. Black answers 17 ... P × P and after 18 P × N P × Q 19 P × Q P × N obtains a marked advantage.

16 ...   N–B3
17 P–B4

A necessary measure – Black was threatening by 17 ... P–B5 to finally destroy White's K-side pawn struc-ture.

17 ...   P–K5
18 KR–Q1

Bogoljubow eases his opponent's task. By playing 18 P–Q5 ! he could have maintained freedom of action for his pieces, and could have hoped for active play on the Q-side. Now Alekhine fully seizes the initiative.

18 ...   P–R3
19 N–R3   P–Q4!

The first part of the general strategic plan has been completed – White's K-side pawns have been weakened. With the advance of his QP Black begins the second stage; initiating lively play on the Q-side, he finally breaks through from the rear to the white king's position.

20 N–B1   N–K2
21 P–R4

Black was threatening by ... P–R5 followed by ... QP × P and ... N2–Q4 to take possession 'for ever' of the very important central Q4 square.

21 ...   N–B3!

But now the black knight breaks through with great force into the white position via ... QN5 and ... Q6.

22 R–Q2   N–QN5
23 B–R1 *(38)*

38
B

23 ...   Q–K1!

The struggle transfers to the Q-side. Black's threat is clear – he intends to capture on ... Q B5, leaving his opponent with an unpleasant choice – should he give up the Q RP, or the important central square Q5? Bogoljubow decides to give up the pawn.

24 R–KN2   P × P
25 P × P   B × P
26 N–B2   B–Q2
27 N–Q2   P–QN4!

Once again the struggle for the ... Q4 square. At the same time an interesting combination is prepared.

28 N–Q1   N–Q6

The first move of a combination with the theme of pawn promotion. If White now plays 29 P × P, then after 29 ... B × P 30 R × P N–Q4 Black obtains a very dangerous attack. In that case the main goal of Alekhine's strategic plan would have been realized: through the open lines on the Q-side Black's forces would have penetrated to White's back ranks, and would have exploited White's weak K-side without difficulty.

Bogoljubow decides to maintain material equality by capturing the Q RP, but a stunning surprise awaits him.

29 R × P   P–N5!
30 R × R

Bad is 30 Q–R1 R × R 31 Q × R Q–R1! 32 Q × Q R × Q, and the rook's intrusion will soon force White to capitulate.

30 ...   P × Q!

Alekhine gives up both rooks, but in return obtains a new queen. In the resulting position the queen together with the knight set up an irresistible attack on the white king, which, within a few moves, decides the game in Black's favour.

It is a fine combination by Black – you will soon be convinced of this, dear reader. For half a century now chess enthusiasts have admired the depth of Alekhine's conceptions, the width of his fantasy, his striking combinations.

A fine combination, and yet ... Almost half a century later a certain chess amateur showed that it was not at all necessary for Black to sacrifice his queen. After the simple 30 ... Q × R 31 Q–N3 (*31 Q–B2 N–K8*) 31 ... Q–R8   32 Q–N1 R–R1 or 32 ... Q × Q 33 N × Q R–R1 Black could have forced his opponent to resign literally within a few moves.

Suppose that Alekhine had found this simple possibility of 'cold destruction'. He would have won the game just the same, and a good deal more quickly. And no one would have been amazed by a wonderful combination ...

Points and art, plain tournament success and the joy of creation – how often do these clash in chess!

Everyone aims for success in tournaments, but a sincere thank you to those who sometimes forgo a certain point for the sake of creating a memorable masterpiece of chess art!

31 R × Q (*39*)

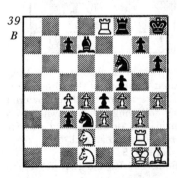

31 ...   P–B7!!

This is the position which Alekhine was aiming for. His opponent cannot prevent the appearance of a new queen.

32 R × R +	K–R2
33 N–B2	P–B8 = Q +
34 N–B1	N–K8!

The black pieces begin to disturb the enemy king. So in a highly original way Alekhine has carried out the final aim of his plan – through White's rear he has broken through at last to the white monarch's residence!

35 R–R2	Q × BP
36 R–QN8	

To meet the terrible threat of 36 . . . B–N4! White has to give up the exchange.

36 . . .	B–N4
37 R × B	Q × R
38 P–N4	

Activity, but alas – clearly belated!

38 . . .	N–B6 +
39 B × N	P × B
40 P × P	Q–K7! (40)

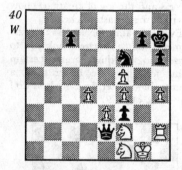

A position of zugzwang has been created – not one of the white pieces can make a move without material losses following. Only pawn moves remain, and Alekhine calmly waits for these to come to an end.

41 P–Q5

Both 41 N–R3 and 41 R–R3 lose to 41 . . . N–N5!

41 . . .	K–N1!
42 P–R5	K–R2
43 P–K4	N × KP
44 N × N	Q × N/K5
45 P–Q6	P × P

46 P–B6	P × P
47 R–Q2 (41)	

47 . . .	Q–K7!

A joke to finish with, but all in the same style. For an instant one more black queen appears on the board. Her rôle is to take play into the simplest of king and pawn endings.

48 R × Q	P × R
49 K–B2	P × N = Q +
50 K × Q	K–N2
51 K–B2	K–B2
52 K–K3	K–K3
53 K–K4	P–Q4+
0–1	

An unusual combination by Alekhine concludes the following game, which was played by him in this same period of intensive preparation for the world championship battle.

16) Grünfeld-Alekhine, Carlsbad 1923

Queen's Gambit Declined

1 P–Q4	N–KB3
2 P–QB4	P–K3
3 N–QB3	P–Q4
4 B–N5	B–K2
5 N–B3	QN–Q2
6 P–K3	0–0
7 R–B1	P–B3
8 Q–B2	

At that time this opening was just as fashionable as are nowadays the Nimzo-Indian Defence with 4 P–K3, or the Rauzer Variation of the Sicilian Defence. At present the classical Queen's Gambit is a rare guest in tournaments, but even so, any player wishing to improve should be acquainted with the opening.

8 ...   **P–QR3**
9 P–QR3   **P–R3**

We have already spoken several times of how certain ideas, or more often individual moves, of Alekhine, have, with the passing of time, aged and gone out of fashion. At the same time, many of Alekhine's suggestions, his accurate appraisals of certain positions, his characteristic observations, should not be forgotten – they have not lost, and will not lose, their value. This speaks for the deep penetration of Alekhine into the secrets of chess.

Here, for example, is Alekhine's comment about Black's move ... P–KR3 in the Queen's Gambit – a comment which retains its significance to this day:

'This move should not be made until Black has definitely decided on his further plan of defence, that is whether he intends ... P × P followed by ... P–QN4 and ... P–QB4, or else ... P × P and ... N–Q4. The move ... P–KR3 weakens White's attack in the Grünfeld Variation, where White transfers his bishop to QN1 via Q3–QB4–QR2, but it is bad in the defence ... P × P and ... N–Q4, since this gives White the possibility of retreating his queen's bishop to KN3, thus avoiding an exchange which would ease Black's defence'.

10 B–R4   **R–K1**
11 B–Q3

'White could have played P–R3, so as not to lose a tempo, since Black would have nothing better than to capture the QBP. However, it is not easy to decide whether or not the move P–R3 would be useful to White' (Alekhine).

11 ...   **P × P**
12 B × P   **P–QN4**
13 B–R2   **P–B4**
14 R–Q1

A significant loss of time. Surely White was not afraid of his QP being isolated? Grünfeld makes a series of passive moves and gradually slips into a bad position.

14 ...   **P × P**
15 N × QP   **Q–N3**
16 B–N1   **B–N2!**

Completing his development with the help of a small tactical finesse. Against 17 N4 × NP Black does not reply 17 ... P × N in view of 18 R × N, but 17 ... Q–B3 18 N–Q4 Q × P, with the better position.

17 0–0   **QR–B1**
18 Q–Q2   **N–K4!**
19 B × N

Grünfeld correctly decides that in the present position White gains no advantage from his bishop on KR4, and exchanges it for Black's good knight.

19 ...   **B × B**
20 Q–B2   **P–N3**
21 Q–K2   **N–B5** (*42*)

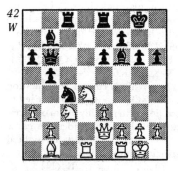

42
W

22 B–K4!

A cunning trap. The careless 22 ... N × RP is now answered by 23 Q–B3! B × B   24 N × B B × N   25 P × B followed by 26 N–B6+, winning the exchange. The Viennese grandmaster plays this part of the game accurately and confidently.

22 ...	**B–N2!**
23 B × B	**Q × B**
24 R–B1	**P–K4**
25 N–N3	**P–K5!**

This creates a strong point at ... Q6, which is quickly occupied by the black knight. Also threatened is 26 ... N × RP, but even so White's position remains quite defensible.

26 N–Q4	**R/K1–Q1!**
27 KR–Q1	**N–K4**
28 N–R2	

Oh, that desire to simplify a position by exchanging! Of how many good positions has it been the ruin! The energetic 28 P–B3 would have given White more possibilities.

28 ...	**N–Q6**
29 R × R	**Q × R**
30 P–B3 *(43)*	

The idea behind this move is correct, but the move itself is premature. By including the moves 30 N–QB3! P–B4, White could have then carried out the undermining pawn advance 31 P–B3. In his preliminary calculations Alekhine had intended then to sacrifice his rook on ... Q5, but, before capturing the knight, would no doubt have noticed that this loses after 31 P–B3 R × N 32 P × R B × P+ 33 K–B1 N–B5 34 Q–Q2 Q–B5+ 35 N–K2 P–K6 36 P–QN3!

Thus White's correct continuation was 30 N–QB3! – it would have led to a position with roughly equal chances. But now Alekhine decides the game by an interesting and far-sighted sacrificial combination.

30 ...	**R × N!**
31 P × P	

Or 31 P × R B × P+ 32 K–B1 N–B5 33 Q × KP Q–B5+ 34 K–K1 N × P+ 35 K–Q2 B–K6+. No better

43
B

in this line is 33 Q–Q2 Q–B5+ 34 K–K1 P–K6!

31 ...	**N–B5!**
32 P × N	**Q–B5!!**

Here it is, the dagger blow which spells immediate catastrophe for White.

33 Q × Q

And this leads to mate.

33 ...	**R × R+**
34 Q–KB1	**B–Q5+**
	0–1

Alekhine concludes the following game with a simple, but nevertheless spectacular combination.

17) Torres–Alekhine, Seville 1922
Ruy Lopez

1 P–K4	**P–K4**
2 N–KB3	**N–QB3**
3 B–N5	**P–QR3**
4 B–R4	**N–B3**
5 0–0	**P–Q3**
6 B × N+	

This move is also played occasionally at the present time. There was a time when the numerous continuations of this opening variation were the subject of study by theorists all over the world.

6 ...	**P × B**
7 P–Q4	**N × P**
8 R–K1	**P–KB4**
9 P × P	**P–Q4**

This is the critical position of the variation. The book recommendations are 10 N–B3 or 10 N–Q4, in both cases promising good prospects for White.

10 N–Q4	B–B4
11 P–QB3	0–0
12 P–KB4	

But this hands the initiative to the opponent. After the correct 12 P–B3 N–N4 13 K–R1 White has a promising position. Now Alekhine sets up dangerous threats by the simple advance of his central pawns.

12 ...	Q–K1
13 B–K3	B–N3
14 N–Q2	B–N2
15 N2–B3	R–Q1
16 Q–B2	P–B4
17 N–N3	P–B5!

Exploiting a tactical opportunity – if 18 B × B, then 18 ... P × N attacking the queen. Black's pawns have become most menacing.

18 N/N3–Q4	P–B4
19 N–K2	Q–B3
20 QR–Q1	P–R3

Intending to open the KN-file for a decisive attack on White's KN2 square. However, things don't get this far: Torres allows an unexpected and carefully concealed combination.

21 R–KB1	K–R1
22 K–R1	Q–N3
23 N2–N1	Q–R4
24 N–R3 (*44*)	

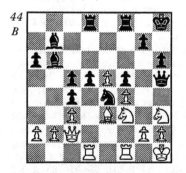

44
B

Thus White prevents the breakthrough P–KN4, but now the lightning strikes from a totally different direction.

24 ...	P–Q5!
25 P × P	

This leads to an immediate loss, but other replies similarly leave White with no hope.

25 ...	P × P
26 B × P	B × B
27 R × B	R × R
28 N × R	Q × N
29 P × Q	N–B7 + +
30 K–N1	N × P mate.

18) Alekhine–Colle, Paris 1925
Chigorin Defence

1 P–Q4	P–Q4
2 P–QB4	N–QB3
3 N–KB3	B–N5

In the first decades of this century the Hypermodernists announced their new principles on the understanding of the role of the centre. They taught that, during the first few moves, the centre should not be occupied by pawns, but should only be attacked by pieces. This led to the appearance of Reti's Opening, the King's Indian Defence, the Nimzo-Indian Defence and the Grünfeld Defence etc., which are popular to this day.

Such an opinion on the problem of the centre was not, however, the discovery of Reti or Nimzowitsch. Before them the great Russian player M. I. Chigorin had used the idea of attacking the centre with pieces. Proof of this is offered by the system of defence which he worked out, and which is adopted by Black in the present game.

4 Q–R4

An interesting idea. Alekhine sacrifices a pawn so as to set up strong pressure along the central files and diagonals.

4 ...	B × N
5 KP × B	P–K3

After 5 ... P×P   6 B×P Q×P
7 N–B3 and 8 B–K3 White rapidly
develops his pieces, which gives him
sufficient positional compensation for
the pawn.

6 N–B3	B–N5
7 P–QR3	B×N+
8 P×B	KN–K2
9 R–QN1	R–QN1
10 P×P	

Exactly the same moves were
played when the two players met in
the tournament at Baden-Baden in
the same year. Then Alekhine continued 10 B–Q3.

10 ...	Q×P
11 B–Q3	0–0
12 0–0	Q–Q3! (45)

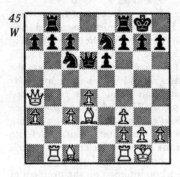

45
W

Colle conducts this part of the
game with subtlety. The queen prevents White from developing his
bishop at KB4, while at the same
time Black vacates his Q4 square for a
knight.

13 Q–B2	N–N3
14 P–KB4	N/B3–K2
15 P–N3	KR–Q1
16 R–Q1	P–N3
17 P–QR4	

A serious inaccuracy, since the QN4
square is weakened. Alekhine recommends 17 B–N2 followed by 18 P–B4.

17 ...	N–Q4!
18 B–Q2	

Now 18 P–B4 would be answered
by 18 ... N–N5.

18 ...	P–QB4
19 P–B5	

The bishops need space.

19 ...	KP×P
20 B×P	P×P
21 P×P	N4–K2
22 B–QN4!	

A purely Alekhine-like, concrete
understanding of the position. He
realizes that, in the given position,
the knights are more important than
the bishops, and immediately carries
out exchanges.

22 ...	Q–KB3
23 B4×N	Q×B/K2
24 R/N1–B1	R–Q4

24 ... P–N4 was stronger.

25 B–K4	R–Q2
26 P–Q5	Q–B3
27 R–K1!	

A cunning move, the meaning of
which becomes clear only at the end
of the game.

27 ...	R1–Q1
28 Q–B6	Q–N4

Colle does not sense the danger,
and falls in with his opponent's
wishes. 28 ... Q–Q5 was stronger.

29 B×N	RP×B? (46)

This allows White to carry out a
decisive combinative blow. Since
Black cannot capture the bishop with
his queen because of 30 Q×R, it
remains to consider 29 ... BP×B.
The struggle could then continue in
the following way:

a) 30 Q–K6+ R–KB2 31 R–B8
R×R   32 Q×R/8+ R–B1, and
White has a pleasant choice between
33 R–K8 Q–B3 34 R×R+ Q×R
35 Q–B6 with a favourable queen
ending, and continuing with the
rooks on the board – 33 Q–K6+
K–R1 34 P–Q6 Q–Q7 35 R–K2
Q–B8+ 36 K–N2 Q–B3+ 37 K–R3.

b) 30 Q–K6+ K–B1 31 R–B4

R–K2 32 R–B4+ K–K1 33 Q–N8+
K–Q2 34 R × R+ Q × R/2 35
Q × RP. Black can defend by 31 . . .
R–KB2, but then follows 32 R4–K4 !
K–N1 33 R–KB4 R1–KB1 34 P–Q6,
and White's advantage is obvious.

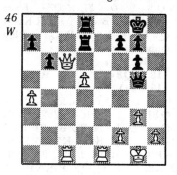

46
W

30 Q × R !

This sacrifice only works because
the black queen blocks her king's exit
on KN4.

30 . . .	**R × Q**
31 R–K8+	**K–R2**
32 R1–B8	**R–Q1**
33 R/K8 × R	**1–0**

At the early stages of his chess
career Alekhine was already an unparalleled master of the attack on the
king. But he achieved especial mastery
of this during the period of his preparations for the world championship
battle.

Alekhine formulated a number of
strategic and tactical principles. One
of these principles, which should be
followed when attacking the king,
will be found by the reader in the
notes to the following game.

19) Alekhine–Bogoljubow, Triberg
1921

Queen's Indian Defence

1 P–Q4	**N–KB3**
2 N–KB3	**P–K3**
3 P–B4	**P–QN3**
4 P–KN3	**B–N2**

5 B–N2	**P–B4**
6 P × P	

Nowadays 6 P–Q5 P × P 7 N–R4
is considered to refute Black's dubious
5th move.

6 . . .	**B × P**

But this is totally bad. After 6 . . .
P × P, bringing one more black pawn
towards the centre, Black could have
faced the future with confidence. Now
his opponent gains a significant lead
in development.

7 0–0	**0–0**
8 N–B3	**P–Q4**

Black hopes to solve all his opening
problems by exchanging on . . . QB5.
Alas, this does not work out: with a
series of energetic moves Alekhine
seizes the initiative.

9 N–Q4 !	**B × N**
10 Q × B	**N–B3**
11 Q–R4	**P × P**
12 R–Q1 !	

A very strong move. Where can the
black queen move to? If 12 . . . Q–K2
13 B–N5 P–KR3 14 B5 × N Q × B
15 Q × Q P × Q 16 R–Q7, and White
wins two pieces for a rook.

12 . . .	**Q–B1**
13 B–N5	**N–Q4**
14 N × N	**P × N**
15 R × P !	**N–N5** (*47*)

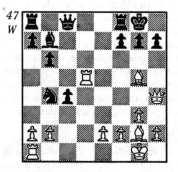

47
W

16 B–K4 !

'This is decisive, as is shown by the
variations given below. I should like

to draw the reader's attention to the similarity of this game to others I have played', – writes Alekhine (he has in mind games No. 20 and No. 26). 'The main peculiarity of these games lies in the unexpectedness of their rapidly successful attacks, which are always prepared far away from the point at which they are really aimed. In each case they are preceded by manoeuvring, of varying degrees of complexity, in the centre or on the Q-side, the aim of which is to lure the opponent's pieces away from the main scene of battle. And only then a lightning blow is struck (in all these games – a bishop move), followed usually by sacrifices, leaving the opponent with no chance of saving the game.

'These attacks based on the same plan, in games of completely different character, are, in my opinion, very significant, and could serve as material from which to form an opinion on a player's style, or at least, on the evolution of his style'.

This reasoning is very instructive. What has been the fate of this method? Have later players used it, have they been able to adopt it in their own games? Of course. The sudden offensive is the guiding principle in the play of a number of practical chess players. It is true that, to a large extent, this creative speciality of Alekhine was inherent in his individuality, but even so the method of veiled preparation for a sudden attack has also instructive significance for players wishing to improve their game.

16 ...   **P–B4**

Other moves also lose:

a) 16 ... P–N3 17 B–B6 N × R (besides *18 Q–R6*, also threatened was *18 Q × RP+* and *19 R–KR5+*) 18 B × N P–KR4 19 B–QB3 Q–Q1 20 Q–Q4 with unavoidable mate.

b) 16 ... P–KR3 17 B × P P–B4 (or *17 ... N × R 18 Q–N5 P–N3 19 B × N Q–KB4 20 Q × Q P × Q 21 B × B*. Also bad is *17 ... P × B 18 R–KN5+ !*) 18 Q–N5 R–B2 (after *18 ... Q–B2 19 B × NP Q × B 20 Q × Q+ K × Q 21 R–Q7+* Black loses) 19 R × P B × B 20 R × R K × R 21 Q × P+ K–K3 22 R–Q1 ! with a winning attack.

17 B × P !   **R × B**
18 R–Q8+   **Q × R**
19 B × Q

The game concluded: 19 ... R–QB1 20 R–Q1 R–KB2 21 Q–N4 N–Q6 22 P × N R × B 23 P × P R1–KB1 24 P–B4 R–K2 25 K–B2 P–KR3 26 R–K1 B–B1 27 Q–B3 R2–KB2 28 Q–Q5 P–KN4 29 R–K7 P × P 30 P × P 1–0.

20) Alekhine-Sterk, Budapest 1921
Queen's Gambit Declined

1 P–Q4	**P–Q4**
2 N–KB3	**N–KB3**
3 P–B4	**P–K3**
4 N–B3	**QN–Q2**
5 P–K3	**B–Q3**

A poor move, which provokes, strangely enough, a poor reply. The bishop is usually developed on K2.

6 N–QN5

A thrust which leads nowhere. After the correct 6 P–B5 B–K2 7 P–QN4 White would obtain serious Q-side pressure in the absence of any counter-play for Black in the centre.

6 ...	**B–K2**
7 Q–B2	**P–B3**
8 N–B3	**0–0**
9 B–Q3	**P × P**
10 B × BP	**P–B4 !**

Threatening to obtain an excellent position by 11 ... N–N3 12 B–Q3 P × P 13 P × P B–Q2. White is forced to exchange on B5, which leads to absolute equality.

11 P × P   **B × P**

12 0–0   **P–QN3**
13 P–K4

Striving to make up for his inaccuracy on the 6th move, Alekhine riskily goes in for a sharpening of the position.

13 ...   **B–N2**
14 B–KN5

Bad is 14 P–K5 N–N5! 15 N–KN5 P–N3 16 N×KP Q–R5 17 P–KR3 Q–N6, and Black wins.

14 ...   **Q–B1!**
15 Q–K2   **B–N5!** (48)

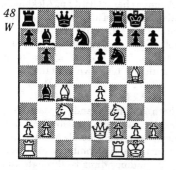

White's KP now appears to be indefensible, since the advance P–K5 is still unfavourable, for example, 16 P–K5 N–N5 or 16 QR–B1 B×N 17 B–Q3! N–B4 18 R×B B×P 19 B×N B×B – in both cases with advantage to Black.

Alekhine initiates double-edged tactical play on the Q-side, and in accordance with his principle of sudden attack, prepares the main blow on the K-side.

16 B–Q3   **B×N**
17 KR–B1!

Intending to answer 17 ... N–B4 – which was Black's best chance – with 18 R×B B×P 19 B×N B×B 20 Q–K3 P×B 21 P–QN4 B–N3 22 P×N P×P 23 R×P and then P–KR4–R5 with a dangerous attack, fully compensating for the pawn sacrificed.

17 ...   **N×P**

But this leads to defeat. For better or worse, Black had to go in for the variation indicated in the previous note.

18 B×N   **B×B**
19 Q×B   **N–B4**
20 Q–K2!   **B–R4**
21 QR–N1   **Q–R3**
22 R–B4   **N–R5** (49)

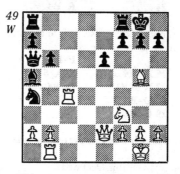

This move appears to save Black, since 23 P–QN4 is answered by 23 ... N–B6. But Alekhine makes a long-foreseen move, which decides the game instantly in White's favour.

23 B–B6

It turns out that the white queen is waiting in ambush; 23 ... P×B is answered by 24 R–KN4+ winning the black queen. On the other hand there threatens 24 R–KN4 Q×Q 25 R×P+ K–R1 26 R–N6 mate. 23 ... P–R4 does not rescue Black – there follows the same reply 24 R–KN4! followed by 24 ... Q×Q 25 R×P+ K–R1 26 N–N5 with inevitable mate.

Perhaps best was 23 ... P–R3, although even then the simple 24 N–K5 sets up a whole series of threats which Black is not in a state to meet.

23 ...   **KR–B1**
24 Q–K5!

The final blow, prepared in advance by White. Before making this move, Alekhine had to consider the following variations:

a) 24 ... Q×R 25 Q–KN5 K–B1 26 Q×P+ K–K1 27 Q–N8+ K–Q2 28 N–K5+ K–B2 29 Q×BP+ and 30 N×Q, winning easily.

b) 24 ... R×R   25   Q–KN5 R–KN5 26 Q×R P–N3 27 Q×N.

c) 24 ... P×B   25 R–KN4+ with mate in two moves.

| 24 ... | R–B4 |
| 25 Q–N3! | |

Simple and precise. White remains a whole piece to the good.

25 ...	P–N3
26 R×N	Q–Q6
27 R–KB1	Q–B4
28 Q–B4	Q–B7
29 Q–R6	1–0

21) Alekhine–Rubinstein, Carlsbad 1923

Queen's Gambit Declined

1 P–Q4	P–Q4
2 P–QB4	P–K3
3 N–KB3	N–KB3
4 N–B3	B–K2
5 B–N5	QN–Q2
6 P–K3	0–0
7 R–B1	P–B3
8 Q–B2	P–QR3
9 P–QR4	

In the 1920s this variation of the Queen's Gambit was highly fashionable, and was naturally subjected to thorough analysis. In particular, a great deal of effort was directed towards appraising the moves P–KR3 and P–QR3 for both White and Black. The matter revolved round the so-called struggle for a tempo: should Black capture the QBP immediately, and carry out the 'relieving' manoeuvre suggested by Capablanca (... N–Q4, and – after the exchange of bishops – ... N×N and ... P–K4), or should he delay the capture until White has developed his KB, thus

winning a tempo? Nowadays, when it is the King's Indian and Sicilian Defences which are popular, theorists are interested in different problems.

The move made by Alekhine, P–QR4, was also a subject for discussion, and had a number of adherents. This energetic thrust hinders Black's Q-side play.

9 ...	R–K1
10 B–Q3	P×P
11 B×BP	N–Q4
12 B–B4!	

A move characteristic of Alekhine's understanding of the problem of the centre. For the sake of including another pawn in the struggle for the central square K5, he agrees to a disruption of his pawn structure.

| 12 ... | N×B |
| 13 P×N | P–QB4 |

Both in play and in analysis, Alekhine successfully combined the specific with the general. Many of his statements and definitions are even today guiding threads through the labyrinth of strategic and tactical possibilities.

'This move, which goes against a basic principle – do not open new lines for your better developed opponent – is provoked by the desire to remove White's cramping pawn on KB4' (Alekhine).

| 14 P×P | Q–B2 |
| 15 0–0! | |

Worse is 15 P–KN3 in view of 15 ... Q–B3 16 B–K2 P–K4! with an excellent game for Black.

| 15 ... | Q×KBP |
| 16 N–K4! | |

Exploiting the fact that his opponent is behind in development, Alekhine initiates an immediate K-side attack. To this end he sacrifices a pawn – a recurrent procedure in chess – since here this is justified by all basic laws.

16 ...   **N × P**

This capture leads Black into serious
difficulties. Better was 16 ... B × P
17 N4–N5 N–B1! with a fully
defensible position.

17 N × N   **B × N**
18 B–Q3   **P–QN3**
19 B × KRP+   **K–R1**

A serious inaccuracy. The position
of the black king on ... R1 gives
White the possibility of inflicting a
number of telling tactical blows. It
was better to play the king to ... B1.

20 B–K4   **R–R2** (*50*)

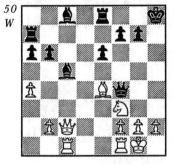

The rook is poorly placed on R2.
After the correct 20 ... R–QN1 play
could develop along the following
lines:

a) 21 P–KN3 Q–Q3 22 KR–Q1
Q–K2 23 N–K5 Q–B2 24 Q–B3
P–R4 25 N–B6 R–N2 26 Q–B3 with
the terrible threat of 27 Q–R5+.

b) 21 P–KN3 Q–B3 22 P–QN4
B–Q3 (otherwise *23 Q–B7* wins
immediately) 23 KR–Q1 Q–K2
(*23 ... R–Q1 24 R × B R × R 25
Q–B7*) 24 B–B6 R–Q1 25 R–Q4
P–N3 26 Q–Q2 K–N2 27 R–Q1
and wins.

The latter of these variations
(suggested by Alekhine) can be
improved for Black. By playing
25 ... K–N1! (instead of *25 ...
P–N3*) Black could still put up a
defence.

Thus moving the rook to ... QN1
would have left Black with hopes of
saving the game, whereas now he
loses by force.

21 P–QN4!

From here to the end of the game
everything is forced. Alekhine's series
of attacking moves, leaving Black no
choice of reply, makes up, in effect, a
forced combination.

21 ...   **B–B1**
22 Q–B6   **R–Q2**
23 P–N3!   **Q–N1**

Where else is there to retreat to? If
23 ... Q–Q3 then White wins by
24 Q–B4! (threatening *25 B–B6 R–B2
26 Q–R4+* and *27 B × R*), and
neither 24 ... K–N1, nor 24 ...
Q–K2 saves Black. After 24 ... K–N1
25 B–B6 R–B2 26 KR–Q1 Q–K2
27 Q–Q3! Black loses the exchange,
while on 24 ... Q–K2 25 N–K5!
R–Q3 26 B–N6! is decisive.

24 N–N5!   **R1–Q1** (*51*)

This allows a tactical stroke long
foreseen by Alekhine. However Black
no longer had a satisfactory defence.

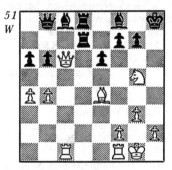

25 B–N6!

Gaining a tempo to transfer the
queen to KR7, which 25 ... B–N2
does not prevent, since White has
26 Q–B4. The whole depth of
Alekhine's far-sighted combination is
seen in the variation: 25 ... P × B
26 Q–K4 B × P 27 Q–R4+ K–N1

28 Q–R7+ K–B1 29 Q–R8+ K–K2
30 Q×P+ K–K1 31 Q–N8+ B–B1
32 Q×NP+ K–K2 33 Q×P mate.

25 . . .   **Q–K4**

Black prefers to give up the exchange, but he is lost just the same.

26 N×BP+	**R×N**
27 B×R	**Q–KB4**
28 KR–Q1!	**R×R+**
29 R×R	**Q×B**
30 Q×B	**K–R2**
31 Q×RP	**Q–B6**
32 Q–Q3+	**1–0**

The following game of Alekhine,
played more than forty years ago,
is considered to be a classical example
of an attack with pieces. The concluding stages are particularly effective.

22) Alekhine-Marshall, Baden-
Baden 1925
Queen's Gambit Declined

1 P–Q4	**P–Q4**
2 P–QB4	**N–KB3**

Marshall should hardly have tried
this dubious variation against such a
powerful strategist as Alekhine. White
gains a pawn centre which he can
defend without particular trouble.

3 P×P	**N×P**
4 P–K4	**N–KB3**
5 B–Q3	**P–K4**

This is the opening surprise that
Marshall had prepared. But it does
not help: with a series of accurate
and energetic moves Alekhine achieves
a decisive positional advantage.

6 P×P	**N–N5**
7 N–KB3!	

But not 7 P–B4? B–QB4 8 N–KR3
Q–R5+ with advantage to Black.

7 . . .	**N–QB3**
8 B–KN5!	**B–K2**
9 B×B	**Q×B**
10 N–B3	**N3×P**
11 N×N	**Q×N**

A serious mistake, for which the
most probable explanation is that

Marshall did not see White's following
elastic manoeuvre with his queen.
Otherwise he would have captured
with the knight: 11 . . . N×N, after
which 12 B–K2 0–0 13 P–B4 N–N5
14 B×N Q–R5+ 15 P–KN3 Q×B
16 Q×Q B×Q 17 K–B2 QR–Q1
18 P–KR3 would have given White
the better endgame, although all the
struggle would still be to come. But
now the white pawns begin an irresistible storm.

12 P–KR3   **N–B3** (*52*)

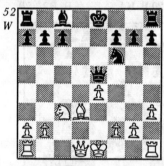

52
W

13 Q–Q2!

By two small advances the queen
transfers herself from Q1 to K3.
But what meaning there is behind
these insignificant steps! The queen
prevents Black from casting Q-side,
while at the same time preparing her
own king's castling, and, what is most
important, consolidates White's pawn
mass on the K-side, uniting it for the
decisive storm.

13 . . .	**B–Q2**
14 Q–K3!	**B–B3**

Poorly played. Had Marshall
played his queen to . . . QR4 he could
have then taken his king over to
the Q-side, thus sparing him his sad
fate. After 14 . . . Q–QR4! 15 0–0–0
Black would play 15 . . . 0–0–0, while
if White tried to keep the black king
in the centre by 15 B–B4, then the
pawn sacrifice 15 . . . 0–0–0 16 B×P

KR–B1 and 17 ... N × P would give him a splendid game.

15 0–0–0   0–0

Even here he could have tried to escape to the Q-side with his king by playing 15 ... Q–QR4. On the K-side the black monarch meets his fate literally within a few moves.

16 P–B4   Q–K3

16 ... Q–QR4 is bad in view of 17 P–K5 N–Q4 18 N × N B × N 19 B × P+ K × B 20 Q–Q3+ and 21 Q × B.

17 P–K5   KR–K1
18 KR–K1   QR–Q1

18 ... N–Q2 would be answered by 19 P–KN4, and the white pawns are irrepressible.

19 P–B5   Q–K2
20 Q–N5   N–Q4
21 P–B6   Q–B1 (*53*)

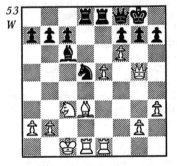

53
W

The swift advance of the KBP has placed Black under the threat of mate. Alekhine conducts the concluding part of the storm with utmost energy.

22 B–B4!

Black's knight has become an obstacle in the path of the white pieces. This move not only drives it from its favourable post, but also puts under fire the important point KB7.

22 ...   N × N
23 R × R   R × R

24 P × P!

This intermediate capture is an important detail in Alekhine's general plan to destroy the enemy king position. Black cannot capture on KN2, since his rook will be undefended, while after 24 ... Q–K1 White can win by 25 B × P+ K × B 26 R–B1+ K–K3 27 R–B6+ K–Q4 28 R–B8.

24 ...   N × P+
25 K–N1!

A further subtlety. Black must not be given a breathing-space: 25 B × N? Q–B4+.

25 ...   Q–K1
26 P–K6!

This is even stronger than 26 B × P+.

26 ...   B–K5+
27 K–R1!

Alekhine is accurate to the end. After 27 R × B R–Q8+ 28 K–B2 Q–R5+ 29 P–QN3 N–N5+ White might encounter certain difficulties.

27 ...   P–KB4

Or 27 ... P × P 28 B × P+ Q × B 29 Q × R+ K × P 30 Q–Q4+, winning in addition the bishop.

28 P–K7+   R–Q4
29 Q–B6

The most accurate.

29 ...   Q–B2
30 P–K8=Q+   1–0

and mates in two moves.

In his notes to the game with Bogoljubow, Alekhine talks about his attacks which are prepared far from the scene of the coming battle, and which suddenly spring on the opponent in places where he least expects them. There are a number of examples of such attacks in Alekhine's games; however, in his rich chess heritage there is a multitude of examples of different types of attack. Like many other masters of attack, Alekhine was able to systematically prepare an offensive, slowly mobilizing his forces until that moment when the superiority in number and mobility of the attacking pieces allowed him to carry out a decisive break-through of the front.

Here is one of these examples – a game, which was also played during his preparations for storming the chess throne.

23) **Alekhine-Asztalos,** Kecskemet 1927
Queen's Gambit Declined

1 N–KB3	P–Q4
2 P–B4	P–K3
3 P–Q4	N–KB3
4 B–N5	P–KR3
5 B × N	Q × B
6 N–B3	P–B3
7 Q–N3 !	

One of the variations which was studied and practised in tournaments in the 1920s and 1930s. White gains a significant amount of space, and at the same time has domination of the centre. These positional advantages are more important than Black's possession of the two bishops.

7 ...	N–Q2
8 P–K4	P × KP
9 N × P	Q–B5
10 B–Q3	B–K2

Passivity is the forerunner of defeat. The centre in chess always plays an important role, and in the present game it has decisive significance. Black should here have staked his claim in the centre by 10 ... P–K4. This would have given him the possibility of gaining space for his bishops, whereas now he is doomed to complete passivity.

11 0–0	0–0
12 KR–K1	R–Q1
13 QR–Q1	Q–B2
14 N–N3	N–B1

14 ... P–QB4 will not do, if only because of 15 P–Q5.

15 Q–B3	P–QR4
16 P–QR3	P–R5
17 N–K5	Q–R4
18 Q–B1	B–Q2
19 P–B5 !	

Completely restricting Black's forces, which now have only the two back ranks in which to manoeuvre. Alekhine clearly intends to transfer his knight from K5 via QB4 to Q6, where it will be invulnerable. Asztalos takes measures against this, but in doing so is forced to weaken his pawn structure.

19 ...	P–QN4
20 B–K4	Q–B2
21 Q–B3	B–K1
22 N–K2 !	

Alekhine demonstrates his mastery of positional play. One white knight is firmly entrenched on a central square, and now his colleague undertakes a lengthy raid via K2–QB1–QR2 to QN4, from where it will support the offensive operations of the white army.

22 ...	R–R3
23 N–B1	N–Q2

Urgent measures must be taken against the menacing set-up of the white pieces.

24 N × N	R × N
25 N–Q3	

But now this knight replaces his colleague, who has just left the battlefield, and aims for K5.

25 ...	R–Q1
26 N–K5	B–B1
27 P–R4 !	

White's pieces are ideally placed – while the black forces are confined to the edge of the board. Asztalos was planning to play 27 ... P–N3 and 28 ... P–R4, with some hope of disentangling his pieces, but Alekhine energetically prevents this. If now 27 ... P–N3 then 28 P–R5 P–N4 29 P–B4 ! with great advantage to White.

27 ...	R3–R1
28 B–N1 !	

White's threat is clear – to place his queen on QB2, and in answer to 28 ... P–N3, play 29 P–R5. This does not suit Black, of course, and he attempts to hold the onslaught of the white pieces.

28 ...	P–R4
29 Q–B3	P–N3
30 P–KN4 (*54*)	

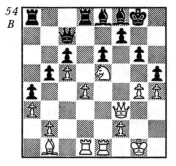

54
B

Slowly and methodically Alekhine has been accumulating positional advantages, and has achieved a great deal. He has an enormous advantage in space, and the activity of his pieces is at a maximum. Besides, he has managed to weaken Black's pawn structure on both flanks, especially on the K-side.

The period of building up his forces is completed, and Alekhine sets about destroying the defences around the black king.

30 ...	P × P
31 Q × NP	B–N2
32 B–R2 !	

Alekhine correctly decides that his bishop has better prospects on the QR2–KN8 diagonal. Thus the careless 32 ... Q–K2 is immediately refuted by 33 N × NP ! P × N 34 R × P.

32 ...	P–N5
33 B–B4 !	

He does not give his opponent the slightest chance. After 33 P × P P–R6 34 P × P R × RP Black's rooks could become unpleasant.

33 ...	P × P
34 P × P	Q–R4
35 Q–K4	Q–B2
36 Q–B4	QR–N1
37 P–R5	

Destroying one further obstacle on the path of the white pieces to the enemy king.

37 ...	P × P
38 K–R1	R–N2
39 R–KN1	Q–K2 (*55*)

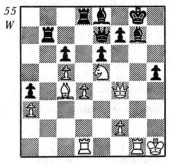

55
W

White has complete domination of the open KN-file – Alekhine's correct strategy of methodical concentration of his forces has given him a menacing K-side attack. The time has come for the realization of his positional advantage – and with his next move the sacrifices start.

40 R × B + !	K × R
41 R–KN1 +	K–R2
42 N × KBP !	1–0

Here Black resigned, thus cutting short this tense game at its most interesting point. After 42 ... Q × N 43 B–Q3 + Q–N3, it seems at first glance that White wins by 44 B × Q + B × B 45 R × B K × R 46 Q–K4 + K–N2 47 Q–K5 +, and one of the black rooks is lost. However, after 46 ... K–R3 ! (instead of *46 ... K–N2*) it is not immediately obvious how White can pick up one of the rooks.

It is probable that in answer to 43 ... Q–N3, Alekhine would have decided to continue the attack by 44 Q–N5 ! !, attacking the queen, the KRP and the rook on Q8. Black has only one reply – 44 ... Q × B (*44 ... R–N2 45 Q × P+* or *45 B × Q+ B × B 46 Q × R*). Then the following sequence leads to victory: 45 Q–N8+ K–R3　46 Q–R8+! Q–R2 (*46 ... R–KR2　47 Q–B8+*)　47 Q–B8+ Q–N2 (*47 ... R–N2　48 Q–B4+*) 48 R × Q R × R　49 Q–B6+ and 50 Q × R/Q8.

And here is one more example in which Alekhine concludes his attack with an elegant combination. In the main variation is hidden an unexpected and most refined piece of tactics.

24) **Kmoch-Alekhine,** Kecskemet 1927
Queen's Gambit Declined

1 P–Q4	P–Q4
2 N–KB3	P–QB3
3 P–K3	B–B4

White intends to adopt the so-called Colle System, in which the main role is played by the white bishop on Q3. Alekhine opposes in advance this bishop with his own.

4 B–Q3	P–K3
5 0–0	N–Q2
6 P–B4	KN–B3
7 Q–B2	

Kmoch correctly reasons that exchanging on B5 would only include Black's KP in the attack on the centre. He therefore forces the bishop to exchange or to retreat to N3.

7 ...	B × B
8 Q × B	N–K5
9 N3–Q2	N2–B3
10 N–QB3	

'After 10 N × N N × N　11 P–B3 N–B3　12 P–K4 P × BP　13 Q × P Q–N3　14 N–B3 R–Q1　15 R–Q1 B–K2 and then 16 ... 0–0, the centre White has acquired would require constant defence' (Alekhine).

10 ...	N × N/Q7
11 B × N	B–K2
12 P–K4	P × KP
13 N × P	0–0
14 B–B3	Q–B2
15 QR–Q1	QR–Q1
16 R–Q2	

Kmoch has played the opening stage of the game well, and now has an excellent position. But, beginning with this move, he gradually loses the thread of the correct plan, and finally gives up the initiative to his powerful opponent. White's best plan was to further strengthen his central position, and to prevent the freeing moves ... P–QB4 and ... P–K4. This aim was best served by the energetic advance 16 P–B4 !, cardinally preventing ... P–K4, and giving the possibility in some cases of P–B5. At the same time White would prevent the unpleasant advance of the black queen to ... KB5.

Alekhine exploits his opponent's inaccuracies with admirable accuracy and energy, and soon fully seizes the initiative.

16 ...	Q–B5
17 N × N+	B × N
18 R1–Q1	R–Q2
19 Q–N3	Q–B4
20 P–B4	

Played not with strategic aims, but with defence in mind – at the first opportunity Black would have played the dangerous move ... B–N4. The advance P–B4, which not so long ago was favourable to White, now weakens his position in the centre, and assists the development of his opponent's attack.

20 ...	R1–Q1
21 Q–K3	P–KR4!

The standard move for blocking the position; now 22 P–KR3 is answered by 22 ... P–R5!

22 P–QN4

But this is already a bad strategic oversight – after Black's reply the white squares in the centre become hopelessly weak. Kmoch should have continued manoeuvring inside his own camp, carefully watching out for any tactical threats.

22 ...	**P–QN4!**
23 Q–B3	

Capturing on N5 and advancing P–B5 were equally cheerless. This is why Kmoch seeks chances in tactical complications.

23 ...	**P × P**
24 Q × BP	**Q × P**
25 Q × BP	**P–K4!**
26 Q–K2	**P × P**
27 R–Q3	

White hopes, at the cost of a pawn, to block the position in the centre. But it turns out that Alekhine has completely different plans.

27 ...	**P × B!**
28 R × R	**R × R**
29 R × R	

Once again, and how many times has this happened, Alekhine's opponent does not allow him to demonstrate the full depth of his combinative thought. The strongest defence was 29 Q–K8 + K–R2 30 Q × R, to which Alekhine planned to play 30 ... Q–K5!! (*56*)

Despite the apparent profusion of possible defences, White's position is hopeless, as was foreseen by Alekhine when he made his exchange sacrifice. There threatens 31 ... P–B7 and 32 ... Q–K6+, and the attempt at perpetual check fails: 31 Q × BP P–B7 32 Q × KRP+ K–N1.

29 ...	**B–Q5 +**
30 K–R1	

30 R × B also loses after 30 ...

56
W

Q × R + 31 K–B1 Q–KB5 + 32 K–K1 Q × NP.

30 ...	**Q–QB8 +**
0–1	

Every great player introduces to chess something special, something new, which was previously unknown. For one player this innovation may be in the opening stage of the game – he discovers some new variations and systems, while sometimes he may give his name to an opening. Another may discover and formulate laws of strategy and tactics not known until that time. A third may surprise the world by his unparalleled technique. History also knows of those chess thinkers, who carry out their research in the field of chess psychology. They study and compare the state of a grandmaster after both a victory and a defeat, they analyse the data, and from it give conclusions and advice which are of great value to the practical player.

The greatness of Alexander Alekhine lies, in our opinion, in the fact that his chess genius embraces all aspects of chess mastery. The number of new moves, variations and systems which he discovered is considerable, he gave the world many wonderful endgames, he researched into many of the laws of chess psychology. And he formulated a number of important strategic principles. Alekhine the strategist played an abundance of games astonishing for the depth of their plans, for the precise formulation of their goals, and for their striking consistency of manoeuvre. In a number of cases Alekhine's strategic principles differed sharply from all that had been said by his great predecessors. His new, original laws and formulations have been studied by his successors.

In the field of strategy the greater part of Alekhine's discoveries and his practical achievements occur during the period of his preparations for the match with Capablanca.

While startling the chess world with his art of conducting combinative battles, Alekhine at the same time grew and perfected himself as a strategist.

In the following game we see Alekhine carrying out, with admirable precision and consistency, a broad strategic plan of squeezing his opponent on both flanks.

25) **Alekhine–Chajes,** Carlsbad 1923
Queen's Gambit Declined

1 P–Q4	N–KB3
2 P–QB4	P–K3
3 N–KB3	P–Q4
4 N–B3	QN–Q2
5 B–N5	B–K2
6 P–K3	0–0
7 R–B1	P–B3
8 Q–B2	P–QR3
9 P–QR3	R–K1
10 P–R3	

We have already spoken about opening set-ups of the type met in this game, and we will mention them several times later. Usually one meets here either Capablanca's relieving method (... P × P and ... N–Q4), or else the extended fiancetto (... P × P and ... P–QN4). Chajes adopts a further, perfectly possible,

system of development, which leads to the pawns being locked, leading to play of a closed, and hence slow, character.

10 ...	P–N4
11 P–B5	

On the exchange on Q5 Black's plan would have become clear – to attempt to place his knights on ... K5 and ... QB5. Alekhine's blockading move has a small tactical motif: White's P–KR3 prevents the freeing manoeuvre 11 ... P–K4 12 P × P N–N5 !, which would otherwise give Black an excellent game.

11 ...	N–R4
12 B–KB4 !	

Otherwise the freeing advance ... P–K4 cannot be prevented.

12 ...	N × B
13 P × N	P–QR4
14 B–Q3	P–N3
15 P–KR4 !	

Tactics serving strategic aims. Since Black cannot play 15 ... P–R4 because of 16 B × KNP, he is forced to allow the opening of lines by P–R5.

15 ...	B–B3
16 P–R5	N–B1
17 P–KN3	R–R2
18 N–Q1 !	B–KN2
19 N–K3	P–B4

The knight on K3 was preparing to move to N4, from where it would have been threatening a terrible check on R6 (after the exchange of pawns).

20 Q–K2	P–R5 ? (57)

This is unexpected. Alekhine was planning to carry out a lengthy re-arrangement of his pieces, with the aim of provoking the weakening ... P–R5, when suddenly Chajes makes this move voluntarily.

With this pawn on ... R4 Black could have initiated, at the appropriate moment, lively play on the Q-side, and thus distracted White's

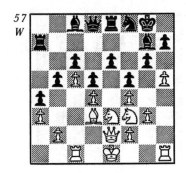

57
W

pieces from their K-side attack. Now, however, Alekhine can without fear turn his whole attention to the the K-side, since there is nothing to threaten him on the Q-side or in the centre. Moreover, the existence of the 'black-squared road' from K1 to QR5 gives Alekhine the possibility of creating threats from this side too, forcing Black to keep a permanent guard there.

White's first task is the following: he must open the KR-file, and try to do this when the object of attack – the KRP – must remain on the file. Then, combining the attack along this file with the threat of breaking through with the king via QR5 (in the endgame), or with a knight via QN4, he will have the chance to 'worry' the opponent on both flanks, and also in the centre.

21 N–B2!

Instantly changing course – the knight heads for QN4 instead of KN4.

21 ...	R2–K2
22 K–B1	B–B3
23 N–K5	B × N
24 Q × B	Q–B2
25 Q–B6!	R–B2
26 Q–R4	Q–K2

A serious mistake. After 26 ... R–N2 Black would be able to capture on N3 with his pawn. Now however, Alekhine at last has the chance to

leave his opponent with a weak pawn on ... R2.

27 P × P	N × P
28 Q–R5	Q–B3
29 B–K2	R–KN2
30 Q–B3	N–B1
31 Q–K3	R1–K2
32 N–N4	B–Q2
33 B–R5!	(*58*)

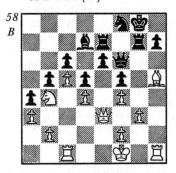

58
B

'This move leads to an amusing position, in which Black's queen, bishop, and both rooks have no move.

'However, White's task is far from solved, since not only doubling, but even tripling, of heavy pieces on the KR-file gets nowhere.

'The rather complicated plan which White intends to follow (with modifications, of course, depending on the opponent's manoeuvres), can be summarized as follows:

'1st part. Transfer the king to the centre, from where it is ready to quickly break through into the opponent's camp via QR5 in the event of the rooks and queens being exchanged on the KR-file. This will, of course, induce the black king to move to a new position, especially since he is needed for the defence of the KP and QBP.

'2nd part. Force the opponent's pieces one by one to leave the K-side by setting up tactical threats against the king and the enemy pawns (39th and 41st moves).

'White's threat to occupy K5 with his knight will tie down Black's knight to his Q2 square, which will make the harmonious interaction of Black's pieces, already hampered by lack of space, even more difficult.

'3rd part. Finally, at the appropriate moment – when the opponent's pieces are furthest removed from the K-side – double rooks on the KR-file, so that they can penetrate into the opponent's position following the forced exchange of queens and bishops.

'As will be seen, the implementation of this strategic plan took White no less than 28 moves !' (Alekhine).

33 . . .	**N–N3**
34 N–Q3	

Care is required even in such a blocked position. The unwary 34 K–K2 would lead to difficulties after 34 . . . P–K4 !

34 . . .	**B–K1**
35 K–K2	**K–B1**
36 K–Q2	**R–N2**

Since the main events are coming to a head on the K-side, both kings make for the Q-side where it is safer.

37 B–B3	**K–K2**
38 KR–K1	**N–B1**
39 N–N4	**K–Q1**

40 B × P ! was threatened.

40 K–Q3	**R/KN2–K2**
41 Q–Q2 !	**R–R2**
42 R–KR1	**R/K2–QB2**
43 R–R2	**B–N3**
44 Q–K3	**K–B1**
45 R1–KR1	**K–N2**
46 K–Q2	**R–K2**
47 N–Q3	**N–Q2** (59)

At first glance it appears that Black has defended successfully, and that there is nowhere for the white pieces to break through. In such positions the exchange of a particular piece can

59
W

have a decisive effect. In the given position it is sufficient to remove Black's bishop from the board for White to immediately either capture the KRP, or else penetrate into the heart of his opponent's position.

In the light of these considerations it is not difficult to find the next very strong move.

48 B–R5 !

This incursion on the K-side has become possible after Black has diverted several of his pieces towards averting the possible break-through via QN4 and QR5, and also towards keeping his . . . K4 square under control.

48 . . .	**R–R1**
49 B × B	**P × B**

If Black had captured with the queen, then White would have also transferred his queen to the KR-file, and would have settled matters either by the attack on the KRP, or by a break-through on the sixth rank.

50 R–R7	**R1–K1**
51 N–K5 !	**N–B1**

This cedes the important square K5 to the white knight, but after 51 . . . N × N 52 BP × N ! Q–B1 53 Q–N5 Black loses his KNP.

52 R–R8 !

An interesting subtlety. Just now Alekhine offered his opponent the exchange of rooks, whereas now he himself avoids the exchange. Why?

It turns out that the position has changed, and that now White's main task is to exchange queens!

52 ...	R–N2
53 N–B3	R–QN1
54 N–N5	R–K2
55 Q–K5!	

This exchange wins the game. Following it the rampant white rooks inflict on Black some terrible blows.

55 ...	Q × Q
56 BP × Q	K–R1
57 R–N8	P–N5

A desperate attempt to create counter-play on a distant front. Passive defence would be similarly unsuccessful.

58 R1–R8	R2–K1
59 P × P	K–R2
60 K–B3	K–R3
61 N–B7!	

Unexpectedly White gains the opportunity of mating the enemy king.

61 ...	R–R1
62 N–Q6	R/K1–N1 (*60*)

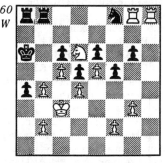

60
W

63 R–R1!	N–Q2
64 R–R1!	1–0

Alekhine, the clever and ingenious tactician, used here, of course, the old strategic principle of transferring his attack from the flank to the centre and vice versa.

In the following game a sharp battle begins in the centre, and then transfers to the vicinity of the white king.

26) Rubinstein-Alekhine, Semmering 1926
Queen's Indian Defence

1 P–Q4	N–KB3
2 P–QB4	P–K3
3 N–KB3	P–QN3
4 P–KN3	B–N2
5 B–N2	B–N5+
6 QN–Q2	

It has been long known that this is a poor move, since it allows Black to carry out without hindrance the two important freeing pawn moves – ... P–QB4 and ... P–Q4. The usual 6 B–Q2 is better.

6 ...	0–0
7 0–0	P–Q4
8 P–QR3	B–K2
9 P–QN4	P–B4!

The apparently active move 9 P–QN4 has only made this counter-thrust even stronger. Alekhine's action in the centre, which is aimed at breaking up the enemy pawns, soon allows him to seize the initiative.

10 NP × P	NP × P
11 QP × P	B × P
12 B–N2	QN–Q2
13 N–K5	N × N
14 B × N	N–N5!

The beginning of an operation which links Black's central action with a K-side offensive. It is difficult now for the white bishop to find a good retreat square; for instance, 15 B–N2 is answered by 15 ... Q–N3!

15 B–QB3	R–N1
16 R–N1	

A serious omission. Had White first exchanged on Q5 he would have been able to face the future with confidence. Now Black's QP becomes the key figure in some very sharp fighting.

16 ...	P–Q5!

17 R × B

And this loses quickly. Only 17 B–N4 B2 × B 18 K × B gave the possibility of a successful defence.

17 ...   R × R
18 B × B (*61*)

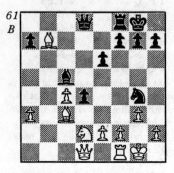

61
B

18 ...   N × BP!!

After originating in the centre of the board, Black's attack now transfers itself to the king's flank. This temporary piece sacrifice allows Alekhine to reach an original position, in which a far-advanced pawn ensures Black a decisive advantage.

19 K × N

In addition, White's king has to move out into the 'open field'. Other defences are weaker, for example:

a) 19 R × N P × B.

b) 19 B–R5 N × Q   20 B × Q P–Q6+ 21 P–K3 N × P.

c) 19 Q–R1 P × B   20 N–N3 N–N5+ 21 N × B Q–Q5+.

19 ...   P × B+
20 P–K3   P × N
21 K–K2   Q–N1
22 B–B3   R–Q1

Black's pawn is strong, while the white king will come under fire from all Black's pieces. It is not surprising that White capitulates within a few moves.

23 Q–N1	**Q–Q3**
24 P–QR4	**P–B4**
25 R–Q1	**B–N5**

26 Q–B2	**Q–B4**
27 K–B2	**P–QR4**
28 B–K2	**P–N4**
29 B–Q3	**P–B5!** (*62*)

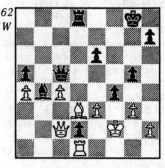

62
W

Here White overstepped the time limit, and just in time! Alekhine gives the following possible continuation: 30 B × P+ K–R1 31 Q–K4 Q × KP+ 32 K–N2 P–B6+ 33 K–R3 Q–K7 34 Q–N6 P–N5+ 35 K–R4 B–K2+ 36 K–R5 Q × RP mate.

27) Alekhine–Rubinstein, The Hague 1921
Queen's Gambit Declined

1 P–Q4	**P–Q4**
2 N–KB3	**P–K3**
3 P–B4	**P–QR3**

Before the present game was played, this advance of the rook's pawn, suggested by grandmaster D. Janowski, was very popular. Alekhine at once spoke out against the move, reckoning that it was merely a senseless waste of time. And yet Alekhine himself refutes the move by the repeated movement of one piece, and by the deep advance of one of his rook's pawns. So where is the logic here? It turns out that there is logic, in that Alekhine's understanding lies not in the mechanical counting of moves, but in the appraisal of the significance of a particular move in a given position.

4 P–B5	N–QB3
5 B–B4	KN–K2
6 N–B3	N–N3
7 B–K3!	

One has the impression that Alekhine's moves do not conform to any sort of logic; he wastes time on pawn moves and on the repeated movement of one piece. And yet, as the reader will soon see, it is profound chess logic that influences the Russian grandmaster.

7...	P–N3
8 P×P	P×P
9 P–KR4!	

'The only(!) way in which White can secure control of the black squares, and increase the scope of his bishop' (Alekhine).

9...	B–Q3
10 P–R5	N/N3–K2
11 P–R6!	P–N3
12 B–N5	0–0
13 B–B6! (*63*)	

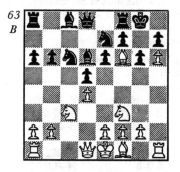

63
B

'A far from normal position after the thirteenth move of a Queen's Gambit. Out of his first thirteen moves White has made three with his KRP, and four with his bishop, after which he has reached a position, which, if not actually won, is very close to being won.

'The original opening of this game caused many to talk about the new "hypermodern" technique, the "Neo-romantic" school, and so on. In fact it can all be explained much more simply.

'In the opening Black made a number of eccentric moves (3 ... P–QR3; 5 ... KN–K2; 6 ... N–N3), which, if the opponent had not reacted to them (for example, if he had played 7 P–K3 instead of 7 B–K3, or 9 P–KN3 instead of 9 P–KR4), would have given him, in the end, a good game.

'And my advance of the KRP was not a preconceived idea; it was necessary to prevent Black gaining the advantage in the centre.

'But, as a rule, such experiments in the opening do not at all suit either my temperament, or my style, as the reader of this book can easily convince himself' (Alekhine).

13...	P–QN4
14 P–K3	B–Q2
15 B–Q3	R–B1
16 P–R4!	

After 'expanding' on the K-side in the very opening, Alekhine now seeks to activate his forces on the Q-side. Black can merely passively await the course of events.

16...	P–N5
17 N–K2 (*64*)	

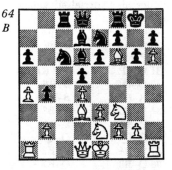

64
B

It is clear which route this knight intends to follow: K2–QB1–QN3–

QB5.

17 ...	Q–N3
18 N–B1 !	R–B2
19 N–N3	N–R4
20 N–B5 !	

Tactics at the service of strategy. The knight cannot be captured: after 20 ... B×N 21 P×B Q×P 22 B–Q4 Q–B3 23 N–K5 Q–Q3 24 N–N4 White wins. Thanks to the accurate calculation of tactical possibilities the white knight is able to remain at its advanced post.

20 ...	N–B5
21 B3×N	P×B
22 N–K5	

The only move of Alekhine's in this game which can be criticized. Stronger was 22 N–K4 ! with two threats: 23 N×B followed by 24 B–K5, and 23 B–N7 followed by 24 N–B6 mate.

| 22 ... | B×N/K4 |
| 23 B×N | B–Q3 ! |

This is the point ! The exchange sacrifice allows Black to put up a lengthy, though admittedly hopeless, resistance.

24 B×R	B×B
25 N×B	R×N
26 P–R5 !	Q–B3
27 Q–B3	R–Q4
28 R–QB1	

Great skill is still demanded of White for his material advantage to be realized.

28 ...	Q–B2
29 Q–K2	P–B6
30 P×P	P×P
31 Q×P	R×RP
32 Q–Q3	B–R6
33 R–B2	B–N7
34 K–K2 !	Q–B3
35 P–B3	P–B4
36 R–QN1	Q–Q3
37 Q–B4	K–B2
38 Q–B8	Q–R3+

Black has to exchange, since the white queen must not be allowed to reach KR8 ! White will find it easier to battle against the active enemy pieces in the endgame.

39 Q×Q	R×Q
40 P–K4	P–N4
41 K–Q3	K–N3
42 P–Q5 !	

Just so ! Black is unable to prevent the advance of this pawn.

42 ...	BP×P+
43 BP×P	P×P
44 P×P	R–R5
45 R–Q1 !	K×P
46 P–Q6	K–R4
47 P–Q7	R–R1
48 K–K4	R–Q1
49 K–B5	K–R5
50 R–KR1+	K–N6
51 R–R3 mate.	

The following game provides an excellent example of the strategic solution of the problems of the position. It was played by Alekhine against the leader of the chess school, which, at the start of the century, was called 'new', and which preached the necessity for strict observance of chess rules.

28) **Tarrasch-Alekhine**, Baden-Baden 1925
Gioco Piano

1 P–K4	P–K4
2 N–KB3	N–QB3
3 B–B4	B–B4
4 P–B3	B–N3
5 P–Q4	Q–K2
6 0–0	N–B3 !

Black has allowed his opponent to set up an apparently strong pawn centre, but this does not imply that he has approached the problem of the centre in a light-hearted way. Black's pieces and pawns are ready at any moment to 'throw themselves' at this centre, to weaken and even destroy it.

| 7 R–K1 | P–Q3 |

8 P–QR4	P–QR3
9 P–KR3	O–O
10 B–KN5	P–R3
11 B–K3 *(65)*	

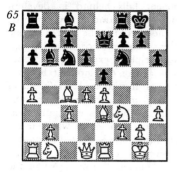

65
B

Everyone knows that a centre has to be attacked by pawns, but to invent a particular, original, and at the same time logically based method of such an attack – this is within the powers only of the elect. Alekhine's following move is one of the deepest made by him during his whole life, and at the same time one of the most unusual in the whole history of chess.

11 ...	Q–Q1!!

The black queen, which not long ago moved from Q1 to K2, moves back again, and we give the move two exclamation marks. A truly unusual occurrence !

'The most difficult move in the whole game', writes Alekhine in his annotations (incidentally, he also gives the move two exclamation marks, a thing which he does comparatively rarely). 'Black forces his opponent to declare the intentions of the well-placed bishop on QB4, since, on the one hand there is threatened (either immediately or a little later) the exchange on ... Q5 followed by ... P–Q4 with complete freedom, while, on the other hand, White's natural 12 QN–Q2 is met by 12 ... N × KP 13 N × N P–Q4, and in each

case Black obtains a very comfortable position. Finally, the move has the advantage that the K-file is left clear for the KR.

12 B–Q3	R–K1
13 QN–Q2	B–R2!

The bishop retreats in anticipation of White's N–B4.

14 Q–B2

Tarrasch, in accordance with the principles which he used to follow, maintains his pawn centre to the last, and even avoids P–Q5, which was, evidently, the best way out. Alekhine accurately weighs up the concrete situation, and within a few moves destroys White's apparently fine pawn centre.

14 ...	P × P
15 N × P	

Necessary, since capturing with the pawn is bad in view of 15 ... N–QN5.

15 ...	N–K4
16 B–B1	P–Q4!

White's centre is finished with. Now Black's pieces obtain great freedom, and start a determined counter-attack.

17 QR–Q1

Poor was 17 P–KB4 N–N3 18 P–K5 N–R4, and Black wins a pawn.

17 ...	P–B4
18 N4–N3	Q–B2
19 B–KB4	

Alekhine considered that more hope was offered by the continuation 19 P × P N × P 20 N–B4 N × N 21 B × N N × B 22 R × N R × R 23 P × R, though even then 23 ... Q–K2 gives Black a marked advantage.

19 ...	N–B6+
20 N × N	Q × B
21 P × P? *(66)*	

And this leads to defeat. The correct continuation was 21 P–K5 B–B4 22 Q–Q2 Q × Q 23 R × Q N–K5 24 R2–Q1 QR–Q1, and White can continue to resist.

66
B

21 ...   **B–B4!**
22 B–Q3

Now on 22 Q–Q2 there follows
22 ... Q × P   23 N–B1 B–B7   24
R × R + R × R   25 R–K1 N–K5   26
Q–B4 P–B5   27 N–Q4 B × N   28
P × B Q–N5! with a marked advantage to Black. But Tarrasch's move is
also no better.

22 ...	**B × P**
23 P × B	**Q × N**
24 R × R +	

Including Black's rook in the attack,
after which the showdown follows
within a few moves.

24 ...	**R × R**
25 B–B1	**R–K4**
26 P–B4	**R–N4 +**
27 K–R2	**N–N5 +**
28 P × N	**R × NP**
0–1	

A sudden finish occurs in the following interesting game, in which Alekhine's correct strategy, of combining
attacks in the centre and on the K-side, triumphs.

It is well known that if the opponent is behind in development, you
should try to engage him in a sharp
piece battle. The opponent will be
forced to attend to immediate threats,
and will not have time to complete
his development. This lack of development will be aggravated, and will
finally lead to the defender's downfall.

This strategic principle is not new,
but Alekhine was able to use it particularly often in his games. Many of
his games are examples in which his
opponent falls behind in development, and is strategically crushed;
the reader will now be able to see one
of these. It is worth commenting that
this principle of exploiting the opponent's lack of development by provoking an immediate battle is one of
the basic means of conducting the
struggle. It becomes especially clear
in certain openings, in which much
theoretical analysis is based on sudden
offensives. As examples one can cite
the bishop sacrifice on QN5 in the
Rauzer variation of the Sicilian
Defence, or the well-known attack on
K6 by B–QB4, N–Q4 and P–KB4–
KB5 in the Sozin variation of the
same defence.

29) Alekhine-Marshall, New York
1927
Queen's Pawn Game

1 P–Q4	**N–KB3**
2 P–QB4	**P–K3**
3 N–KB3	**N–K5**

A dubious move. At the same time
great attention should be paid to the
method by which Alekhine refutes
this premature advance.

4 N3–Q2!	**B–N5**
5 Q–B2	**P–Q4**
6 N–QB3	**P–KB4**
7 N2 × N	**BP × N**
8 B–B4	**0–0**
9 P–K3	**P–B3**

Simple arithmetic shows that White
has three pieces in play, and Black
only two. Besides, the bishop on N5
will have to retreat, or else be exchanged. White has a clear advantage
in development, which is why Alekhine soon provokes a battle in the
centre, beginning with the undermining move P–B3.

10 B–K2   N–Q2

As if it were not enough that Marshall has already wasted time, he now loses several further tempi. White's QB is so strong that Black has to exchange it off; this could have been achieved by 10 . . . B–Q3. Marshall carries out this exchange, but by a different, more lengthy, path.

11 P–QR3   B–K2
12 0–0   B–N4 (67)

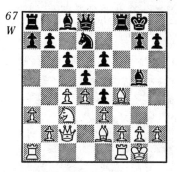

67
W

13 P–B3

White makes this advance while Black's QR and QB are still on their original squares, which seriously weakens the black army. 'Into battle!' – Alekhine orders his central troops, and their activity soon brings its rewards.

13 . . .   B × B
14 P × B   R × P

Marshall does not yet sense the danger. By playing 14 . . . KP × P 15 R × P N–B3 he could have temporarily held his opponent's forces, with the hope of completing his development. Now the centre is opened up, and White's rampant forces break through into the enemy camp within a few moves.

15 P × KP   R × R +
16 R × R   P–K4

Otherwise Black perishes from passivity. Now the game takes on an original character.

17 Q–Q2!

The inventiveness of an Alekhine was required to find this cunning move and to weigh up its consequences. Alekhine sacrifices a piece, after accurately calculating that his pawns, supported by the heavy artillery, can inflict the decisive blow.

17 . . .   P–B4

Marshall falls in with his opponent's intentions. In the case of 17 . . . Q–N3 18 P–B5 Q–R4 19 KP × P KP × P 20 P–QN4 P × N 21 Q–N5 Q–B2 White wins prettily by 22 P–Q6!

18 P × KP!   P–Q5
19 Q–B4!   P × N

19 . . . Q–K2 does not help: 20 N–Q5 Q × P 21 Q × Q N × Q 22 N–K7+ and mates.

20 Q–B7+   K–R1
21 P × P! (68)

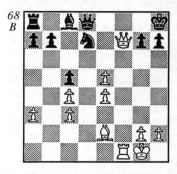

68
B

An original position, accurately weighed up by Alekhine. Black's three pieces still on their original squares are unable to successfully defend their own king. Having based his attack on the principle which we formulated earlier, Alekhine does not for one moment forget about the concrete calculation of possible variations. Thus, he decided to capture the pawn on QB3 only after convincing himself that the immediate 21 P–K6 was insufficient because of 21 . . .

N–B3 22 P–K7 Q–N1 23 R×N
B–N5! 24 Q×Q+ K×Q 25 R–Q6
R–K1 and Black threatens . . . P–B7.

21 ...	Q–N1
22 Q–K7	P–KR3
23 B–R5!	

A curious position. Black cannot
move any of his pieces (23 . . . K–R2
24 B–B7 Q–B1 25 B–N6+), while
the advance of White's KP is a serious
threat.

| 23 ... | P–R4 |

Or 23 . . . Q×P 24 B–B7 with a
swift mate.

| 24 P–K6 | P–KN3 |

No better is 24 . . . N–B3 25 B–B7
Q–R2 26 R×N P×R 27 Q–B8+.

| 25 P×N | B×P |
| 26 R–B7 | 1–0 |

This game was awarded a brilliancy
prize.

Alekhine made a significant contribution to the study, both theoretical
and practical, of positions in which a
pawn is sacrificed for the initiative.
It has long been known how difficult
it is to gauge correctly such sacrifices,
since the positional advantages obtained in exchange for the pawn can
be very small, and a deep understanding of the secrets of the position
is required in order to correctly weigh
them up.

We give two examples which
demonstrate Alekhine's mastery in
playing positions of this type. Both
games were played during the period
of preparation for his match with
Capablanca. Later on the reader will
encounter a number of subtle pawn
sacrifices in games played by Alekhine
in later stages of his chess career.

30) Tarrasch-Alekhine, Pistyan
1922
Blumenfeld Counter-Gambit

1 P–Q4	N–KB3
2 N–KB3	P–K3
3 P–B4	P–B4
4 P–Q5	P–QN4

This gambit was invented by that
outstanding Soviet master B. Blumenfeld. Black gives up a pawn, obtaining
in exchange a very strong pawn
centre. The impression made by the
present game was so strong, that after
it many began to refuse the dangerous
gift.

| 5 QP×P | |

Nowadays it is considered preferable to refuse the sacrifice and to
play 5 N–B3.

| 5 ... | BP×P |
| 6 P×P | P–Q4 (69) |

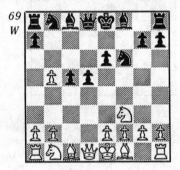

Black's centre is menacing and
invulnerable, while in addition he
has the open KB-file, and good diagonals (QR1–KR8 and QN1–KR7)
for both his bishops. All this gives him
full compensation for his sacrificed
pawn. Alekhine exploits the advantages of his position with great skill.

7 P–K3	B–Q3
8 N–B3	0–0
9 B–K2	B–N2
10 P–QN3	QN–Q2
11 B–N2	Q–K2
12 0–0	QR–Q1

Alekhine has first of all completed
the mobilization of all his pieces, and
now prepares to throw the enemy
ranks into confusion by the advance
of his KP to K5.

13 Q–B2	P–K4
14 KR–K1	

Tarrasch, who was a profound expert of chess, defends himself excellently, which makes the present game even more interesting. By transferring his KN to KB1, he securely defends his KR2 square, while his KB2 will be defended by the other knight from Q1.

14 ...	P–K5
15 N–Q2	N–K4
16 N–Q1	N3–N5
17 B × N/N4	N × B
18 N–B1 (70)	

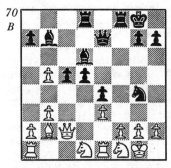

It appears that White has everything in order, but Alekhine discovers a weakness in his opponent's king position.

18 ...	Q–N4!

Two of the points are defended, but as a result the third is insufficiently controlled. Black's thoughts turn to the point . . . KN7, and it is just here that the catastrophe eventually takes place. The method of attack is simple: the knight will be transferred via . . . KR3 and . . . KB4 to . . . KR5.

19 P–KR3!	

Tarrasch reorganizes the forces defending his king. The king will move away to R1 so as to vacate KN1 for the rook.

19 ...	N–R3
20 K–R1	N–B4

21 N–R2	P–Q5!

It turns out that the black knight manoeuvre also had a further aim – Black makes an important pawn break-through in the centre. It is bad for White to capture on Q4 – after 22 P × P P–K6! 23 N × P N × N 24 P × N Q–N6 he loses.

22 B–B1	P–Q6
23 Q–B4+	K–R1
24 B–N2 (71)	

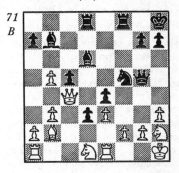

24 ...	N–N6+!

The decisive stroke. Although White's KN3 square is covered by a pawn, Black is complete master of it. Of course, White is unable to capture on N3 either now or later.

25 K–N1	B–Q4
26 Q–R4	N–K7+
27 K–R1	R–B2
28 Q–R6	P–R4!

This takes away from White's knight the square KN4, and at the same time prepares the concluding blow.

29 P–N6	N–N6+!
30 K–N1	P × P
31 Q × NP	P–Q7
32 R–KB1	N × R
33 N × N	B–K3!

This is the point: White is unable to prevent the bishop from capturing on his KR3. In addition the terrible 34 . . . R–B6! is threatened. Alekhine gives the following variation against

34 Q–B6: 34 ... R–B6   35 Q×KP
B–Q4   36 Q–QR4 Q×NP+   37
K×Q R–N6++   38 K–R2 R–N7+
39 K–R1 R–R7++   40 K–N1 R–R8
mate.

34 K–R1	B×RP!
35 P×B	R–B6
36 N–N3	P–R5
37 B–B6	Q×B
38 N×P	R×RP+
0–1	

This game also received a brilliancy
prize.

There was one especially difficult
and important problem among the
many which Alekhine had to solve in
order to win his match with Capablanca. It is well known that the
distinguishing feature of Capablanca's
play was his excellent technique,
based on a deep intuitive understanding of the position. In order to become
world champion, Alekhine had, in a
short space of time, to surpass his
rival in the mastery of playing endgames and simple positions. Alekhine
devoted a great deal of time and effort
to this work, and the results of it are
already noticeable in many games
played during the years 1921–1927.
Alekhine not only analysed the endgame, but also in practice, in tournaments, did not let slip the opportunity
to test himself.

The following games from the pre-
match period illustrate Alekhine's
great mastery in the concluding stage
of the chess battle.

31) Alekhine-Znosko-Borovsky,
Birmingham 1926
Nimzo-Indian Defence

1 P–Q4	N–KB3
2 P–QB4	P–K3
3 N–QB3	B–N5
4 B–N5	

At one time this energetic bishop
move was considered to be one of the
best ways of meeting the Nimzo-
Indian Defence, but then it fell out of
favour. Nowadays the move has once
again begun to be adopted: players
have despaired of refuting the opening, invented by the talented theorist,
by the moves 4 Q–N3, 4 Q–B2 and
4 P–K3, and so have decided to try
out this system of development. Ex-
world champion Spassky is particularly fond of the move 4 B–N5.

4 ...	P–KR3
5 B×N	

But this already gives up all
attempts to obtain an opening advantage. In modern tournament games
White's hopes are associated with
retreating his bishop to R4.

5 ...	Q×B

It was better to first capture White's
knight. Then White's impaired pawn
configuration would give Black good
chances of developing an initiative
on the Q-side, while White, with two
pieces already exchanged, would not
find it easy to make a K-side offensive.

6 R–B1	P–QN3
7 N–B3	B–N2
8 P–K3	0–0
9 B–K2	P–Q3
10 0–0	B5×N

This is necessary, since the bishop
was now misplaced, and, after the
knight had moved away, could have
been in danger. Of course, White now
captures on B3 with his rook.

11 R×B	N–Q2
12 N–Q2!	

'With the aim of exchanging
bishops and then further weakening
Black's already somewhat insecure
Q-side pawn position. Black is unable
to prevent this. One cannot say, of
course, that this plan promises White a
decisive advantage, but he obtains
active play with chances for a win,
while his opponent has the difficult
task of struggling for a draw.

'Every chess player, in my opinion, should exploit similar opportunities and try to solve the problem of winning without 'fear' of simplification. Playing for complications is an extreme measure, which a player should adopt only when he is unable to find a clear and logical plan. In the present case, where White has such a plan, he should try to realize his advantage, even though this may be a far from easy task' (Alekhine).

This important practical advice is based on a subtle understanding both of chess strategy, and of chess psychology, and has not lost its importance in the present day. It is true that nowadays certain leading players go to the other extreme: simplifying the position, striving for the sacred half point, they completely ignore the creative side of chess. And yet Alekhine's advice is valuable, in particular to reckless, desperate players, to those who consider that every exchange of pieces is practically the ruin of their hopes.

Alekhine's teaching to such chess 'dare-devils' is: love the endgame, love the beautiful, deep, quiet, subtle manoeuvres, which are characteristic of the concluding stage of the game.

12 ...	P–K4
13 B–B3	B × B
14 N × B	P–K5
15 N–Q2	Q–K2
16 Q–R4	P–KB4
17 Q–B6	N–B3
18 P–QN4!	

White's offensive on the Q-side threatens to become very dangerous, which is why Znosko-Borovsky hurries to simplify the position even more by further exchanges. The resulting endgame appears to be safe enough for Black, but even so 18 ... KR–Q1 was more accurate.

| 18 ... | P–QR4 |

19 R–R3!	Q–Q2
20 Q × Q	N × Q
21 P × P	R × P
22 R × R	P × R
23 R–N1	R–N1
24 R × R +	N × R (72)

72
W

Let us examine the position reached. Where does White's advantage lie? After a lengthy examination we can come to the following conclusion: White stands better due to the fact that the enemy pawns are too far advanced (in particular his QRP and KP. If these were put back to QR2 and K3 the position would be absolutely level).

This suggests a method by which White may exploit his positional advantages. He should try to combine an attack on the QRP with his king with the undermining operations P–KN4 and P–KB3. Let us suppose that the white king reaches QR4. Then the black king must defend his QRP from QN3, after which Black's king's flank will be without defence. It is just this plan which Alekhine carries out.

| 25 K–B1 | N–Q2 |

'A wrong idea, which is immediately refuted. Necessary was 25 ... K–B2 26 K–K2 K–K2 27 K–Q1 K–Q2, and the further advance of White's king gets him nowhere, for example 28 K–B2 K–B3 29 K–N3 K–N3 30 K–R4 N–Q2 31 N–N3

K–R3, and now 32 N × P? is a mistake because of 32 ... N–N3+ 33 K–N4 P–B4+.

'However, instead of this White has three continuations, each of which would lead to a win: 28 N–N3 (forcing ... P–R5, which further weakens this pawn), 28 P–B3 and 28 P–N4' (Alekhine).

| 26 K–K2 | N–N3 |
| 27 K–Q1 | P–R5 |

The pawn moves closer to the white king, and so becomes even weaker. Znosko-Borovsky naively supposed that Alekhine would allow him to play 28 ... P–B4, which would lead to a complete blocking of the Q-side, and an automatic draw. Alekhine's reply suggests itself, and enables him to win without difficulty the important QRP.

28 P–Q5!

Now the QRP is doomed. Black attempts to recoup his losses among White's K-side pawns.

28 ...	N–Q2
29 K–B2	N–K4
30 K–B3	N–N5
31 K–N4	N × BP
32 K × P	P–B5

A more stubborn defence was 32 ... K–B2 33 K–N5 K–K2 34 K–B6 K–Q1, though even then the breakthrough 35 P–B5! gives White a forced win. For example: 35 ... P × P 36 N–B4! N–N5 37 P–KR3 N–B3 38 P–QR4, or 35 ... N–N5 36 P × P P × P 37 K × P N × KP 38 P–QR4, and Black cannot stop both the QRP and QP.

33 P × P	P–K6
34 N–B3	N–Q6
35 K–N5!	

This is the way: the outside passed pawn is more important than the knight.

| 35 ... | P–N4 |

Or 35 ... P–K7   36 P–QR4

P–K8 = Q 37 N × Q N × N 38 P–R5, and the pawn is unstoppable.

36 P × P	P × P
37 P–QR4	P–K7
38 P–R3!	

Not allowing the chance opportunity 38 P–R5 P–N5! and it is Black who wins.

38 ...	N–B4
39 P–R5	N–N6
40 N–K1	N–Q5+
41 K–R4	1–0

In the following ending Alekhine exploits the strength of his knight with great ingenuity.

32) Alekhine-Yates, London 1922

73
W

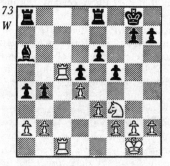

White has mastery of the open file (*73*), which enables him to break through onto the seventh rank. But first of all Alekhine activates his knight.

21 N–K5!

It is easy for the reader to realize the difference in strengths of the knight and bishop in this position. The bishop, which in other positions can be very powerful, here stands timidly on the edge of the board, having only one diagonal QR3–KB8, on which there is nothing for it to do. It cannot reach the K-side, where the main events will develop, since all paths are closed by black pawns. At the same time the knight on K5 is a truly fine piece! He dominates the whole board, no one can threaten him, he is even invulnerable to the black rooks. It is not surprising that, within the next few moves, the great superiority of White's position reaps its rewards.

| 21 ... | R/K1–N1 |

Black could not exchange off all four rooks: after 21 ... QR–B1 22 R×R R×R 23 R×R+ B×R 24 N–B6 he loses a pawn.

22 P–B3!	P–N6
23 P–QR3	P–R3
24 K–B2	K–R2
25 P–R4!	

The KRP joins the attack.

| 25 ... | R–KB1 |
| 26 K–N3 | R/B1–QN1 |

Black can do absolutely nothing.

| 27 R–B7 | B–N4 |
| 28 R1–B5! | |

Intending to double rooks on the seventh rank by 29 R–K7 R–K1 30 R–KB7, and Black cannot further chase the rook on B7.

28 ...	B–R3
29 R5–B6	R–K1
30 K–B4	K–N1
31 P–R5!	

The beautiful final position, in which the main role will be played by the white king, begins to take shape.

31 ...	B–B8
32 P–N3	B–R3
33 R–B7	K–R2
34 R6–B7	R–KN1
35 N–Q7!	K–R1
36 N–B6	R/N1–KB1
	(74)

| 37 R×P! | |

It is this move, foreseen long ago by Alekhine, on which all White's previous play is based.

| 37 ... | R×N |
| 38 K–K5! | 1–0 |

The white king triumphs. The rook is lost, since it cannot retreat to

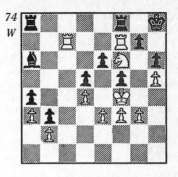

74
W

B1 because of mate by the rooks on KR7 and KN7, while the attempt to defend the rook by 38 ... R1–KB1 meets with the same end.

And now one more example of Alekhine's mastery of the endgame, based not only on a great understanding of the position, but also on the accurate calculation of variations.

33) **Alekhine–Tartakower,** Vienna 1922

French Defence

1 P–K4	P–K3
2 P–Q4	P–Q4
3 N–QB3	N–KB3
4 B–KN5	P×P
5 B×N	

This continuation, which significantly lessens the sharpness of the opening struggle, was sometimes adopted in the 1920s. It is not played nowadays.

5 ...	P×B
6 N×P	P–KB4
7 N–QB3	

It is easy to see that White has achieved nothing from the opening, while Black's bishop from ... KN2 will successfully support the operation to surround and destroy the opponent's insecure centre.

7 ...	B–N2
8 N–B3	0–0
9 Q–Q2	P–B4!

Alekhine's plans included castling long and then developing a K-side attack by P–KR4–R5 and R–KR3–KN3. Therefore Tartakower immediately switches to an endgame, accepting that even there White's chances will be somewhat preferable. In accordance with his often-stated principle, Alekhine does not avoid going into a slightly better ending.

10 P × P	**Q–R4**
11 N–QN5 !	

The exchange is necessary, otherwise Black's strong bishop and active queen, supported by rooks on the open Q B-file, would set up a threatening attack.

11 . . .	**Q × Q+**
12 N × Q	**N–R3**
13 P–QB3	**N × P**
14 N–N3 !	**N × N**

It was better to play the knight to R5, to avoid opening the important file.

15 P × N	**P–QR3**
16 N–Q6	**R–N1**
17 P–QN4	**R–Q1**
18 0–0–0	**B–K4**
19 N × B	**R × R+**
20 K × R	**R × N** (75)

75
W

Let us weigh up the resulting endgame position. A close examination reveals that White has the advantage, based on the following considerations:

1) The black pawns are seriously weakened, and will soon be attacked by White's bishop.

2) White can create a passed pawn on the Q-side by preparing P–N5 and the further advance of his pawns, while Black is unable to do the same on the K-side.

Alekhine's subsequent play is dictated by attempts to exploit these positional advantages.

21 B–K2	**K–B1**
22 K–B2	**R–B2**
23 R–R1	**K–K2**
24 P–R3	**P–B5**

A poor move. Tartakower hopes to throw forward his pawn group on the K-side, but only succeeds in weakening it still further. 24 . . . R–Q2 deserved attention, so as to transfer the bishop to . . . QN3, where it would occupy an excellent position.

25 K–N3	**R–Q2**
26 R–R5 !	

Activating his forces. Now 26 . . . P–B3 is answered by 27 B–B3 K–Q1 28 P–N5 P × P 29 R × P, while 26 . . . R–Q4 ? is very bad because of 27 B–B3 ! So Black has to allow White's rook to attack the KRP.

26 . . .	**B–B2**
27 R–R5	**R–Q7**
28 B–B3	**P–N3**
29 R × P	**R × BP**
30 B–R5 !	

Up to this point White's play has been based on a deep understanding of the endgame, but now precise calculation takes over. After working out the resulting complications, he happily allows his opponent to set up two very dangerous passed pawns.

30 . . .	**R × KNP**
31 R × P+	**K–Q1**

This is the only way, since 31 . . . K–Q3 would lose the KBP.

32 B–N4 !	**P–K4 !**

Black's main hope is the sacrifice of the exchange. One can suppose that Tartakower was in excellent spirits at this time, since his pawns appear to be unstoppable.

33 R–Q7+	**K–B1**
34 R–Q2+	**R × B**
35 P × R	**P–B6!** (*76*)

How can the passed pawns be stopped now? Alekhine gives a number of possible ways, but none of them reach their goal. Come on, dear reader, let us try to stop those passed pawns. Here are several attempts:

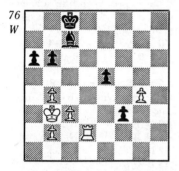

76
W

a) 36 K–B4 P–K5 37 K–Q4 B–B5 38 R–KB2 P–K6 39 R × P P–K7, or 38 R–Q1 P–K6 39 R–QR1 P–K7, and the pawns are irresistible.

b) 36 R–R2 P–K5 37 R–R8+ K–Q2 38 R–KB8 B–N6 39 P–KN5 B–Q3! 40 R–B6 B–K4! 41 R–B7+ K–K3, and Black draws by perpetual attack on the rook, which cannot leave the KB-file. It is interesting that in this variation 39 ... P–K6 does not draw, since after 40 R × P P–K7 White wins by first giving check on Q3 before playing the rook to K3.

c) 36 K–B2 P–K5 37 R–Q4! P–K6 38 K–Q1 P–K7+ 39 K–Q2 B–N6 40 R–K4 B–R5 41 R–K5 B–N6 with a draw.

d) 36 P–KN5 P–K5 37 R–Q5 (37 P–N6 even loses after 37 ... B–K4 and 38 ... P–K6) 37 ... P–B7 38 R–KB5 P–K6 39 P–N6 P–K7 40 P–N7 P–B8 = Q 41 P–N8 =

Q+ K–N2 42 Q–Q5+ K–R2, and White cannot win.

Alekhine was not bound to go in for this position, which means that he must have seen his next move long before. One cannot fail to be astonished at the harmonious thinking of the great Russian player, who was able, like no one else, to adorn his strategic plans with amazing tactical blows and combinations.

The style of Alekhine's future opponent – Capablanca – was also distinguished by the ability to add effective 'little combinations' to his dry strategic planning. The present game shows that Alekhine had decided not to be inferior to him in this respect also.

36 R–Q5!!

A study-like solution to a most difficult problem – only in this way can Black's pawns be stopped. Even to the modern player, armed with whole volumes devoted to the endgame, it will be of interest to study the instructive comments made by the Russian grandmaster about this move.

'The variations which explain this at first sight strange move (the rook attacks the defended pawn, and allows the other to advance), will appear simple if the basic idea is understood. The black pawns are harmless:

1) when they are situated on squares of the same colour as their own bishop, since the white king can easily blockade them. For example: 36 ... P–B7 37 R–Q1 P–K5 38 K–B2 B–B5 39 R–KB1 and 40 K–Q1.

2) when the rook is able to attack them from behind, only without loss of time, for example: 36 ... P–K5 37 R–KB5 B–N6 38 P–KN5 P–K6 39 R × P P–K7 40 R–K3' (Alekhine).

36 ...	**P–K5**
37 R–KB5	**B–N6**

38 P–KN5	K–Q2
39 P–N6	K–K3
40 P–N7	

This is the simplest solution.

40 ...	K × R
41 P–N8 = Q	B–B5
42 Q–B7+	K–N5

Or 42 ... K–K4 43 P–B4.

43 Q–N6+	B–N4
44 Q × KP+	K–N6
45 Q–N6	K–N5
46 Q × P	1–0

In his battle for the world championship Alekhine was to meet a player who was noted for his rare ability to play technical positions, in which his wealth of natural intuition helped him to orientate himself. This is why it was important for Alekhine to train himself to play such positions.

Therefore in games played during the period of preparation we often see Alekhine striving to transfer a complicated battle into purely technical channels. We give below two games which are characterized by this. And it was not in vain that Alekhine set himself these training examples: in both cases we see the great mastery of the future world champion in playing positions, which, though apparently rather dull, are in fact full of deeply hidden subtleties.

34) **Thomas-Alekhine**, Baden-Baden 1925

Alekhine's Defence

1 P–K4	N–KB3
2 P–Q3	

This is not the way to refute Alekhine's Defence. It is not surprising that within a few moves Black seizes the initiative. Thomas attempts, as White, to set up a Dutch Defence type of formation. Such a method of play is adopted at the present time, for example by playing the King's Indian Defence as White. However modern masters always have a general idea behind their moves. Without such a guiding thread, the choice of random moves can quickly lead to disaster.

2 ...	P–B4
3 P–KB4	N–B3
4 N–KB3	P–KN3
5 B–K2	B–N2
6 QN–Q2?	

And here, for example, is such a move. What is the point of it? By playing 6 P–B4 and 7 N–B3, White could have prevented the advance P–Q4. ... Now this move becomes especially strong.

6 ...	P–Q4
7 0–0	0–0
8 K–R1	P–N3
9 P × P	Q × P

There is no point in giving White's QN the K4 square.

10 Q–K1	B–N2
11 N–B4	N–Q5
12 N–K3	Q–B3
13 B–Q1	

White's pieces paint a sorry picture – grouped in disorder on the back ranks. Now with some energetic thrusts Alekhine creates gaping weaknesses in the opponent's camp.

13 ...	N–Q4!
14 N/B3 × N	

Bad was 14 N/K3 × N Q × N 15 Q × P KR–K1 with great advantage to Black.

14 ...	P × N
15 N × N	Q × N
16 B–B3	Q–Q2
17 B × B	Q × B
18 P–B4	

White prefers to have two relatively weak pawns on Q3 and QB3 instead of one absolutely weak one on QB2.

18 ...	P × Pep
19 P × P	QR–B1
20 B–N2	KR–Q1
21 R–B3	B–B3
22 P–Q4	

In the end White would have been forced to make this move. Now Black's winning plan is associated with exploiting the weakness of the white squares.

22 ...	Q–Q4
23 Q–K3	Q–QN4
24 Q–Q2	R–Q4
25 P–KR3	P–K3
26 R–K1	Q–R5
27 R–R1	P–QN4
28 Q–Q1	R–B5!

All Black's pieces strive to establish themselves on white squares.

Sooner or later White will be forced to exchange queens, after which it will be even more difficult to defend the white squares.

29 Q–N3	R–Q3
30 K–R2	R–R3
31 R3–B1	B–K2
32 K–R1	R5–B3!

Since White is in no hurry to exchange queens, Alekhine tries to force the exchange. For this purpose he intensifies the pressure on the QRP, by the following regrouping of his pieces: ... Q–B5, ... R–R5 and ... R3–R3.

33 R/B1–K1	B–R5!
34 R–KB1	Q–B5
35 Q × Q	

In any case Black would have forced the exchange of queens two moves later. Now we have an ending with rooks and like-coloured bishops.

| 35 ... | R × Q |
| 36 P–R3 | B–K2 (77) |

The position is won for Black. He has a simple plan for achieving victory: his king will move to ... Q4, from where it threatens to advance further to ... K5 or ... QB5. If White at this moment places his king on Q3, then the pawn thrust ... P–K4 will be decisive.

| 37 R/B1–QN1 | B–Q3! |

Alekhine takes every opportunity

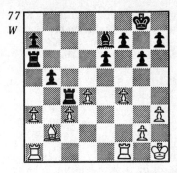

77
W

to force another pawn onto a square of the same colour as White's bishop. It would be justified in a possible bishop ending.

38 P–N3	K–B1
39 K–N2	K–K2
40 K–B2	K–Q2
41 K–K2	K–B3
42 R–R2	

With Black's king defending his QNP, ... R5–R5 was now threatened.

42 ...	R5–R5
43 R1–QR1	K–Q4
44 K–Q3	R3–R4
45 B–B1	P–QR3
46 B–N2	P–R4

47 ... P–R5 threatens. So one more white pawn is forced onto a black square.

| 47 P–R4 (78) | P–B3! |

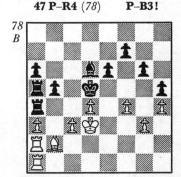

78
B

The break-through ... P–K4 will give Black's rook on ... R5 the chance to make a decisive raid to . . . KN5. White is faced by inevitable disaster.

48 B–B1	P–K4
49 BP × P	P × P
50 B–N2	

Or 50 P × P B × KP 51 B–B4 B × B 52 P × B R × BP.

50 . . .	P × P
51 P × P	P–N5!
0–1	

The exceptionally accurate manoeuvres by Alekhine in the following game make its final stage a classical example of the realization of microscopic positional advantages.

35) **Alekhine-Spielmann,** New York 1927

French Defence

1 P–K4	P–K3
2 P–Q4	P–Q4
3 N–QB3	N–KB3
4 B–KN5	B–K2
5 P × P	

Alekhine carries out this exchange of pawns, although he himself demonstrated on a number of occasions that it was favourable for Black. How can we explain this? The explanation is simple: Spielmann was a player with a sharp combinative style, and it was easier to fight him in the endgame. Also, Alekhine was in need of endgame practice; the match with Capablanca was not far away. As the reader will see later, it turned out to be excellent practice.

5 . . .	N × P
6 B × B	Q × B
7 Q–Q2	Q–N5
8 N × N	Q × Q+
9 K × Q	P × N
10 R–K1+	B–K3

Alekhine is proved right. In the much-simplified position Spielmann already makes his first mistake. Correct was 10 . . . K–B1.

1 N–R3!

From KB4 the knight will have a number of possible paths: to exchange on K6, to manoeuvre to K5 or QB5 via Q3, or to move to KR5.

11 . . .   N–B3

And it was better to refrain from making this move, since now Black's pawns are significantly weakened. The correct method of defence was 11 . . . P–QB3 12 N–B4 K–K2 with 13 . . . N–Q2 to follow.

12 B–N5	K–Q2
13 N–B4	QR–K1
14 P–B4!	K–Q3

The only defence against catastrophe on his Q4 square. Now play goes into a complicated, but most interesting, rook ending.

15 P–B5+	K–Q2
16 R–K5	P–B3
17 R × B	R × R
18 N × R	K × N
19 B × N	P × B (79)

79
W

Alekhine considers this ending to be won for White. The main advantages which White holds are his favourable pawn structure, and the activity of his rook which, within a few moves, penetrates to QR6 to attack Black's weak broken pawns.

20 R–K1+   K–Q2

'This is better than 20 . . . K–B2, after which White would win by 21 K–B3! R–QN1 22 R–K3. Black's rook must now stay on the QN-file, and he is unable to prevent the following moves by his opponent: P–QR3!, K–B2, P–B3! and R–QN3; then after Black's ... R–K1 White plays K–Q2, and his rook intrudes into the enemy camp.

'It should be mentioned that even with White's king on QB2 Black can not go in for the exchange of rooks, since the resulting pawn ending is lost, for example: ... R–K1 2 R × R K × R 3 K–N3 K–Q2 4 K–N4 K–B1 5 K–R5 K–N2 6 P–B3! (or *P–QN4!*, if the pawn already stands on KB3). After Black's pawn moves on the K-side are exhausted, he will be forced to play ... P–QR3, on which there follows 1 P–QN3! K–R2 2 P–QN4 K–N2 3 P–QR4 K–R2 4 P–QN5 RP × P 5 P × P P × P 6 K × P K–N2 7 P–B6+ with an easy win for White. An instructive ending!' (Alekhine).

21 K–B3	R–QN1
22 R–K3	R–KB1
23 R–N3	R–B2
24 K–N4	

Before finding the correct offensive plan, Alekhine suffers a short 'period of searching'.

24 ...	R–K2
25 K–B3	R–B2
26 R–R3	P–KR3
27 K–Q2 (*80*)	

80
B

The correct path to victory is found: Black is unable to defend the QRP with his king – 27 ... K–B1? 28 R–R3 K–N2 29 R–K3! with an intrusion along the K-file – and in the end this weak pawn will perish. True, the play would still conceal a number of subtleties.

| 27 ... | R–K2 |
| 28 R–R3 | |

Here 28 R–K3! led to a win, by forcing the opponent into a pawn ending, since 28 ... R–B2 loses immediately to 29 R–QR3. The battle of kings and pawns could develop in the following way: 28 ... R × R 29 K × R K–K3 30 K–B4 P–N3 (*30 ... P–N4+? 31 K–N4*) 31 P–KN4. Alekhine gives the following lengthy variation: 31 ... P–N4+ 32 K–K3 K–Q2 33 K–Q3 K–B1 34 K–B3 K–N2 35 K–N3 K–R3 36 K–R4 K–N2 37 K–R5 P–R3 (after *37 ... K–B1 38 K–R6* followed by the advance of the QNP and QRP is decisive) 38 P–QR4 K–R2 39 P–N3! K–N2 40 P–N4 K–R2 41 P–N5 RP × P 42 P × P K–N2 43 P–N6! (*43 P × P+? K–N1–R1* with a draw) 43 ... P × P+ 44 P × P K–N1 45 K–R6 P–QB4 46 P × P K–Q5 47 P–N7 P–Q6 48 K–N6 P–Q7 49 P–B6 P–Q8 = Q 50 P–B7 mate.

In working out this variation, Alekhine did not notice the move 43 P–N6! (a rare occurrence), and so avoided going into the pawn ending.

| 28 ... | R–K5 |

But now Black's rook is able to make a fairly successful counterattack.

29 R–R4	K–B1
30 P–B3	R–R5
31 P–KR3	K–N2
32 K–K3	P–B4!
33 R–N4+	K–B1
34 P–R4	P–N4?

Spielmann lets slip his opportunity to exploit Alekhine's mistake on the 28th move. After 34 ... P–B5+!

35 K–B2 R–R4 followed by transferring the rook to . . . KB2, Black could entertain hopes of achieving a draw. Now he is lost.

35 P–R5	P–N5
36 RP × P	P × P (*81*)
37 P–R6!	

81
W

Black loses his QRP, which signifies the end of the contest.

37 . . .	P × P
38 P × P	R–R8
39 R–N7	R–K8+
40 K–B4!	R–Q8
41 K–K5	R–K8+
42 K–B5	R–Q8
43 R × RP!	

Having committed one inaccuracy, White once again exploits his advantage with great mastery. Now Black gains two dangerous passed pawns – on . . . Q4 and . . . KR3, but Alekhine has accurately calculated that his QRP will be the decisive factor.

43 . . .	R × P
44 R–R8+	K–Q2
45 P–B4	R–R5
46 P–R7!	P–R4
47 P–N3!	

This modest pawn move allows White's king to reach the 'control square' Q4. This could not be done immediately – 47 K–K5 R–K5+!

47 . . .	R–R8
48 K–K5	R–K8+
49 K–B6	R–QR8

50 K–K5	R–K8+
51 K–Q4!	

The path to victory is found. Now the KBP can advance.

51 . . .	R–Q8+
52 K–B3	R–QR8
53 P–B5!	K–K2

Otherwise White would win immediately by advancing this pawn to B6 and B7.

54 K–Q4	P–R5
55 K–K5	R–K8+
56 K–B4!	

The king manoeuvres to great effect. After reaching KN5 he will eliminate a dangerous enemy – the KRP.

56 . . .	R–QR8
57 K–N5	R–KN8+

He has to give up the pawn, since after 57 . . . P–R6 White wins by 58 R–R8! R × P 59 R × P R–R8 60 P–B6+ K–B2 61 R–R7+ K–B1 62 R × P.

58 K × P	R–QR8
59 K–N5	

The final stage of the plan – the king moves over to the Q-side, so as to personally support the white pawn storm.

59 . . .	R–KN8+
60 K–B4	R–QR8
61 K–K5	R–K8+
62 K–Q4	R–QR8
63 K–B3	R–R6
64 K–N2	R–R3
65 P–N4	K–B2
66 K–N3	R–R8
67 P–B6! (*82*)	

Zugzwang. The black rook is forced to move to R3.

67 . . .	R–R3
68 P–N5	P × P
69 K–N4	1–0

On 69 . . . P–B3, 70 R–R8! decides.

Thus we have seen how Alekhine played during the years when he was

82
B

carefully preparing for his match with Capablanca. Let us now examine some of the games from that historic match.

36) Capablanca-Alekhine,

1st match game, 1927
French Defence

1 P–K4	P–K3
2 P–Q4	P–Q4
3 N–QB3	B–N5
4 P × P	

The exchange variation of the French Defence – in those days this opening provoked arguments: should White take away the tension in the centre or not? Nowadays this problem has found an undisputed solution: simplification in the centre is not favourable to White, and the sharp positions resulting from 4 P–K5 are to be preferred. The present game was, to a great extent, responsible for this conclusion being reached. With convincing accuracy Alekhine discloses the drawbacks to White's set-up.

4 ...	P × P
5 B–Q3	N–QB3
6 KN–K2	KN–K2
7 0–0	B–KB4

This is one of Black's trumps – he is able to exchange off White's active KB.

8 B × B	N × B
9 Q–Q3	Q–Q2
10 N–Q1	

Exchanging off Black's knight on ... B4 costs White a lot of time. Simpler was 10 B–B4.

10 ...	0–0
11 N–K3	N × N
12 B × N	KR–K1
13 N–B4	

While this is already a serious inaccuracy, which Alekhine exploits by combinational means. By playing 13 B–B4 and then 14 P–QB3, Capablanca could have maintained equality.

13 ...   B–Q3!

Inviting the opponent to tread along a slippery path – 14 N × P B × P+ 15 K × B Q × N 16 P–QB4 Q–KR4+ 17 K–N1 QR–Q1 18 P–Q5 R–Q3 and Black's attack may soon become irresistible. Capablanca does not accept the challenge, but is soon faced by even more unpleasant complications.

14 KR–K1

A further inaccuracy. It is bad to allow the knight to reach ... N5, and so he should have played 14 P–QB3.

14 ...   N–N5
15 Q–N3

And here the Cuban commits a serious tactical oversight. Correct was 15 Q–Q2, defending for the second time both his knight and his rook on K1.

15 ...   Q–B4
16 QR–B1? (*83*)

A blunder, although it was already difficult for White to find a defence. Alekhine indicates the following variations, which confirm, in his opinion, that, even on the opponent's best defence, Black's advantage is beyond question.

a) 16 R/K1–QB1 P–QR4! 17 P–QR3 P–R5 18 Q–B3 N–B3 19 N–Q3 R–K3 with ... QR–K1 to follow.

b) 16 N–Q3 N×N   17 Q×N
Q×Q 18 P×Q B–N5 19 R/K1–QB1
P–QB3, and then . . . P–QR4! with
the better ending.

83
B

16 . . .   N×BP!

The indicated move, which involves, it is true, a small subtlety.
Perhaps it was just this subtlety that
the world champion had not foreseen,
otherwise how can his oversight in a
comparatively elementary combination be explained?

17 R×N   Q×N!

Here it is, this subtlety. After 17 . . .
B×N 18 R–B5 White would easily
win back his pawn, whereas now he
has to attend to the threat of mate.

18 P–N3   Q–B4

The result is that Black has won a
pawn, while keeping an excellent
position. Nevertheless, Capablanca
puts up a stubborn resistance, which
gives the game interest right to the
finish.

19 R2–K2	**P–QN3**
20 Q–N5	**P–KR4**
21 P–KR4	**R–K5!**

Threatening a mating attack by
sacrificing this rook on . . . KR5.

22 B–Q2!

An excellent defence, based on
counter-attack.

22 . . .	**R×QP**
23 B–B3	**R–Q6**
24 B–K5	**R–Q1**
25 B×B	**R×B**

26 R–K5	**Q–B6**
27 R×RP!	

White's pieces have become very
active, and already mate on the move
is threatened. It is interesting to
follow how skilfully Alekhine wrests
the initiative from his powerful
opponent, until he once again dominates the board.

27 . . .	**Q×R**
28 R–K8+	**K–R2**
29 Q×R+	**Q–N3**
30 Q–Q1	**R–K3!**

Black returns his extra pawn in
order to be able to throw his remaining forces at the enemy. The queen
ending would be won without difficulty by Black, so Capablanca prefers
to keep his rook.

31 R–QR8	**R–K4**
32 R×P	**P–QB4**
33 R–Q7	

This lightens Black's winning task.
Stronger was 33 K–N2, though even
then the clear superiority in activity
of Black's forces would tell in the end.

33 . . .	**Q–K3**
34 Q–Q3+	**P–N3**
35 R–Q8	**P–Q5**
36 P–R4	**R–K8+** *(84)*

84
W

Once again the weakness of the
first rank has a deciding word in this
game. Now the white king comes
under an irresistible attack, and yet
an exclamation mark cannot be
attached to this move. Only the tension

in the first game of a match for which he had been striving all his life can explain why Alekhine overlooked an immediate win by tactical means – 36 ... Q–K2 37 R–QN8 Q–B2 38 R–QR8 Q–B3, and White must resign.

37 K–N2	Q–QB3+
38 P–B3	R–K6
39 Q–Q1	Q–K3
40 P–KN4	R–K7+
41 K–R3	Q–K6
42 Q–KR1	Q–B5

White cannot meet the threat of 43 ... R–KB7.

43 P–KR5	R–KB7
0–1	

The following game, the eleventh in the match, marked a turning point; it showed Capablanca just how much Alekhine's mastery had grown, both in the solution of strategic problems, and in endgame manoeuvring.

37) Capablanca-Alekhine,
11th match game, 1927
Queen's Gambit Declined

1 P–Q4	P–Q4
2 P–QB4	P–K3
3 N–QB3	N–KB3
4 B–N5	QN–Q2
5 P–K3	P–B3
6 N–B3	Q–R4

The well-known Cambridge-Springs variation, analyses of which occupied the pages of many journals in the 1920s. Black's counter-play based on the pin on White's knight and the advance of the black knight to ... K5, looks very dangerous. But, as often happens, good ways of meeting this opening sortie were discovered, and the Cambridge-Springs variation practically disappeared from tournament practice. Is this for long? Will not some enterprising grandmaster return to this opening, which contains so many interesting nuances?

7 N–Q2	B–N5
8 Q–B2	P×P
9 B×N	N×B
10 N×P	Q–B2
11 P–QR3	B–K2

Any judgement of the Cambridge-Springs variation must be made on the appraisal of this fundamental position. White controls a large amount of space, and his opponent's pieces are considerably cramped. On the other hand, Black has two dangerous bishops, which may become active after the opening of the centre. Black faces a prolonged defence with hopes of counter-play after preparing a pawn advance by ... P–QN3 and ... P–QB4. The reader can follow the ingenuity and accuracy with which Alekhine prepares this break-through, which in the end enables him to seize the initiative.

12 B–K2

At a later stage of the match Capablanca successfully adopted the flank development of this bishop by 12 P–KN3.

12 ...	0–0
13 0–0	B–Q2
14 P–QN4	P–QN3
15 B–B3	QR–B1
16 KR–Q1	KR–Q1
17 QR–B1	B–K1
18 P–N3	

Black is still extremely cramped. With this pawn move Capablanca prevents the possibility of a black knight moving from ... Q4 to ... KB5 after P–K4 by White.

18 ...	N–Q4
19 N–N2	Q–N1
20 N–Q3	B–N4

This prevents P–K4, and prepares to carry out ... P–QB4 in the most convenient circumstances.

21 R–N1	Q–N2

| 22 P–K4 | N × N |
| 23 Q × N | Q–K2 |

More accurate was 23 ... R–B2 24 B–N2 B–B3 25 P–K5 B–K2 26 R/N1–B1 Q–B1.

24 P–KR4	B–R3
25 N–K5	P–N3
26 N–N4	

Here it is, Capablanca's first omission. By playing 26 N–B4 followed by 27 P–K5, White could have obtained an excellent post for his knight on Q6. This inaccuracy by White allows Alekhine to make a breakthrough and initiate a counteroffensive.

26 ...	B–N2
27 P–K5	P–KR4
28 N–K3 (*85*)	

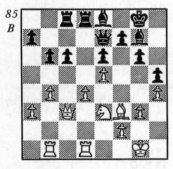

85
B

| 28 ... | P–QB4! |

The long-awaited freeing move. Now Black's bishops gain their freedom, and have the chance to become very dangerous. The pawn sacrifice is a temporary one, since after the plausible 29 QP × P P × P 30 R × R Q × R 31 P × P Black wins the pawn back by 31 ... Q–B2. Capablanca chooses a different path, but even so Black keeps the better position.

| 29 NP × P | P × P |
| 30 P–Q5 | |

This only results in trouble for White. By playing 30 R–N7 R–Q2 31 R × R B × R 32 P–Q5 P × P 33

N × P Q–K3 34 N–B4, the world champion could have simplified the position, and easily gained a draw.

30 ...	P × P
31 N × P	Q–K3
32 N–B6+	

White should have refrained from making this move, after which he has a weak pawn on B6, and should have continued the struggle by 32 R–N7 B × P 33 Q–R5.

32 ...	B × N
33 P × B	R × R+
34 R × R	B–B3!

Taking play into a favourable heavy-piece ending.

35 R–K1

White cannot capture on B6, since then he simply loses his KBP.

35 ...	Q–B4
36 R–K3	P–B5
37 P–R4	P–R4!

Avoiding the cunning trap which Capablanca had set. 37 ... B × P? would be a mistake, since after 38 B–K4 Q–Q2 (better *38 ... Q–N5*) 39 R–B3 K–R2 40 Q–K5 White has a winning attack on the enemy king.

| 38 B–N2 | B × B |
| 39 K × B | Q–Q4+ |

We have reached a heavy-piece ending, which usually demands from the players great endgame mastery, and also the ability to carry out combinative attacks. As the reader will already have seen, Alekhine was well endowed in these qualities. This is why, despite a number of mistakes, the following realization of a positional advantage is marked by both the beauty, and accuracy, of the manoeuvres.

40 K–R2	Q–KB4
41 R–B3	Q–B4
42 R–B4	K–R2
43 R–Q4	Q–B3?

Heavy-piece endings are very difficult to play; the present game, played by two grandmasters of the highest class, demonstrates this. The unsuccessful queen move could have led to the game being drawn, while after the correct 43 ... Q–N3! 44 R–B4 K–N1 Black would have every chance of winning.

44 Q × RP	**P–B6**
45 Q–R7	**K–N1**
46 Q–K7!	

An excellent move. There threatens 47 R–Q8+ R × R 48 Q × R+ K–R2 49 Q–K7 Q–K3 50 P–R5 P–B7 51 Q–B7 Q–N6 52 P–R6 with a draw.

46 ...	**Q–N3**
47 Q–Q7?	

Following his good move Capablanca immediately makes a losing one. By 47 R–Q7! Q × P/B7+ 48 K–R1! White could have reached a drawn position, for example: 48 ... Q–QR7 49 R–Q8+ R × R 50 Q × R+ K–R2 51 Q–KB8.

47 ...	**Q–B4!**
48 R–K4	

Otherwise Black would advance his pawn to B7.

48 ...	**Q × P+**
49 K–R3	**Q–B8+**
50 K–R2	**Q–B7+**
51 K–R3	**R–B1**
52 Q–B6!	**Q–B8+**
53 K–R2	**Q–B7+**
54 K–R3	**Q–B8+**
55 K–R2	**K–R2**

Threatening, with decisive effect, to bring out the rook to ... Q1 or ... QN1.

56 Q–B4	**Q–B7+**
57 K–R3	**Q–N8!**

A spectacular winning manoeuvre. After 58 P–N4 Black wins by 58 ... P–B7! 59 Q × QBP R–K1!! 60 R × R P × P mate.

58 R–K2	**Q–KB8+?**

58 ... Q–KR8+ 59 R–KR2 Q–B6 led to a win.

59 K–R2	**Q × P**

60 P–R5? (*86*)

Yet another mistake – Capablanca simply has not seen the effective end to the game. He could have exploited Alekhine's mistake by playing simply 60 R–QB2!

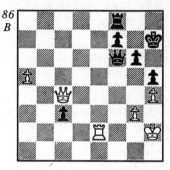

86
B

60 ...	**R–Q1!**

This leads to a wonderful finish. In the first instance White has to meet the threat of 61 ... R–Q7.

61 P–R6	**Q–B8!**

This threatens both 62 ... R–Q7 and 62 ... R–Q8.

62 Q–K4	**R–Q7**
63 R × R	**P × R**
64 P–R7	**P–Q8=Q**
65 P–R8=Q	

It seems that the outcome is still unclear, but Alekhine has long before seen the possibility of an unusual mating finish.

65 ...	**Q–KN8+**
66 K–R3	**Q/Q8–KB8**
	+!
0–1	

White resigns, since on 67 Q–N2 there follows 67 ... Q–KR8 mate.

38) Capablanca-Alekhine,
21st match game, 1927
Queen's Gambit Declined

1 P–Q4	**P–Q4**
2 P–QB4	**P–K3**
3 N–QB3	**N–KB3**
4 B–N5	**QN–Q2**

5 P–K3   B–K2
6 N–B3   0–0
7 R–B1   P–QR3
8 P–QR3

The typical struggle for a tempo: White does not develop his bishop on Q3 until Black has captured the QBP. At one time a number of works by chess theorists were devoted to this theme. And then they came to the conclusion, that all the same no win of a tempo ensures White an opening advantage.

And the theorists decided that it is better for White himself at an early stage of the game to exchange on Q5. From that time and to the present day the best method of play for White has been considered to be the 'minority attack' – after exchanging on Q5 White advances his QRP and QNP against the static enemy pawn position.

8 . . .   P–KR3
9 B–R4   P × P
10 B × P   P–QN4!

This method of developing the queen's bishop, called the 'extended fianchetto', allows Black to both conveniently place his bishop on . . . N2, and start lively play on the Q-side.

11 B–K2

A passive move, which allows Alekhine to seize the initiative. After the energetic 11 B–R2, intending to transfer the bishop to N1 and the queen to Q3 with mating threats on R7, White would be able to put pressure on his opponent's position.

11 . . .   B–N2
12 0–0

White is unable to prevent 12 . . . P–B4 by 12 P–QN4, since there follows 12 . . . P–QR4!, and Black attacks the weak white pawns on QR3 and QN4.

12 . . .   P–B4

13 P × P

White finally refrains from any attempt to obtain an opening advantage. Usually White allows the exchange on his Q4, resulting in an isolated QP, but such risky set-ups were not to Capablanca's taste.

13 . . .   N × P

Accurately calculated, which is characteristic of Alekhine. If now White attempts to exploit the poorly-defended position of the knight on . . . B4 and plays 14 B × N B × B 15 N × P, then Black replies 15 . . . Q × Q 16 KR × Q N–N6, and after 17 R–B7 B × N 18 B × B P × N 19 B × R R × B obtains the better game.

14 N–Q4   R–B1
15 P–QN4 (*87*)

87
B

15 . . .   N4–Q2!

This indicates a subtle understanding of the position. In such positions, with fixed pawns on the Q-side and an open QB-file, the initiative usually goes to the player who can first occupy the outpost on this file with a knight – the respective QB5 squares. Alekhine therefore avoids the plausible 15 . . . N4–K5 and takes the knight via . . . Q2 to . . . QN3 and . . . QB5.

16 B–N3

While Alekhine plays this game with invention and artistry, Capablanca is content to make natural, plausible moves, and so further worsens his position. By playing 16 N–N3, intending to answer 16 ... N–N3 with 17 N–R5, the world champion would have had equal chances in the difficult struggle to come. But it was hard for Capablanca to decide to move his knight from its excellent central square to one on the edge of the board.

16 ...	**N–N3**
17 Q–N3	**N/B3–Q4**

All Black's pieces help in the attempt to establish a knight on ... QB5. He hopes to exchange White's knight on B3, after which the black bishop can also attack ... QB5 from ... Q4.

18 B–B3	**R–B5!**
19 N–K4	**Q–B1**
20 R × R?	

This is a serious positional mistake. By continuing 20 Q–N1, White could have put up a long fight both for his QB4 square, and for the QB-file, with the possibility of such exchanging moves as N–Q6 or N–Q2. With the N3 square freed, the knight on Q4 would once again have the possibility of N–N3–R5. In general, after 20 Q–N1 the white pieces would still show signs of life, whereas the hasty exchange renders them half dead.

20 ...	**N × R**
21 R–B1	**Q–R1!**

Threatening to capture the QNP or KP with his knight on ... Q4.

22 N–B3	**R–B1**
23 N × N	**B × N**
24 B × B	**Q × B**
25 P–QR4	**B–B3**
26 N–B3 (*88*)	**B–N7!**

A splendid move, which fits in with several plans, and sets up a number of tactical threats. The bishop remains master of the long diagonal, even after Black plays ... P–K4, and this plays a deciding role in the coming complications.

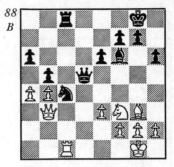

88
B

The varied possibilities in this position are best illustrated by the variations given by Alekhine.

a) 27 R–Q1 P × P! 28 Q × P N–N3 29 R × Q N × Q 30 R–Q1 N–B6 31 R–K1 R–B5 32 B–Q6 N–K5 33 B–K7 P–B3 34 R–N1 K–B2 35 K–B1 B–B6, and Black wins the ending without difficulty.

b) 27 R–N1 N–R6 28 Q × B N × R 29 Q × N Q–N6 30 Q–KB1 P × P 31 P–R3 P–R6, also with an easy win.

27 R–K1	**R–Q1**
28 P × P	**P × P**
29 P–R3	**P–K4**
30 R–N1	

This hastens White's defeat. Capablanca has overlooked an unusual tactical stroke for Alekhine. Better defensive chances were offered by 30 P–K4.

30 ...	**P–K5**
31 N–Q4	

Other knight moves are no better. After 31 N–K1, decisive is 31 ... Q–Q7! 32 Q–B2 (*32 K–B1 Q–B6!*) 32 ... Q × Q 33 N × Q R–Q7 34 N–K1 N–R6, while 31 N–R2 also loses: 31 ... Q–Q6! 32 R × B Q × Q 33 R × Q R–Q8+ 34 N–B1 N–Q7 35 R–R3 N × N.

31 ...	**B × N**
32 R–Q1 (*89*)	

Not noticing Black's brilliant reply, which immediately decides the game.

However, 32 P × B Q × P would have held out only a little longer.

89
B

32 ...	N × P!
0–1	

White resigns, since he comes out a piece down.

The following game is the final one from the 1927 match, and decided the outcome of this historic encounter. It gives evidence of Alekhine's great mastery of all stages of the game of chess.

39) Alekhine-Capablanca,
34th match game, 1927
Queen's Gambit Declined

1 P–Q4	P–Q4
2 P–QB4	P–K3
3 N–QB3	N–KB3
4 B–N5	QN–Q2
5 P–K3	P–B3
6 P–QR3	

One of the subtleties of the Queen's Gambit. Since Black has already made the move ... P–QB3, there is no need for White to develop his rook on QB1. Besides, he also has no need to struggle for a tempo, and soon develops his KB.

6 ...	B–K2
7 N–B3	0–0
8 B–Q3	P × P
9 B × BP	N–Q4
10 B × B	Q × B
11 N–K4	

The pawn on QR3 makes this move possible – the black queen does not have the square ... QN5.

11 ...	N4–B3
12 N–N3	P–B4

This is a serious opening mistake, since now the development of Black's QB is held up for a long time. He should have developed it on N2, and followed the plan which Alekhine carried out as Black in the eleventh game (see No. 37).

13 0–0	N–N3
14 B–R2	P × P
15 N × P	P–N3

Black naturally wishes to play ... P–K4, and first makes his ... KB4 square unavailable to the white knights.

16 R–B1

White seizes the open file, which provokes an immediate reaction from Capablanca, who strives to neutralize the rook on QB1.

16 ...	B–Q2
17 Q–K2	QR–B1
18 P–K4	P–K4
19 N–B3	K–N2

For some reason Capablanca suddenly avoids exchanging off all four rooks on the QB-file. His play was evidently influenced by the hopeless state of the match.

20 P–R3	P–KR3 (*90*)

90
W

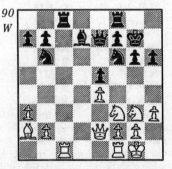

21 Q–Q2!

From this moment onwards

Alekhine carries out a series of amazingly subtle manoeuvres, combining them with sharp tactical blows. There are two aims to this move. The first is clear and understandable – to advance the queen to QR5, where it will immediately attack two pawns, on QR7 and K5. The second aim is unexpected. The opponent's plausible reply 21 ... B–B3 is refuted by the stunning 22 N–R4!! For example, 22 ... N×P (*22 ... B×P 23 Q–K3!* or *22 ... B–Q2 23 Q–R5*) 23 N4–B5+ P×N 24 N×P+ K–N3 25 Q×P+ K×N 26 P–KN4 mate.

21 ...   B–K3?

But even so, there was no need to capitulate so meekly. After the game Lasker showed that Black had an adequate defence – 21 ... N–R5! In this case Black's counter-attack against the QNP would give him the chance to successfully repulse White's attack. Now he simply loses a pawn.

22 B×B   Q×B
23 Q–R5

Capablanca's attempts to interrupt the logical course of events by small tactical blows do not disturb Alekhine.

23 ...   N–B5
24 Q×RP   N×NP
25 R×R   R×R
26 Q×P   N–B5
27 Q–N4   R–QR1
28 R–R1   Q–B3! (*91*)

Perhaps Capablanca hoped that by 29 ... R–R5 he would be able not only to blockade the QRP, but even to win it, but he has not taken everything into account.

29 P–QR4!

A small tactical finesse. It turns out that White is not making a present of his KP.

29 ...   N×P
30 N×P!

And once again White is a pawn to the good. But Capablanca resists

91
W

stubbornly. After all, the loss of this game would cost him the chess throne.

30 ...   Q–Q3!

Taking play into a heavy-piece ending, where, as is well known, it is very difficult to realize the advantage of an extra pawn.

31 Q×N   Q×N
32 R–K1   N–Q3
33 Q–QB1!   Q–B3
34 N–K4   N×N
35 R×N   R–QN1

There begins a wonderful battle of heavy pieces, worthy of concluding this historic encounter. At first glance it appears difficult for White to advance his extra passed pawn, but ingenuity and fine technique enable Alekhine to achieve the impossible.

Here is what Alekhine writes about the winning plan which he drew up in this position. 'The winning method here consists of combining threats created by the passed pawn with an attack on the somewhat weakened position of the black king. White first gains control of the important diagonal QR1–KR8'.

36 R–K2   R–QR1
37 R–R2   R–R4
38 Q–B7   Q–R3
39 Q–B3+!

In order to prevent the advance of the QRP, Black was forced to abandon the long diagonal, and so, of course, the white queen occupies it.

Combinative play, in which White's mating threats are very real, now begins.

39 ...	**K–R2**
40 R–Q2	

Here is the first threat – R–Q8.

40 ...	**Q–N3**
41 R–Q7	**Q–N8+**
42 K–R2	**Q–N1+**
43 P–N3	**R–KB4** (*92*)

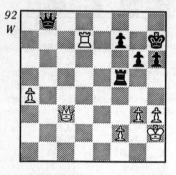

44 Q–Q4!

The strength of this move lies in its simplicity. White's threat to advance his QRP forces Capablanca to agree to further piece exchanges, which hastens White's victory.

44 ...	**Q–K1**
45 R–Q5	**R–B6**

The queen ending would be hopeless for Black.

46 P–R4!

The threat to open the black king's position and begin an attack by P–KR5 forces Capablanca to seek exchanges.

46 ...	**Q–KR1**
47 Q–N6!	

The queens must not be exchanged yet, since the black rook would have time to occupy the important defensive position behind the QRP.

47 ...	**Q–R8**
48 K–N2	**R–B3**
49 Q–Q4	

This is the correct time to exchange.

49 ...	**Q × Q**
50 R × Q (*93*)	

The third stage of this 'multi-episode' game begins. Alekhine conducts the rook ending with great mastery.

50 ...	**K–N2**
51 P–QR5	**R–R3**
52 R–Q5	**R–KB3**
53 R–Q4	**R–R3**
54 R–R4	**K–B3**
55 K–B3	**K–K4**
56 K–K3	**P–R4**
57 K–Q3	**K–Q4**
58 K–B3	**K–B4**
59 R–R2	**K–N4**
60 K–N3	**K–B4**
61 K–B3	**K–N4**
62 K–Q4!	

The place for the white king is among the black pawns, while the black pieces are tied down by White's rook and QRP.

62 ...	**R–Q3+**

Or 62 ... K–N5 63 R–R1 !, and the black king is unable to organize a perpetual attack on the rook.

63 K–K5	**R–K3+**
64 K–B4	**K–R3**
65 K–N5	**R–K4+**
66 K–R6	**R–KB4**
67 P–B4	

White could have chosen a swifter road to victory: 67 K–N7 R–B6 68 K–N8 R–B3 69 K–B8 ! R–B6 70

K–N7 R–B4 71 P–B4, and Black is in zugzwang. But can we reproach Alekhine, who was on the threshold of realizing his life's dream . . .

67 . . .	R–B4!
68 R–R3	R–B2
69 K–N7	R–Q2
70 P–B5	P × P
71 K–B6	P–B5
72 P × P	R–Q4
73 K–N7	R–KB4
74 R–R4	K–N4

75 R–K4!

White gives up his QRP, but wins in return both Black's K-side pawns.

75 . . .	K–R3
76 K–R6	R × RP
77 R–K5	R–R8
78 K × P	R–KN8
79 R–KN5	R–KR8
80 R–KB5	K–N3
81 R × P	K–B3
82 R–K7	1–0

3 Intoxicated by Vacillating Fame

VICTORIES, VICTORIES . . .

A storm of ecstasy greeted the new chess king. Letters and telegrams arrived in Buenos Aires from countries all over the world, but in particular – from Russia. They were sent by friends and chess enthusiasts from Moscow, Leningrad, Siberia. Their delight was sincere – they were acclaiming the glorious victor who had won the throne from the formidable Capablanca, previously thought to be unbeatable. Perhaps it was just this unexpectedness of the victory, against all the predictions, which impressed people, even those who knew nothing about chess.

And Alekhine's fellow-chess players were delighted by the mastery shown by Alekhine in the titanic battle at Buenos Aires. The six splendid wins demonstrated forcefully and convincingly Alekhine's mastery of all three stages of the game. These artistic works have remained for many years as examples of chess creativity. Those who had predicted Alekhine's victory – Lasker and Reti – unashamedly praised him, while even the most fervent supporters of Capablanca sharply changed their tune.

From Buenos Aires Alekhine and his wife visited Chile, and then set off for Europe by sea. They were met by an exultant crowd of chess enthusiasts at the port of Barcelona. There were speeches, toasts, meetings with delighted admirers, outings. During one trip to the mountains Alekhine was almost hurt in a car accident, but fortunately everything turned out well in the end, and soon the couple were aboard the Barcelona–Paris express, bound for home.

And then came the first blow – the herald of coming misfortunes. There were only a few people to meet Alekhine at the station in Paris. There were practically no French people, only a few close acquaintances and reporters. This was a terrible blow after the triumph in Barcelona! What was the reason? Surely it wasn't that no one in France was bothered about the World Chess Champion? Already at the station questions began to arise, the answers to which Alekhine was to seek for years to come. . . .

In the French newspapers there were practically no articles about Alekhine. 'Such a greeting gave the world champion the chance to rest', – this was the caustic remark in one of the emigré newspapers the following day.

Of course, Russian emigrés were greatly interested in Alekhine's victory. A. I. Kuprin wrote an excellent congratulatory article; even those who had nothing to do with chess expressed their opinions. One felt that Alekhine's victory had given the Russian people living in Paris, far from their homeland, and struggling for their existence, occasion to start arguments with the French:

'He is one of us Russians! Just see if you can do anything like that.'

There was no lack of invitations, and of course, a banquet was held in the Russian club of Paris in honour of the chess king.

This was a splendid occasion. Those who came to the dinner paid twenty-five francs, and those who only came to dance – ten francs. Alekhine was presented with presents which were modest, but close to his heart, such as a copy of the first edition of Philidor's book. And then came Alekhine's answering words. . . . It would have been better if he had kept quiet that evening!

The following morning the emigré newspapers gave an account of the banquet, and singled out the desire, apparently expressed by Alekhine, that 'the myth of the invincibility of the Bolsheviks should be dispelled, just as the myth of Capablanca's invincibility had been dispelled'.

Did Alekhine actually speak these words? Was this the meaning of his speech? While preparing material for the novel *Byeliye i Chorniye*, I read over all the emigré newspapers of those days: in each of them Alekhine's speech was reported in a different way, and some of them made no reference at all to 'the myth'.

Knowing the habits of the reactionary section of the White Guards, I sought advice from people who knew closely the life of Russians in Paris. No one was firmly convinced that it was Alekhine who spoke these words. An important fact, which to a certain extent exonerates Alekhine, is that following this he never said anything of a similar nature. Conviction has its own logic: if you firmly hold an opinion, then you will certainly repeat and defend it. In all the following years Alekhine not once returned to these ideas which were attributed to him. In fact, it was just the opposite; there was not a single bad word about his homeland and Soviet power, only a longing desire to return and see his native land.

But the deed was done, and the reaction was immediate. The chess organization of the Soviet Union could naturally only go by the material published, and Alekhine's action received the following response. 'After his speech in the Russian club, we are finished with citizen Alekhine – he is our enemy, and from now on we will regard him only as an enemy'. This was the official point of view of Soviet chess players, expressed by N. V. Krilenko. While brother Aleksey wrote this letter to Soviet papers:

'I condemn any anti-Soviet demonstration, whatever the source, even if, as in the given case, it is my brother. I am finished for ever with Alexander Alekhine. Aleksey Alekhine'.

Thus was broken the thread which connected Alekhine with his homeland, with the people, opinions and friendship which he so valued. Articles in chess journals also terminated: Grekov sent a telegram to the effect that the journal *Shakhmaty* was ceasing all co-operation with Alekhine.

So what was there left? There was still his beloved Nadya from his homeland, his beloved chess was always with him. Here he was the sovereign, everyone listened to him, everyone obeyed him.

All the thoughts, all the actions of Alexander Alekhine were to be devoted to chess. It is true that in the next few years he did make attempts to study something besides chess (Alekhine even joined a Masonic Lodge in Paris, the amusing habits of which were described to me by Lev Dmitrievich Lyubimov, who joined the order at the same time as Alekhine). But he soon finished with all this.

CHESS ALONE

There remained only chess, and this brought him the joy of victory, of creativity, and a feeling of his own greatness and superiority. Indeed, only Lasker had enjoyed such an untroubled reign. Alekhine had no dangerous rivals.

Emanuel Lasker immediately rejected any attempts to organize a match between him and the new world champion. 'If the match had been won by Capablanca, I would have taken the opportunity to cross swords with him' – wrote Lasker. 'But to battle with youth in chess, thank you – no !'

Capablanca gradually became accustomed to his new position. At first he could not sit quietly for one minute. How soon could he win back his lost title ! In a return match he would easily beat Alekhine.

And Capablanca became amazingly active, forgetting for the moment that Alekhine now had the deciding word, that he could, and would, demand postponements and dictate conditions, just as Capablanca had done for six years.

Yes, in all probability the Cuban did not appreciate this, otherwise how can one explain his demand for a change in the conditions of world championship matches. 'I defeated you fairly by winning six games', was Alekhine's answer to the ex-world champion, 'and I will accept that someone is stronger than me, if he wins six games against me'.

The defeated champion began to prophesy the death of chess due to drawing, thus repeating what Lasker had said when he had lost his title. Capablanca even played a match with Maroczy on an enormous board – sixteen squares by twelve. Nothing became of this venture, except that its popularity suffered.

However, all this was not the main point. The cause of Capablanca's crisis lay elsewhere. A defeat has to be endured, lessons must be learned from it, readjustments made, and only then should one once more go forth into battle. Capablanca's character was such that he could not tolerate such waiting and deliberation, and he straight away threw himself into new chess battles. Arriving in Europe, the former champion, who up till then had rarely taken part in tournaments, began to play in one after another. But his strength was not the same – the infallibility of the former chess machine had gone: it has long been known that the brain works accurately only in youth, and that in later years infallibility in chess disappears. Besides, his opponents, who had formerly been overawed by the champion's reputation, now began to play more boldly against him, and he found wins more hard to come by.

'Despite the loss of his title, Capablanca still retains too much self-confidence, but his superb intuition is beginning to betray him' – so wrote one of the experts after the tournament in Kissingen (1928). After losing hope of achieving anything definite by correspondence with Alekhine, Capablanca soon realized that patrons would be even less willing to give him money for a return match, than they were to give money to Alekhine for a match several years previously. After this the Cuban began playing chess less frequently. Supported by the small island of Cuba, which had provided him with a comfortable diplomatic post, Capablanca would still appear at the 'Régence' cafe in Paris, but only to play . . . bridge.

The remaining challengers did not threaten to disturb Alekhine's composure. Nimzowitsch, with his lack of practicability, would never have been able to raise the fifteen thousand dollars (Alekhine inherited the 'tradition' of demanding this sum from his predecessor), and there remained only Bogoljubow and Euwe. Neither was dangerous – he could rule in peace, and play and play . . . 'My task', Alekhine decided, 'is to demonstrate everything of which I am capable in chess'.

'AS WITH MERE NOVICES'

And during the years 1929–1932 Alekhine showed the world what he was capable of.

After winning a match with Bogoljubow 'on the way', as it were, Alekhine began to display unprecedented, record results in tournaments, all against strong opposition. During this period Alekhine took part in ten international tournaments, and in all ten won first prize! Chess brought him fame, chess bowed to his will, chess opened to him its innermost secrets.

Two tournaments were especially memorable: at San Remo in 1930, and at Bled in the following year. At the picturesque resort of San Remo the tournament was particularly strong; of the likely contenders for the world title there was Nimzowitsch, Bogoljubow and Rubinstein; only Lasker and Capablanca were missing. But Alekhine's dealings with Capablanca were abnormal; their quarrel had continued, and relations had worsened to such an extent that one would leave a room if the other should enter it. Capablanca once demanded that the judge should remove the 'foreigner' to outside the barrier, behind which the competitors in a tournament were playing. 'But he is the world champion!' was all the judge could say, with a helpless gesture.

Alekhine was asked by the organizers of one tournament: 'What is your appearance fee?'

'Five thousand.'

'And if Capablanca is playing?'

'Then ten thousand'.

The tournament in San Remo finished as one of the greatest triumphs of the Russian champion. Only two players managed to draw with him, all the rest lost. Up to that time the tournament record was held by Lasker for his performances in London in 1899, where he was $4\frac{1}{2}$ points ahead of Janowski, and in Paris in 1900, where Nimzowitsch was two points behind (Lasker scored $23\frac{1}{2}$ out of 28, and $14\frac{1}{2}$ out of 16 in the respective tournaments). At San Remo Alekhine came ahead of his nearest rival, Nimzowitsch, who took second place, by $3\frac{1}{2}$ points.

Even more impressive than Alekhine's results was the style of his victories. In this tournament he played a number of brilliant games, and many of his opponents were defeated at a very early stage of the game.

'He deals with us, as if we are mere novices', exclaimed Nimzowitsch after losing to Alekhine in the tournament at Bled (1931).

The tournament at Bled was played in two cycles (each contestant played a total of 26 games). Besides well-known grandmasters, the most talented representatives of chess youth had been invited: Flohr, Kashdan and Stoltz. Alekhine defeated his opponents in crushing style – $20\frac{1}{2}$ points out of 26! Bogoljubow, who came second, finished $5\frac{1}{2}$ points behind him! In the history of tournament play the like had never been seen. And once again outstanding games, full of deep strategic plans, bold attacks, and unexpected tactical ideas.

In the London tournament of 1932, and in the same year in Berne, Alekhine once again came first. At the tournament in Zurich (1934) a tactical oversight in his game against Euwe forced Alekhine to begin with a loss. And what came of it? Nothing. The world champion concluded the tournament with a series of wins, and as a result scored 13 points out of 15, finishing a point ahead of Flohr and Euwe.

Alekhine had convinced the chess world of his great strength, and when Bogoljubow began seeking means to organize a second match, the sceptics only smiled. Why was he bothering! And the sceptics were proved right: Alekhine crushed without difficulty his persistent opponent.

His tremendous results and splendid creative achievements aroused the admiration of even his closest rivals. 'Alekhine, it seemed, used to infuse his pieces with the features of his own striking personality', wrote the English master Sir George Thomas in answer to my request in 1956. 'Against no one else did I sense so keenly that I was playing against a man'. 'Alekhine is the absolutely ideal chess player, he is equally outstanding in all stages of the game', was Flohr's reply to the same request. 'Alekhine, in my opinion, is the greatest player of all time. Alekhine is the outstanding phenomenon in chess history'.

And this is the opinion of his opponent in three matches, the man who won the world title from Alekhine for two years – ex-world champion Euwe. 'The Alekhine of Buenos Aires 1927, of San Remo

1930, and of many other chess battles, showed the world delightful combinations and excellent play in all stages of the game, in short, all that comes easily to a genius from the grace of God'.

I WANT TO GO HOME !

It was in this brilliant fashion that the 1930s started for Alekhine. And then suddenly around 1932–1933, admirers of Alekhine, when playing over his games, began to occasionally shrug their shoulders in perplexity. What is the world champion doing, why is he playing so strangely? He will suddenly spoil his pawn structure voluntarily, lose tempi, allow his opponent a dangerous attack . . .

Only those who were close to Alekhine, who knew his frame of mind, could guess at the truth. The world champion was experiencing a period of depression, dissatisfaction, at times despair.

All that a chess player could wish for, Alekhine had achieved. He had a clear superiority over all his contemporaries, he was firmly established on the chess throne. Patrons would simply wave aside anyone who asked for money for a match with Alekhine. Why throw money down the drain? Who has even the slightest chance of defeating such a Titan? The chess king had every right to be satisfied: he could reign in peace, revel in his greatness and fame, and enjoy being admired by everyone. . . . What more could a champion want?

The champion, perhaps, wanted nothing, but the man was in need of much. Alekhine needed friends, who would sincerely appreciate his talent, he needed a homeland, which would be proud of him, and which would come to his aid in difficult times. Did he have all this? Who was excited by his achievements, his victories, who was interested in his beautiful games? The French? They were not particularly fond of chess, and he was, in effect, a foreigner to them. The Russians in France? They were living from hand to mouth, and were constantly searching around for work. They had no need of chess, not even of the world champion himself!

It seemed that he was striving to create, suffering, spending sleepless nights in analysis, and all for whom? Not for anyone! There was, it is true, a country, a people, to which his name belonged, where he would be loved, famous, where he would be regarded as one of them, but he had lost that country, to everyone there he was an enemy. . . .

And what was happening there in chess! Flohr had told him – it was a real chess El Dorado! They played in theatres, on the stage.

Long articles were written about chess in the press, there were broadcasts on the radio: every piece of news was instantly sent to all corners of the country by telephone and telegraph. Thousands took part in tournaments. These thousands were his supporters, his friends.

'Alekhine questioned me for a long time about Moscow, about Leningrad' wrote Salo Flohr in reply to my questionnaire, 'and even I – no psychologist – understood and read in Alekhine's eyes that he was greatly missing Moscow'.

'I very much wanted Alekhine to visit Moscow. If they warmly applauded me in the Hall of Columns when I isolated my opponent's pawn, or obtained the two bishops, then what would happen, I thought, when Moscow saw the brilliant, inimitable combinations of Alekhine! In 1933 and 1935 I was convinced that Alekhine was incredibly popular in the USSR. Whatever had happened, Alekhine was Alekhine!

'Unfortunately for me, for Alekhine, and for Soviet chess players, the Russian champion never managed to get to Moscow, and my strongest desire to see him greeted in the Hall of Columns in Trade Union House was not realized'.

Salo Flohr is echoed by his friend – Andrei Lilienthal:

'On one occasion Flohr and I were sitting in a cafe, when Alekhine came in. We got into conversation, and he said that he was thinking of returning to his homeland. He spoke on this theme on a number of occasions, it was his cherished dream. The last years of this outstanding chess player burned with thoughts about his country of birth, and it is a great pity that this dream of his was never fulfilled'.

It was during this period that Alekhine began to take steps to return to his homeland. In 1933 Salo Flohr, who was then champion of Czechoslovakia, set off to Moscow for a match with Mikhail Botvinnik. Alekhine asked him to have a word with the USSR envoy in Prague, Ilyin-Zhenevsky, who was an old partner of Alekhine from the 1920 Olympiad. Zhenevsky said that everything should be discussed with Moscow. Later in Moscow Flohr spoke to Krilyenko, who replied: 'First let Alekhine write a letter to the press. We were too offended by that stupid speech of his!' The question of him coming to the Soviet Union was deferred . . .

'In 1933 I first noticed sadness in Alekhine's eyes', writes Flohr. 'When I left Prague for the match with Botvinnik in Moscow, Alekhine saw me off from the station. He himself remained in Prague, from where he was to go on tour. Only my youth and inexperience of life could explain why I failed to understand how tragically sad this parting was for Alekhine'.

DECLINE

But at this point an encounter occurred which was to leave its mark on Alekhine, and to change his life to a great extent. During one of his regular tours with simultaneous displays, Alekhine met the widow of the Governor of Morocco, Grace Wishaar, an Englishwoman. He left Nadezhda Semyenovna and married Grace. She was a well-educated woman, and she keenly understood and shared the interests of her husband. 'She understands me perfectly', said Alekhine on a number of occasions. His new wife had some private means, and owned a house in Dieppe. For the first time since leaving Moscow Alekhine had found a refuge in the case of illness and old-age. . . .

It was just at this time that Alekhine received a challenge from Max Euwe. The Dutch Government and patrons guaranteed the financial side of the event, and Alekhine agreed, although he was complaining about his health. Why did he do this? Perhaps he simply underestimated Euwe?

Not at all! Alekhine considered that Euwe was a dangerous tactician, an expert on theory, and one of the five strongest grandmasters in the world. He was particularly dangerous in match play. True, Capablanca had been able to beat him by two points in a ten-game match, but in their first match, in 1927, Alekhine had only finished one point ahead. Alekhine knew that the Dutch champion's supporters would do everything to ensure that their favourite was prepared for the match in the best possible way. Some of the strongest grandmasters in the world would be his trainers. But Alekhine was not afraid of trainers!

'During the match between Alekhine and Euwe in 1935 I became involved in Alekhine's "internal affairs" with Euwe. As a strong player at that time, I should have avoided siding with either of the players, and this I did in 1937. I do not wish to imply by this that I was responsible for Alekhine's defeat in 1935, but my presence would, in any case, have had an adverse effect on his humour.

'In fact, during the 1935 match the relations between us worsened somewhat, but they became normal again within two or three months after the match'.

Here Flohr talks about Alekhine's poor material circumstances prior to this match with Euwe. He writes: 'Often I was asked: was Alekhine rich? No, as yet no one had become rich from chess. With his boundless love for the game, Alekhine felt a certain "chess fatigue" during the last period of his life. He said that he was tired of having to struggle for his means of existence, and dreamed of organizing tournaments himself, of being the judge, or, still better, the patron who would give brilliancy prizes.'

Alekhine began the match with Euwe in his usual brilliant fashion. Although he lost the second game, three wins in the first, third and fourth games gave him the lead, which he further consolidated by winning the seventh. 4–1 was a convincing score, and seemed to promise Alekhine an 'easy life'. The Dutch were beginning to regret that they had subjected their favourite to such a trying ordeal, and it was expected that the match would soon finish.

And then, suddenly, amazing news began to arrive from the various Dutch towns where the games were being played. Alekhine began to lose. But it wasn't just the fact that he was losing – you can't expect to avoid a single defeat in a match of thirty games! What was important was the character of the defeats. Instead of a grandmaster of extra class, as had been seen during the first ten games, the spectators suddenly found a completely different player sitting across the board from Euwe. In one game he castled into mate, and in another he played the opening so absurdly weakly that he could have easily resigned after only a few moves.

What was happening? – the chess world asked in bewilderment. How was such a sudden change possible, what was the cause? After many suggestions, the following conclusion, confirmed by reports from correspondents in Holland, was reached: Alekhine had played these games in a drunken state. It was written that, for one of the games, Alekhine arrived in such a condition that he was unable by his own efforts to climb onto the stage. 'Perhaps we should postpone the game?' suggested the always sporting Euwe. 'Definitely not!' came Alekhine's mumbled reply.

Alekhine's play during the middle part of the match was of a very poor standard. The result was four losses, and by the fifteenth game the scores had become level. Menaced by the threat of losing his title, Alekhine decided to take a grip on himself, and called on all his mastery.

But here a part was played by the imprecisely determined law of form, inspiration, and other incompletely understood ideas. Even earlier it had not been easy for Alekhine to beat Euwe, and now the Dutch champion, inspired by his series of wins, played the rest of the match with great verve.

By not keeping to a routine, and by scornfully disregarding the basic strategic laws of chess, Alekhine seemed to have, as it were, offended his beloved art, and it appeared to decide to make him pay for this. In any case, whenever he needed just the slightest bit of luck, it didn't happen: when the position was better for Alekhine, and he was on the point of chalking up a point, an exceptional, problem-like draw would be found. Practical players will be acquainted with this alternation from one tournament where one is lucky to another where nothing goes right.

During the match Alekhine sent the following telegram to Moscow: 'Not only as a chess player of many years standing, but also as a person who understands the significance of all that is being done in the USSR for culture, I send my sincere congratulations to the chess players of the Soviet Union on the 18th anniversary of the October Revolution. Alexander Alekhine'.

This telegram was printed in *Izvestia*. The reaction was stormy. Emigres, who had no special liking for Alekhine because of his exceptional position – world champion, able to travel all round the world ! – attacked him in a series of articles. In one of the papers was printed a fable, the concluding lines of which expressively indicate the atmosphere which at that time surrounded Alekhine. 'Have morals, reader, in your head, and in this, do not forget Alekhine, who, beaten by Euwe, went over to the Soviets'.

The concluding part of the 1935 match was a real tragedy for a great player who had come into conflict with himself, with the merci-lessness of fate, with the surrounding world, and with chess itself. Euwe had an advantage of two points, which Alekhine then reduced to one. Just one more win would save him, but this he could not manage. In the twenty-eighth game, Alekhine won a pawn, went into an ending, the win was almost there, but the pieces were so placed that there was a draw in the position, and Euwe found it.

Just the two final games remained.

The twenty-ninth game, and once again Alekhine has an extra pawn. The position promises the win, which will save the match. But . . . the pieces group themselves in such a cunning way that a win is impossible. Once again a draw.

And at last, the final, thirtieth game. Oh, these final encounters !

Alekhine had been playing them with exceptional strength, though this had demanded tremendous efforts on his part. But now he seemed somehow broken. In Alekhine's soul there was still hope, but he was conscious that he was not going to win this game.

'Alekhine appeared in a dress-coat, white tie, and patent-leather shoes', writes Truda Kmoch, the wife of Euwe's former trainer, about this final encounter 'and with the words "I am wearing this dress-coat in honour of Doctor Euwe" took his place. It appeared that he was trying to play a rehearsed role, but he was barely able to do this. Soon he became nervous, began to put out cigarettes which he had only just lit, and to consult with his doctor. Several times he took something, evidently a stimulant, then once again smoked and smoked. In the whole hall I doubt whether there was even a handful of people who at that moment were hoping for Alekhine to win'.

In this game there was never a glimmer of hope for Alekhine; from the very start things went badly for him. 'I am prepared at any moment to agree to a draw', Euwe told his opponent before the start of the game. The world champion, enjoying the last few hours of his reign, declined the offer. Although, as might be expected, Euwe also became nervous during the game, he nevertheless played with commendable accuracy. The time control was reached. Alekhine was two pawns down in an ending.

'I will agree to a draw', said Alekhine, not believing that his offer would be accepted. Just so as to test Euwe. The Dutchman agreed and stretched out his hand.

'Hurrah for the new world champion ! Long live Dutch chess players !' exclaimed Alekhine, rising from his chair.

When the notice with the word 'draw' appeared, the hall almost exploded. Pushing each other about, and shouting wildly, grown-ups rushed either to the exit or to the stage. All semblance of order and decorum was lost. Euwe was embraced and kissed, and the new chess king arrived home on the shoulders of his friends. There they shouted for him to appear on the balcony. There was general rejoicing until late into the night.

... Abandoned by everyone, the overthrown chess king sat for a long time on the stage of the empty hall, then walked slowly back to his hotel, his patent-leather shoes squelching through the autumn puddles. In his hotel room he took out a bottle of whisky, but he didn't want to drink.

Soon an invitation to the 3rd Moscow International Tournament arrived.

'He said that his trip to Moscow would have to wait a little', writes Flohr. 'I want to go to Moscow only as Champion of the World . . .'.

GAMES FROM THE YEARS
1927–1935

The following game illustrates Alekhine's great mastery of appraising a position, and also his irreproachable accuracy in the calculation of lengthy variations.

40) Alekhine-Koltanowski, London 1932

Ruy Lopez

1 P–K4	P–K4
2 N–KB3	N–QB3
3 B–N5	P–QR3
4 B–R4	P–Q3
5 B × N+	P × B
6 P–Q4	P × P

The players have chosen the so-called Steinitz Defence Deferred, which was popular at the start of the century, and which has not lost its importance even today. The only difference is that in modern tournaments Black does not hurry to give up the centre, but tries to reinforce his K4 square by 6 . . . P–B3.

7 N × P	B–Q2
8 0–0	P–N3
9 N–QB3	B–N2
10 R–K1	N–K2
11 B–B4	0–0
12 Q–Q2	P–QB4
13 N–N3	N–B3

Black has played the opening well, and now has a perfectly defensible position, with hopes of counter-play associated with occupation of his . . . Q5 and . . . K4 squares, together with the open QN-file and the powerful KB.

For this reason he should not have allowed White to exchange off his fine bishop. The elastic 13 . . . R–K1 would have allowed the bishop to retreat to R1 at the appropriate moment.

14 B–R6	B–K3
15 B × B	K × B
16 N–Q5	P–B3
17 QR–Q1	R–QN1
18 Q–B3	Q–B1
19 P–QR3	R–B2
20 P–R3!	Q–N2
21 R–K3	Q–N4 (*94*)

In making this move, Koltanowski apparently had no suspicion that there was any danger threatening him. And in fact, White's sacrifice is somewhat unexpected.

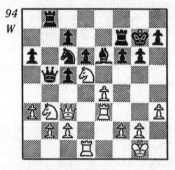

94
W

22 N × QBP!

A positional sacrifice. Alekhine obtains strong pressure along the open central file, and then transfers this pressure to the K-side, in particular to the KBP.

'As a rule so-called positional sacrifices are more difficult to find, and should therefore be rated more highly, than those which are exclusively based on the exact calculation of tactical possibilities'.

True, in presenting a large number of concrete, combinational variations, Alekhine to some extent contradicts himself: if so many variations were calculated, it means that it was not a 'pure' positional sacrifice.

22 ...   **R×N**
23 R×P   **B–B5**

Besides this move, Alekhine considers the following possible defences:

a) 23 ... B×N?   24 Q×KBP+ and then 25 R×B with an easy win.

b) 23 ... N–Q5?   24 N×N etc.

c) 23 ... Q–B5   24 N×P! etc.

d) 23 ... N–Q1   24 R–B3 R–B2 25 N×P etc.

e) 23 ... R–K1   24 N×P N–Q1 25 P–QN4 N–B2   26 R×B etc.

f) 23 ... R–K1   24 N×P N–Q1 25 P–QN4, 'after which 25 ... R–B3 enables Black to avoid an immediate debacle, although the three pawns foɪ a bishop promise White good winning chances'.

g) 23 ... K–B2   24 R–B3 K–K2 25 P–QR4 Q–N3 26 R×B+ K×R 27 N×P+   K–Q3 (or *27 ... K–B2 28 Q×P+ K–N1 29 N–K6!* etc.) 28 Q×P+ K×N 29 R–B3+ K–N5 30 Q–Q6+ and wins.

24 P–QR4!   **Q×P**

The only move – the queen must continue to defend both the knight and the bishop.

25 N×P   **Q–N4**
26 Q×P+   **K–N1**
27 N–Q7!   **R–Q1** (*95*)

Here also White is able to throw all his pieces at the unfortunate enemy king.

28 R–KB3   **Q–N5**
29 P–B3   **Q–N4**
30 N–K5!   **R1–QB1**
31 N×N   **1–0**

On 31 ... R×N there follows 32 R–Q8+ and mate in two moves. For this game Alekhine was awarded a special brilliancy prize.

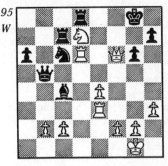

41) Alekhine–Molina, Buenos Aires, 1926,
Simultaneous, Danish Gambit

1 P–K4   **P–K4**
2 P–Q4   **P×P**
3 P–QB3

The romantic Danish Gambit, which won a number of glorious victories in tournaments during the last century and at the beginning of this century. On observing some of the colourless draws in present-day tournaments, one cannot help wishing that our grandmasters and masters should be forced, if only on 'festival days', to give the spectators some pleasure by playing games with gambit openings.

3 ...   **P–Q4**
4 KP×P   **N–KB3**
5 N–B3   **N×P**
6 Q×P   **N–QB3**
7 B–QN5   **B–K2**
8 0–0

After 8 Q×NP B–B3 and 9 ... Q–K2+ with Q-side castling soon to follow, the game could be far from in White's favour.

8 ...   **0–0**
9 B×N   **P×B**
10 R–K1   **B–N2**
11 N–R3   **R–K1**
12 N–B4   **P–QB4**
13 Q–Q1   **Q–Q2**
14 N–R5   **Q–N4**
15 N×B   **Q×N**

16 P–B4

This move provokes doubled-edged complications, in which White outplays his opponent.

16 ...	N–N5
17 Q–N3	QR–Q1
18 B–K3	Q–R3

This denies the white queen her QR4 square, and threatens the deadly 19 . . . R–Q6.

19 P–QR3!   **N–Q6**

Of course 19 . . . R–Q6 now loses to 20 P × N!

20 R/K1–Q1	Q–KN3
21 R–Q2	R–Q2
22 Q–R4	P–QB3
23 R1–Q1	R1–Q1
24 P–R3!	

Now Black should also have given his king a loophole by 24 . . . P–KR3. In passing over this chance, Alekhine's opponent allows a combination of rare beauty, while 24 . . . P–KR3 would have led only to a better ending for White after 25 Q–B2 B–B3 26 N–K1 N–K4 27 Q × Q.

24 ...   **N × NP** (*96*)

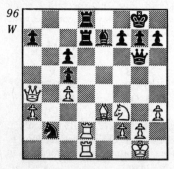

96
W

25 Q × RP!!

This queen sacrifice is based on far-seeing and precise calculation. Black now has several possibilities:

a) 25 . . . R × R 26 R × R R × R 27 N × R, and White has, in effect, an extra pawn (on QR3).

b) 25 . . . N × R 26 R × R N × B

27 P × N R × R 28 Q × R B–B1 29 N–K5 etc.

c) 25 . . . B–Q3 26 Q × R R × Q 27 R × N Q–K3 28 R2–Q2, and the pin on the bishop decides (Alekhine).

25 ...	R × Q
26 R × R+	B–B1
27 B × P	P–R3
28 R × B+	K–R2
29 R1–Q8	Q–N8+
30 K–R2	R–N2
31 N–R4!	1–0

Here it is, the finishing stroke. Only the advance of the NP can prevent mate on KR8, but does this save the game? If 31 . . . P–N3, then White mates by the simple 32 B–Q4, while 31 . . . P–N4 is answered by 32 R–KR8+ K–N2 33 R/Q8–N8+ K–B3 34 R × RP+ K–K4 35 R–K8+ with mate on the following move. Black therefore resigned.

Alekhine was able to discover and foresee the most fantastic hidden possibilities in chess, and not only when he was attacking, but also in defence. The following game is a wonderful example.

42) Johner–Alekhine, Switzerland 1928

Grünfeld Defence

1 P–QB4	N–KB3
2 N–QB3	P–B4
3 N–B3	P–Q4
4 P × P	N × P
5 P–KN3	P–KN3
6 B–N2	B–N2
7 0–0	0–0
8 P–Q4	

By transposition, one of the variations of the Grünfeld Defence has been reached. Black can, if he wishes, achieve a quick draw by 8 . . . P × P 9 N × P N × N 10 P × N N–B3 11 N × N P × N, as occurred in the seventh game of the Korchnoi-Petrosian match in 1971. But Alekhine never used to choose a path which led to wholesale exchanges.

8 ...	**N × N**
9 P × N	**N–B3**
10 P–K3	**Q–R4?**

But this is a serious inaccuracy, which allows White to significantly improve the distribution of his forces by the manoeuvre N–Q2–B4. The simple 10 ... B–K3 would have allowed Black to complete his development, with a roughly equal game.

11 B–N2	**R–Q1**
12 N–Q2!	**Q–B2**
13 Q–B2	**N–R4**

And this display of activity only worsens Alekhine's position. By continuing 13 ... P–K3 followed by 14 ... P–N3 and 15 ... B–N2 Black could still have put up a solid defence against his opponent's offensive operations in the centre. Now, however, Johner develops a dangerous initiative.

14 QR–B1	**B–K3**
15 B–QR3!	**N–B5** (*97*)

In a difficult position Alekhine decides to sacrifice a pawn in order to gain some possibility of active play. Bad were both 15 ... P–B5 and 15 ... P × P 16 BP × P.

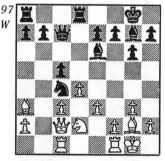

16 N × N	**B × N**
17 KR–Q1	**P × P**
18 BP × P	**QR–B1**
19 Q–K4?	

M. Botvinnik has shown that by 19 B–B1 P–QN4 20 B × B White could have won a pawn while keeping an excellent position, for example: 20 ... P × B 21 B–B5, or 20 ... Q × B 21 Q × Q R × Q 22 R × R P × R 23 B × P. The Swiss master hopes for more, but has overlooked an amazing finesse.

19 ...	**R–Q2**
20 P–Q5	**P–QN4**
21 B–R3	**P–K3!**

It is probable that Johner considered only 21 ... P–B4, after which 22 Q–K6+ and 23 P–K4 would give White a decisive advantage. The defensive plan which Alekhine has worked out is highly original and completely unexpected.

22 P × P	**R × R+**
23 R × R	**P–B4**

Without doubt Johner had foreseen this move, and had prepared in reply a surprising combinative blow. But can you imagine his surprise, when he saw Alekhine's next move!

24 P–K7!	**R–K1!**

Cunning against cunning. White wins after 24 ... P × Q 25 B × R K–B2 26 R–Q8, whereas now the natural 25 R–Q8 is met by the stunning rejoinder 25 ... R × R 26 P–K8=Q+ B–B1!! (*98*)

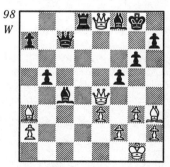

A unique position – the two white queens are unable to hold their own with the markedly weaker black forces. White's best would be 27 Q4–K5 Q × Q 28 Q × Q B × B, when the threats of advancing the Q-side pawns, together with 29 . . . R–Q8+, would decide the game in Black's favour.

25 Q–R4	B × P
26 R–Q8	B–B2
27 R × R+	B × R
28 B–KN2	Q–B6
29 B–Q5+	K–R1
30 B–Q6?	

30 Q–QN4 would have continued the resistance. Now he is lost.

30 . . .	Q–Q7!
31 P–K4	P–N4!
32 Q–R3	P–KN5
33 Q–R4	B–Q5
0–1	

In the game which the reader can now play over, one is delighted by Alekhine's ability to combine a logical plan with small, elegant, and precisely calculated combinations, which immediately decide the issue.

43) Alekhine–Flohr, Bled 1931
Queen's Gambit Accepted

1 P–Q4	P–Q4
2 P–QB4	P × P
3 N–KB3	N–KB3
4 P–K3	P–K3
5 B × P	P–B4
6 0–0	N–B3
7 Q–K2	P–QR3
8 R–Q1	

In those days this was considered to be the best. Later the theorists decided that 8 N–B3 was stronger, and this opinion is held at the present time.

8 . . .	P–QN4
9 P × P	Q–B2
10 B–Q3	B × P
11 P–QR4	P–N5?

A mistake which gives White complete control of QN3 and QB4.

The best chance was to capture on . . . R5.

12 QN–Q2	0–0
13 N–N3	B–K2
14 P–K4	N–Q2
15 B–K3	N2–K4

This move allows Alekhine, by precise play, to take control of the open QB-file, and fully seize the initiative. More stubborn was 15 . . . B–N2 16 QR–B1 Q–N1, with some resistance against the attacking white pieces.

16 N × N	N × N
17 QR–B1	Q–N1 (99)

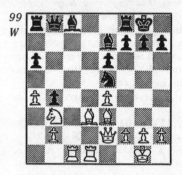

99
W

White's pieces are active, and they control most of the squares in the centre and on the Q-side. White's task is to further cramp the opposing forces, and then search for an object on which to strike the decisive blow.

18 B–B5!

The first of a series of offensive manoeuvres. After the exchange of the black-squared bishops the weakened black squares on the Q-side become points of intrusion for the white pieces.

18 . . .	B × B
19 N × B	Q–N3
20 Q–R5	N–Q2

Yet another passive move. Had Flohr supported his knight by 20 . . . P–B3, he would have had some chance of saving the game. Now all his pieces will be passively placed.

21 B–K2	P–N3
22 Q–N5	N × N
23 R × N	P–QR4

White was threatening to separate Black's Q-side pawns by 24 P–R5.

24 P–R4	B–R3
25 B–B3!	

This move has three simultaneous threats: 26 P–R5, 26 R × P and 26 R–Q7.

25 ...	P–B3
26 Q–K3	QR–Q1
27 R × R	R × R
28 P–K5!	

As a result of logical play White has set up a perfectly 'normal' position, in which, however, is concealed a cunning tactical stroke. In Alekhine's games sound strategy is closely interwoven in this way with tactical blows and traps. But the world champion did not search for these traps, he did not play specially for them; rather they somehow arose out of the peculiarities of the position, thus further confirming the correctness of Alekhine's overall strategy.

The pawn move to K5 appears plausible; in this way White breaks up the opponent's pawns, controls his Q6 square, and induces a weakening of the black squares on the K-side. Alekhine does not seem to be even thinking about a trap or tactics, and Black's reply appears perfectly natural. Why should he play 28 ... P × P, when his K-side pawn structure will be spoiled?

28 ...	P–B4 *(100)*
29 R–B8!	1–0

Q3 is no longer available to the Queen, and so Black suffers heavy material losses.

In the following famous game Alekhine carries out an ingenious piece attack.

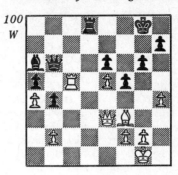

100
W

44) **Alekhine–Lasker,** Zurich 1934
Queen's Gambit Declined

1 P–Q4	P–Q4
2 P–QB4	P–K3
3 N–QB3	N–KB3
4 N–B3	B–K2
5 B–N5	QN–Q2
6 P–K3	0–0
7 R–B1	P–B3
8 B–Q3	P × P
9 B × BP	N–Q4
10 B × B	Q × B

This is the typical position of the Queen's Gambit when Black adopts the defensive system named after Capablanca. In Alekhine's time this position was very popular, and in the Alekhine–Capablanca match this opening was almost exclusively played, the contestants being happy to adopt it either as White, or as Black. Many moves have been suggested by the theorists, but the main continuations are considered to be 11 N–K4 or 11 0–0.

11 N–K4	N4–B3
12 N–N3	P–K4

Alekhine considered this move to be the initial cause of Lasker's defeat, although subsequent analysis has shown that he could have still defended himself at a later stage. Even so, it looks safer to first exchange queens by 12 ... Q–N5+ 13 Q–Q2 Q × Q+ and only then think about freeing moves such as ... P–K4 or ... P–QB4.

13 0–0	P×P
14 N–B5	Q–Q1
15 N3×P	N–K4
16 B–N3	B×N
17 N×B	Q–N3? *(101)*

This incautious move, which takes the queen far away from the K-side, seriously affects Black's chances of putting up a successful defence. It is simply astonishing that such a splendid master of defence as Lasker should underestimate this circumstance. After the correct move 17 ... P–KN3, a complicated struggle with equal chances could develop, whereas now Black loses quickly.

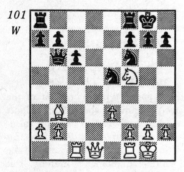

101
W

18 Q–Q6	N4–Q2!

Lasker comes to his senses, and makes some excellent defensive moves, but alas, it is already too late!

19 KR–Q1	QR–Q1
20 Q–N3	P–N3
21 Q–N5!	K–R1

Other moves were no better, since White would simply play 22 R–Q6 and 23 R1–Q1.

22 N–Q6	K–N2
23 P–K4!	N–KN1
24 R–Q3	P–B3

Black allows a spectacular finish to the game, but he had no way of meeting the terrible threat of 25 R–KB3. The misplaced black queen makes a sad sight, apparently unaware that her king is being taken prisoner on the other side of the board.

25 N–B5+	K–R1 *(102)*

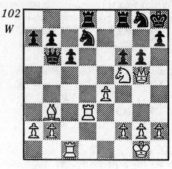

102
W

26 Q×NP!!	1–0

The following curious miniature is used even today as an example of the sudden storming of the king's position.

45) **Alekhine–Mindeno,** Holland 1933
Ruy Lopez

1 P–K4	P–K4
2 N–KB3	N–QB3
3 B–N5	P–Q3

The ancient Steinitz Defence, which is occasionally adopted nowadays.

4 P–Q4	P×P
5 Q×P	B–Q2
6 B×N	B×B
7 N–B3	N–B3
8 B–N5	B–K2
9 0–0–0	0–0
10 P–KR4	P–KR3
11 N–Q5	P×B?

An obvious oversight. Black was hoping for 12 P×P N×N 13 P×N B×NP+, but overlooked the intermediate capture of his KB.

12 N×B+!	Q×N
13 P×P	N×P
14 R–R5!	

For the sacrificed piece White has good compensation in the form of the open KR-file, along which his pieces can break through into the enemy camp.

| 14 ... | Q–K3 |
| 15 R1–R1 | P–B4 (*103*) |

16 N–K5!!

A brilliant combinational solution. White's task is to deny, by any means, the black king his KB2 square. To this end he has to prevent the opponent from playing ... P–Q4 in answer to a check on QB4.

| 16 ... | P × N |
| 17 P–N6 | 1–0 |

On 17 ... Q × NP there follows 18 Q–B4+.

Among the strategic achievements of the new world champion, in the period when he was at the height of his powers, mention should be made first of all of several games in which he settled the outcome in the opening itself.

In the following game Black's poor play, which entails a serious weakening of his black squares, is convincingly refuted.

46) Alekhine-Bogoljubow,
1st match game, 1929, Wiesbaden
Slav Defence

1 P–Q4	P–Q4
2 P–QB4	P–QB3
3 N–KB3	N–B3
4 N–B3	P × P

| 5 P–QR4 | P–K3 |

A poor, and what is more important, very passive move, which allows Alekhine to quickly gain a decisive superiority in the centre. Correct is 5 ... B–B4.

6 P–K4	B–N5
7 P–K5	N–Q4
8 B–Q2	B × N

And this exchange is responsible for the resulting debacle. Some hold could still be made on the position by 8 ... P–QN4 9 N–K4 B–K2 10 P–QN3 N–Q2 11 NP × P P × BP 12 B × P N2–N3 13 B–N3 B–R3 or 13 B–K2 P–QR4 followed by 14 ... N–N5. Now however, the black squares in Black's position become so weak that White is able to exploit this positional factor almost by forced means. True, Alekhine's ingenuity is required in order to do this.

| 9 P × B | P–QN4 |
| 10 N–N5! (*104*) | |

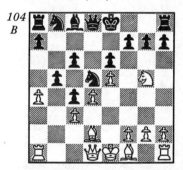

White's plan is simple: he intends to transfer this knight via K4 to Q6, which would immediately render Black's position hopeless. So Bogoljubow adopts extreme measures, so as to at least hinder the knight from establishing itself at Q6.

| 10 ... | P–B3 |

Of course, Black cannot capture on ... QB6 because of 11 Q–B3.

| 11 KP × P | N × KBP |

Or 11 ... Q × P 12 N–K4 Q–Q1
13 B–N5, and Black stands badly.

12 B–K2	P–QR3
13 B–B3 !	

How can Black defend against
14 P × P? Bad are both 13 ... N–Q4
14 Q–B2 P–N3 15 N × RP R × N 16
Q × P+, or 13 ... R–R2 14 B–B4
Q–N3 15 B–Q6, and Black can
hardly move a piece.

13 ...	P–R3
14 B–R5+	N × B
15 Q × N+	K–Q2
16 N–B7	Q–K1
17 Q–N6 !	R–N1
18 B–B4 !	

The black king cannot last out for
long against the fire of so many
enemy pieces. With a series of precise
moves the world champion forces the
win in the shortest possible time.

18 ...	B–N2
19 B–N3	K–K2
20 B–Q6+	K–Q2
21 0–0	P–B4
22 QP × P	B–Q4
23 P × P	P × P
24 R × R	B × R
25 R–R1	N–B3 (*105*)

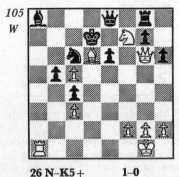

105
W

26 N–K5+	1–0

On 26 ... N × N there follows
27 R–R7+ K–B3 28 Q–K4 mate.

No less convincing is the rout
inflicted on the opponent in the
following game.

47) Alekhine-Euwe, 27th match
game, 1935
Vienna Game

1 P–K4	P–K4
2 N–QB3	N–KB3
3 B–B4	N × P
4 Q–R5	

In Alekhine's hands this ancient
variation of the Vienna Game takes
on a new meaning. The reader can
follow how the world champion
skilfully brings a new positional
content into old forms of sharp tactical
variations. At the same time the
reader may involuntarily regret that
such variations, which appear to
hide much that is unexplored, are not
played nowadays.

4 ...	N–Q3
5 B–N3	B–K2

The variation 5 ... N–B3 6 N–N5
P–KN3 7 Q–B3 P–B4 8 Q–Q5
Q–K2 9 N × BP+ K–Q1 10 N × R
P–N3 has been subjected to much
analysis, but without a final decision
being reached as to which of the two
sides gains the advantage from the
resulting complications. In any case,
one can understand Euwe's reluctance
to go in for such a line without preparatory home analysis.

6 N–B3	N–B3
7 N × P	N × N?

Unexpectedly this leads to a very
difficult position for Black. Better
was 7 ... 0–0 8 N–Q5 N–Q5.

8 Q × N	0–0 (*106*)
9 N–Q5 !	

A splendid solution to a most difficult strategic problem. Had Alekhine
delayed this by one or two moves –
by first castling or developing his
QB, Black would soon have equalized
by playing ... B–B3, ... P–B3, ...
N–K1 and ... P–Q4. As always, the
world champion's plan is precise, and
takes into account apparently small,
but very significant details. In the

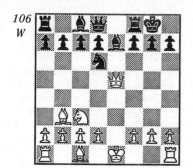

106
W

given position White must do everything to prevent Black's bishop from reaching ... KB3, and it is this main problem that Alekhine puts ahead of all others.

9 ...	R–K1
10 0–0	B–B1
11 Q–B4	P–QB3

In contrast, Euwe makes moves according to general considerations. But concrete analysis shows that he is unable to achieve the ideal set-up of ... P–QB3 and ... P–Q4, and so he should have developed his QB on N2.

12 N–K3	Q–R4
13 P–Q4	Q–R4

13 ... R–K5 did not work because of 14 B × P+, and many other moves by Black are refuted by this tactical blow.

14 P–QB3	N–K5
15 P–B3!	

An elegant solution to the problem! Now the harmony between Black's pieces is destroyed. 15 ... B–Q3 is answered by 16 Q × P+ Q × Q 17 B × Q+ K × B 18 P × N+. The knight is forced to retreat, which soon leads to confusion in the black ranks.

15 ...	N–N4
16 P–Q5!	

The threat of 17 P–KR4 forces Euwe to capture this pawn, as a result of which he is left with a completely shattered pawn position.

16 ...	P × P

17 N × P	N–K3
18 Q–KN4	Q–N3

Black does not agree to the opening of the KB-file, since his KBP would then be under fire from White's rook.

19 B–K3	P–N3
20 QR–Q1	B–N2
21 Q × Q	

Black has a poor pawn structure, and this weakness can be best exploited in the endgame. Thus Alekhine's opening strategy is linked, via a short middlegame, with the endgame. One can admire only a few high-class games played in the present era, which have such a precise strategic connection linking all three stages of the game.

21 ...	RP × Q
22 KR–K1	QR–B1
23 K–B2	B–B4
24 B × B	B × N

It is most probable that Euwe incorrectly appraised the resulting rook ending, otherwise he would have kept his strong bishop, and played 24 ... R × B.

25 B × B	N × B
26 R × R+	R × R
27 P–QN4!	

A convincing decision. Since after 27 ... N–R5 28 B–N3 N × P 29 R × P White hits the KBP, while 27 ... N–R3 is answered by 28 R–Q4 with threats of 29 R–KB4 and 29 R–QB4, Black is virtually forced into the rook ending.

27 ...	N–K3
28 B × N	QP × B (*107*)

This is the reward for the world champion's patient strategy: 'only' a better rook ending. But this is quite sufficient – Alekhine's fine technique enables him to exploit the advantages of his position: the shutting off of the black king in the corner, and the possibility of creating a passed pawn on the Q-side.

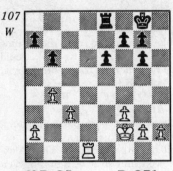

107
W

29 R–Q7	R–QB1
30 R × RP	R × P
31 R–R8 +	K–R2
32 P–QR4	R–N6

Against the alternative plan, 32 ...
R–B7+ 33 K–K3 R × P Alekhine
would have quickly decided the game:
34 R–R6 R–R7 35 K–Q4, and after
his king reaches QN3 White obtains
two irresistible connected passed
pawns. Black's best move was 32 ...
P–K4!

33 P–N5	P–N4
34 K–K2	P–K4
35 K–Q2	P–B3
36 K–B2	R–N5
37 K–B3	R–Q5
38 R–R6!	K–N3

Now a single passed pawn proves
sufficient.

39 R × P	R × P
40 R–B6	R–Q5
41 P–N6	1–0

The break-through of the white
king to QB5 will make the QNP
unstoppable.

While in this last game the advantage gained in the opening was
realized only deep into the endgame,
the following game could serve as a
classical example of a middlegame
attack over the whole chess front.

48) Alekhine–Euwe, 3rd match
game, 1935
French Defence

1 P–K4	P–K3
2 P–Q4	P–Q4
3 N–QB3	B–N5
4 P–QR3	

At that time Alekhine considered
this move to be the best. The practice
of the following years has not confirmed his opinion, and nowadays the
more solid strategic methods of
strengthening the centre by 4 P–K5
are preferred.

4 ...	B × N+
5 P × B	P × P
6 Q–N4	N–KB3

A quiet game results from 6 ...
K–B1; it was just this move that
Alekhine himself recommended. It is
strange, however, that few tournament
players have followed the champion's
advice. The most probable explanation of this is that players who choose
such a variation do not usually aim
for a quiet position, but prefer everything to be complicated and double-
edged.

7 Q × NP	R–N1
8 Q–R6	P–B4
9 N–K2	QN–Q2
10 N–N3	R–N3?

A serious mistake, after which
Black's position becomes difficult.
Stronger was 10 ... Q–R4, leaving
the white queen on R6. Besides, as
the reader will see later, the position
of the rook on ... N3 provides White
with a motif for a number of dangerous tactical blows.

11 Q–K3	N–Q4
12 Q × P	N × P
13 Q–Q3	N–Q4

Or 13 ... P × P 14 Q × P Q–B3
15 Q × Q N × Q 16 B–Q3 R–N2
17 B–Q2, with an excellent position
for White.

14 B–K2	Q–B3
15 P–QB3	P × P
16 P × P	N2–N3 (*108*)
17 B–R5!	

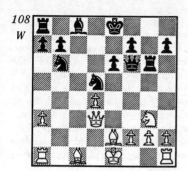

108
W

The commencement of an energetic attack, which gradually envelops the whole front. After arising on the K-side, it transfers to the Q-side, and finally the white forces strike through the centre to the black king's position.

17 ...	R–N2
18 B–B3	Q–N3
19 B–K4!	P–B4
20 B–B3	K–B1
21 P–QR4!	

Now the QB, which has long been inactive, joins the attack. At the same time, the further advance of this pawn looks dangerous for Black.

21 ...	R–QB2
22 0–0	B–Q2
23 B–R3+	K–N1
24 P–R5	R–B6

This leads to the loss of a pawn, but even the best defence – 24 ... N–QB5 25 B–B5! N–K4 26 P×N R×B 27 KR–B1 R1–QB1 28 R×R R×R 29 Q–Q4! was similarly cheerless for Black.

25 Q–N1!	N–R5
26 B×N	P×B
27 Q×NP	Q–QB3
28 P–R6	N–N3

No better was 28 ... Q×Q 29 P×Q R–N1 30 KR–N1 N–N3 31 B–N4 followed by 32 R×P.

29 B–B5	P–B5
30 N–B5	K–R1
31 N–K7	Q–K3

32 B×N

Now Black's position is hopeless, but Euwe still tries to find a way out by tactical tricks.

32 ...	B–B3
33 N×B	R–KN1
34 N–K5!	R–N2
35 Q–N8+?	

This makes the win more difficult, whereas 35 B×P! would have finished the game immediately.

35 ...	R–B1
36 N–N6+	R×N
37 Q×BP	Q×B
38 Q–K5+	

However, even here White's advantage is quite sufficient.

38 ...	R–N2
39 Q×P	R–Q1
40 Q–K5	Q×QP
41 Q×Q	1–0

In the games examined so far, Alekhine's strategy has been of a 'normal' character – his plans have enveloped the whole board, and have involved exploiting a number of elements of the position. But from the period when Alekhine was at the height of his powers, we find a number of 'model' strategic games, in which the strategic plan is based on just one positional element. See, for example, how the world champion exploits the one open file in the following game.

49) Alekhine-Nimzowitsch, San Remo 1930
French Defence

1 P–K4	P–K3
2 P–Q4	P–Q4
3 N–QB3	B–N5
4 P–K5	P–QB4
5 B–Q2	

This move is too cautious. More energetic is 5 P–QR3 or 5 Q–N4.

5 ...	N–K2
6 N–N5	B×B+

7 Q × B	0–0
8 P–QB3	P–QN3

This exceedingly careless move by Nimzowitsch is a serious error. The preacher of prophylaxis in chess for some reason forgets about the most elementary prophylactic measures. Since the white knight is aiming for Q6, he should have guarded this square by 8 . . . N–B4.

9 P–KB4	B–R3

Nimzowitsch intends to transfer his knight from N1 to QR4, after first provoking the move P–QR4. He fails to fulfil this idea due to the deeply-devised strategic plan which Alekhine carries out with rare energy and conviction.

10 N–B3	Q–Q2
11 P–QR4	QN–B3 (*109*)

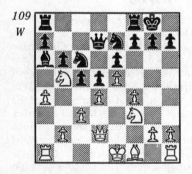

109
W

12 P–QN4!

'It is somewhat strange' – writes Alekhine – 'that this move, which is more or less dictated by the situation (it prevents the manoeuvre . . . N–R4, and at the same time forces a clearing of the position in the centre) caused a sensation at the time. Tarrasch, for example, in his notes to this game, called it "highly original". What seems surprising to me is not the move itself, but the fact that a player of grandmaster class did not seriously consider the possibility of such a

reply, when he conceived the plan commencing with 8 . . . P–QN3'.

This is an interesting comment, which characterizes Alekhine the strategist. These words, which objectively assess both his own play and that of his opponent, should be an example to those players who are insufficiently critical towards their own achievements, and are always ready to praise the play of a defeated opponent.

12 . . .	P × NP
13 P × P	B–N2
14 N–Q6	P–B4?

This prevents the opponent from advancing his K-side pawns, but there was an urgent necessity to somehow weaken White's onslaught on the Q-side. By playing 14 . . . P–QR4 15 P–N5 N–N5 or 15 B–N5 P × P, Nimzowitsch could have ensured his knight a good future on . . . QN5 or . . . QR4, whereas now it is pinned down in its own camp.

15 P–R5!

This is just at the right time, since 15 . . . P × P fails to 16 P–N5!

15 . . .	N–B1
16 N × B	

The proud knight sacrifices itself to allow the white army to completely constrict the enemy pieces.

16 . . .	Q × N
17 P–R6	Q–KB2
18 B–N5! (*110*)	

110
B

The QB-file is the most important section of the whole front. It is along this file that White's heavy pieces will break through decisively into the enemy camp.

18 ...	N1–K2
19 0–0	P–R3
20 KR–B1	KR–B1
21 R–B2	Q–K1

The black queen voluntarily places herself vis-a-vis the white bishop – does not this signify the loss of all hope? However, Nimzowitsch had nothing better. If 21 ... N–Q1, then 22 R1–QB1 R × R 23 R × R R–B1 24 R × R N × R 25 Q–B3, and the white queen penetrates to QB7.

22 R1–QB1	QR–N1
23 Q–K3	R–B2
24 R–B3	

White intends to triple heavy pieces on the QB-file, with the queen behind the rooks.

24 ...	Q–Q2
25 R1–B2	K–B1
26 Q–B1	R1–B1
27 B–R4!	

The terrible threat of 28 P–N5 forces Black to sacrifice a pawn, but this fails to improve his position.

27 ...	P–QN4
28 B × P	K–K1
29 B–R4	K–Q1
30 P–R4 (*111*)	1–0

111
B

Although he has defended against the advance of the QNP, Black, with almost all the pieces still on the board, finds himself in a position of complete zugzwang. Not one of his pieces is able to move without material being lost.

Alekhine's last move 30 P–R4! accentuates the zugzwang position, and he simply intends to wait for the opponent's pawn moves to run out. Nimzowitsch decided not to give his opponent any more enjoyment, and resigned the game.

In the following game Alekhine carries out a crushing attack on the enemy king position, only on this occasion the offensive is directed not just along one file, but simultaneously along three.

50) Stahlberg-Alekhine, Hamburg 1930
Nimzo-Indian Defence

1 P–Q4	N–KB3
2 P–QB4	P–K3
3 N–QB3	B–N5
4 Q–N3	

For many years attempts have been made to refute the Nimzo-Indian Defence in various ways, which include this queen move. Nowadays 4 Q–N3 is rarely adopted, since simple means have been found to give Black equality.

4 ...	P–B4
5 P × P	N–B3

This is how they played in the 1930s, but then Soviet players discovered the best arrangement for the black pieces – ... N–R3, ... B × P–K2, ... P–QN3, ... N–B4 and ... P–Q4.

6 N–B3	N–K5
7 B–Q2	N × QBP
8 Q–B2	P–B4
9 P–QR3	B × N
10 B × B	0–0
11 P–QN4	N–K5
12 P–K3	P–QN3

All these moves for Black and White can be found in opening manuals.

13 B–Q3	**N × B**
14 Q × N	**B–N2**
15 0–0	**N–K2**

This retreat, which significantly weakens his black squares in the centre, is directed against active operations by White, in particular P–B5.

16 B–K2

Grandmaster Stahlberg prepares to initiate play on the Q-file, but nothing comes of this. Alekhine energetically seizes the initiative.

16 ...	**Q–K1**
17 KR–Q1	**R–Q1**
18 P–QR4	

This is too slow. More dangerous to Black was 18 Q–K5 with the threat of 19 Q–B7.

18 ...   **P–B5!**

'From here until the end all Black's moves are very precisely worked out. It is doubtful if any one of them could be improved upon' (Alekhine).

19 P–R5	**BP × P**
20 Q × KP	**N–B4**
21 Q–B3	**P–Q3**
22 P × P	**P × P**
23 N–K1	**P–K4**

Black's knight obtains an excellent strong point at ... Q5, while the rooks will have ... KB5 as a 'transfer' point. From these squares the black pieces make their final storm.

24 R–R7	**N–Q5**
25 Q–K3	**R–Q2**
26 R–R2	**R2–KB2**
27 P–B3 *(112)*	**R–B5!**

Black's pieces have taken up ideal positions. It only remains for the queen to take up the best position from which to command the coming offensive.

28 B–Q3   **Q–R4!**

Here it is, the command post! There threatens 29 ... P–K5! 30

112
B

Q × N P × P winning immediately, and so the bishop must retreat at once.

29 B–B1   **Q–N4!**

Alekhine conducts the attack brilliantly. The black rooks strike along the KB-file, while the queen commands the neighbouring files. The threat is not difficult to spot – 30 ... R × P! 31 Q × Q R × B mate.

30 R–KB2 *(113)*

113
B

30 ...   **P–R3!**

This 'small' advance of a pawn decides the outcome of a mighty battle. White has no satisfactory defence to the threat of 31 ... R × P 32 Q × Q R × R. Alekhine planned to answer 31 Q–Q2 with 31 ... B × P 32 N × B N × N+ 33 R × N R × R 34 Q × Q R × B+ 35 R × R R × R+ 36 K × R P × Q 37 K–K2 K–B2 38 K–B3 K–K3 39 K–K4 P–N4! with an easy win in the pawn ending.

The move chosen by Stahlberg leads to an immediate loss.

31 K–R1   R×P
0–1

Among Alekhine's games we have seen those in which he sacrifices a pawn in the opening for the initiative. During the period of his greatest achievements the Russian champion also employed this, his favourite method of play. We invite the reader to play over two games on this theme.

51) Alekhine–Colle, Bled 1931
Queen's Gambit Declined

1 P–Q4	**N–KB3**
2 P–QB4	**P–K3**
3 N–QB3	**P–Q4**
4 B–N5	**QN–Q2**
5 N–B3	**P–B3**
6 P–K4	

The Cambridge-Springs Variation, which Black was intending to play – 6 P–K3 Q–R4 – is not to everyone's taste. And so a number of ways of avoiding this variation have been devised. Alekhine employs one of these ideas; this bold advance involves the sacrifice of a pawn.

6...	**P×KP**
7 N×P	**Q–N3**
8 B–Q3 *(114)*	

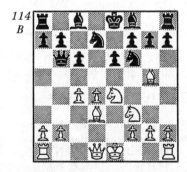

114 B

White sacrifices a pawn for the initiative. It should be pointed out that this is an example of a real

sacrifice, that is, the pawn is not recovered within the next few moves. There is only one way for White to demonstrate the correctness of his sacrifice – he must set up and maintain pressure on his opponent's position until such time as he is able to obtain in exchange some advantage which fully compensates for the pawn.

8...	**Q×NP**
9 0–0	**N×N**
10 B×N	**N–B3**
11 B–Q3	**Q–N3**
12 R–K1	**B–K2**
13 Q–B2	**P–KR3**
14 B–Q2	**P–B4**

Colle commits his first inaccuracy – he should not have allowed the opening of the long black-squared diagonal, since White's bishop is able to exploit it.

15 B–B3	**P×P**
16 N×P	**0–0**
17 N–B5!	**Q–Q1**
18 N×B+	**Q×N** *(115)*

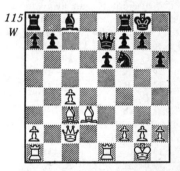

115 W

Let us examine the position, and give an answer to the question: what has Alekhine obtained for his sacrificed pawn? First of all, his pieces are excellently placed. The bishops are ideally positioned, while the rooks are already in play, and can be quickly transferred to the K-side. Meanwhile Black has not yet completed his development, and this gives White time to increase the pressure on the enemy king position.

19 Q R–N1 !

This threatens 20 B–N4, and prepares to include the second rook in the attack on the K-side.

19 . . .	R–Q1
20 R–K3	P–QN3
21 Q–K2	B–N2
22 R–KN3	N–K1
23 R–K1	K–B1
24 Q–N2 !	

The white queen manoeuvres behind her own lines, forcing weaknesses in the enemy position.

24 . . .	P–B3
25 B–N4	N–Q3
26 R3–K3	K–B2
27 P–B4	Q–Q2
28 Q–K2 !	

The pressure mounts, and now White threatens not only 29 R × P, but also 29 Q–R5 +.

28 . . .	R–K1
29 Q–R5 +	K–N1

The attempt to run away to the Q-side would have cost material: 29 . . . K–K2   30 R × P + Q × R 31 R × Q + K × R 32 Q–N4 +.

30 Q–N6	P–B4
31 B × N	Q × B
32 B × P	Q × P
33 Q–R7 +	K–B1
34 B–N6	

Black could have resigned here. 35 R–KB1 is threatened.

34 . . .	Q–Q5
35 B × R	R × B
36 K–R1	Q–B3
1–0	

Here Colle noticed that after 37 Q–R8 + K–B2   38 Q × R + K × Q 39 R × P + he would be the exchange down in the ending, and so, without waiting for White's reply, he resigned.

In the following celebrated game, Alekhine sacrifices two pawns in the opening, gaining in exchange an active position. The storm by the white pieces is so furious that by the 19th move it is all over. This lightning rout made a strong impression on Alekhine's opponents.

52) Alekhine-Nimzowitsch, Bled 1931
French Defence

1 P–K4	P–K3
2 P–Q4	P–Q4
3 N–QB3	B–N5
4 KN–K2	P × P
5 P–QR3	B × N +
6 N × B	P–KB4

'This breaks all the principles of sound strategy' – this is how this move is judged by Alekhine, who then explains: 'The black squares in Black's position become very weak due to the absence of his KB.' Better was 6 . . . N–QB3 ! His belief in the seriousness of Nimzowitsch's strategic error gives Alekhine the basis for starting an attack by sacrificing a second pawn.

7 P–B3	P × P
8 Q × P	Q × P

When this game was played it was declared that 8 . . . Q–R5 + 9 P–KN3 Q × QP was stronger. But this is incorrect – 10 N–N5 would give White an irresistible attack.

9 Q–N3 !	N–KB3

Or 9 . . . N–K2   10 B–K3 Q–B3 11 0–0–0 with great advantage to White.

10 Q × NP	Q–K4 + ?

Black would still have had some hopes after 10 . . . R–N1, whereas now he goes down without a fight.

11 B–K2	R–N1
12 Q–R6	R–N3
13 Q–R4	B–Q2
14 B–KN5	B–B3
15 0–0–0	(*116*)

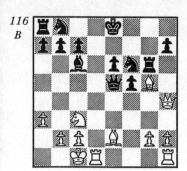

116
B

It is not difficult to imagine that Black will quickly lose: in addition to the usual bad features of such positions, his QN and QR are still completely undeveloped.

15 ...   **B × P**

Black's game was already beyond saving.

16 KR–K1	**B–K5**
17 B–R5	**N × B**
18 R–Q8+	**K–B2**
19 Q × N	**1–0**

4 After the Downfall

It is grievous for a king to lose his crown, and this applies also to a chess king. Public sympathy had changed. The public becomes tired of continual victories, it constantly demands new names, interesting happenings. And also Euwe's persistance had been acknowledged.

Only a few remained on the side of the Russian chess king in his exile. Emanuel Lasker retained his belief in Alekhine and in his previous appraisal of Alekhine's talent: 'I think that, after a necessary rest, he will once again give the world a number of interesting games'. In Moscow they did not believe that this was the downfall of his great talent, while Alekhine had a number of supporters in Prague, Warsaw, London and Vienna. But even his staunchest supporters doubted whether their favourite could regain his health, and, most important, rid himself of the addiction which had been the most terrible cause of his defeat.

For Alekhine this was the beginning of a difficult period, and it is time for us to talk about his human qualities, and of how they displayed themselves during these difficult times.

Much has been written about Alekhine's unsociableness, his shyness and irritability, and his desire to withdraw into himself. Appearances in tournaments over a number of years enabled me to meet a number of Alekhine's colleagues, enthusiasts who had seen him, and people who had known him. From their reports I was able myself to gain an impression of the great player.

But first of all let us see what documents have to say. 'A representative of the Slav nations, over six feet in height, fair-haired and with blue eyes', writes Capablanca about Alekhine, 'Alekhine always makes a striking impression when he appears in the tournament hall. He is fluent in six languages, has the title of Doctor of Law, and has a general education well above that of the average person. Alekhine appears to possess the most outstanding chess memory that has ever existed. It is said that he can remember by heart all the games played between masters or very strong players during the last 15–20 years'.

And other colleagues of Alekhine speak about his outstanding intellect and broad education. I have read a number of articles and books written by Alekhine, and I must confess that I envy the precision of his language and the breadth of his views.

Among his fellow chess players Alekhine was courteous and sympathetic, and always prepared to render assistance. I heard about this on a number of occasions from Andrey Lilienthal, who was warmly met by Alekhine in Paris when the young Hungarian first travelled to a strange city. And here is another extract: 'Alekhine was a very likeable person, was always prepared to give advice to his colleagues, and did not begrudge sharing his knowledge and experience. Not everything that was written about him was good, but this staunch admirer will testify to the fact that Alekhine was of a sympathetic, sensitive nature' (Ernst Grünfeld).

It would be interesting, of course, to know of the impression gained of Alekhine by the player who played three matches with him, and who saw more of him, perhaps, than any other grandmaster. And I asked Dr. Euwe about this.

'As a person Alekhine was something of an enigma. He was so engrossed in his chess and in himself, that in our countries he was jokingly called "Alein-ich" (in German "I am alone"). With such an attitude of mind he could not have any real friends, only admirers and supporters. He liked to hear friendly words, especially when things were going badly for him; there was something rather childish in his nature. . . . If you look at Alekhine in this light, then you can excuse him a great deal; at the chess board he was mighty, away from chess, on the other hand, he was like a little boy, who would get up to mischief and naively think that no one was watching him.'

Thus we see a shy, withdrawn person, not always able to correctly weigh up his actions, and so to avoid mistakes. Such people are not particularly well liked, and this is one more reason why the defeated chess king remained alone, without the support of friends. . . .

While all around the experts were praising the new champion. Practically all asserted – some openly, others merely hinted – that the age of the beautiful Alekhine combination was over, and that the era of the mathematically precise Euwe had begun.

NO HOPE . . .

A chess player can find consolation only in new tournament battles. And in the two years following the loss of his title Alekhine played in ten tournaments. These included some extremely strong tournaments, such as the one at Nottingham in 1936, but in the main the opposition was fairly modest. Alekhine's poor form is shown by the fact that he won only two of these, while in two others he shared first prize. The player who only a short time previously had been finishing a long way ahead of his rivals – 3½ and 5½ points – had forgotten, as it were, how to win.

He was hindered by blunders, oversights, and confused thinking. And lack of confidence, terrible lack of confidence in his own powers, and in the correctness of his plans. The reader will be able to play over a number of games played by Alekhine during this period, and he will find this admission by Alekhine himself: 'At another time I would have gone into the ending, and would have easily won it, but during this period I was unsure of my endgame mastery'.

Significant are the results of the two main tournaments of this period – at Nottingham in 1936, and at Kemeri in 1937. Both of these had strong entries, and in neither did Alekhine do well. At Nottingham he was sixth, while at Kemeri he shared fourth and fifth places. Not only was his play no longer of extra-class, but he had also lost his superiority over ordinary opponents.

The result at Nottingham was especially disappointing. Alekhine played brilliantly in several games – he crushed Tartakower, he had an interesting draw with Botvinnik, and won an important victory in a long queen ending against Euwe. Let the world champion know how well Alekhine can still play! But at the same time there was a loss to Reshevsky, and a vexing defeat against Capablanca.

What a lot of trouble was caused by this game between the two former world champions with a grudge against each other! The opening and middlegame went in Alekhine's favour, but, as often happened at this time, he spoiled everything with a few poor moves. Alekhine's advantage disappeared, and the judges were already discussing the disturbing question: 'How will they offer each other a draw? After all, they don't speak to each other!' But the question decided itself: Alekhine made some further mistakes, and as adjournment approached his position became hopeless. Then Alekhine made a move after the judge had indicated that the game should be adjourned, and the tension which hung in the atmosphere over this game blew up into conflict. . . .

Nottingham produced a new name – Mikhail Botvinnik. They had already begun talking about him playing a match with Euwe – after the latter had won his return match with Alekhine. What a question, of course he would win ! It was sufficient to just look at the depressed Russian to realize that he would soon be forgotten in the chess world. . . .

THE IMPROBABLE HAPPENS

In the conditions for the match in 1935 between Alekhine and Euwe the following point was included: in the event of Euwe winning, Alekhine should have the right to a return match which should take place within two years. I have always admired the sporting attitude of Euwe, who fulfilled this agreement without the least delay. After all, many of those who had held the title would without doubt have delayed the start of the return encounter, if they had not rejected it altogether. Had we not seen other challenges met by various excuses, such as being too busy, in the past ?

Not long ago I told Max Euwe that the promptness with which he fulfilled his obligation demonstrated his sporting nature, and had raised his prestige in the chess world. And I also asked him why he hadn't put off the start of the match, so as to have at least one extra year as champion ?

'Why should I have delayed matters ?' said the ex-world champion. 'I was absolutely convinced that I would easily beat Alekhine the second time. In those days it was sufficient to simply look at Alekhine to come to this conclusion'.

So what exactly happened ? How was it that two years later Alekhine appeared in Amsterdam in the brilliant form of his best days ? The imperturbable Dutch waiters, who were well acquainted with the Russian champion's habits, were astonished on receiving the order for a glass of Dutch milk – the best milk in the world ! Alekhine had given up smoking, he had gained several pounds in weight, and appeared fresh and rested.

His preparation had also been different. Alekhine had arrived for the first match without sufficient opening preparation, and without a second (he had had to entrust the Dutch master Landau with the duties of his second). Now he had a good second – grandmaster Eliskases – and had made considerable theoretical preparation. If only the Dutch customs had known about all the chess 'bombs' concealed in the suitcase of the smiling Russian !

Just how did this all come about ? How could a man who, a short time before, had been depressed and suffering from a heart complaint, fight off illness, regain his health, and arrive for a most difficult battle in his very best form? How had he overcome his depression? Not long ago there had been misfortune, blunders, oversights, but now deep plans and precise calculations. What strength had caused this amazing transformation?

The answer can be found in the peculiarities of Alekhine's character.

'During the eleven years of our acquaintance I came to know many of Alekhine's characteristics', Romanovsky writes about him. 'The most important of these, in my opinion, was his amazingly strong sense of purpose. He always needed a goal in life. It is interesting that his famous victory over Capablanca in 1927 brought him great joy – his goal had been achieved – but also his first disappointment. How could he go any further? There was no longer any goal, and from this moment Alekhine's life began to become enshrouded in a haze of drama.

'He began to speak and write about the new tasks which supposedly stood before him, and of his new responsibilities. Along with interesting new thoughts and ideas, the symptoms of experiment began to creep into his play. This finally led to him losing the 1935 match with Euwe, which he failed to take sufficiently seriously. However, even this, perhaps the only serious setback in his chess career, had its brighter side: once again he had a goal – to once more demonstrate that he was the strongest player in the world'.

Splendid words! They show an excellent understanding of the Russian grandmaster's character. Composure during success, a redoubling of effort after failure. The correctness of this assertion is demonstrated by a simple analysis of tournament tables. How many special brilliancy prizes did Alekhine win for games played when he had suffered a defeat the previous day! Strength of will, the ability to intensify his efforts, staunchness of character – over his whole life these are what distinguished Alekhine in his chess battles. In the history of chess he remains one of the very few grandmasters who was not demoralized by a defeat, but, just the opposite, was made even more formidable.

In 1937 Euwe was in no worse form than he had been two years previously. Certainly, he has never made any complaint, either then or today, that he was out of condition. Simply Alekhine stepped into the chess ring in such excellent form, and his blows were so strong, that the Dutch champion was faced by defeat from the very first rounds.

Everything about the revitalized 45-year-old Alekhine was

surprising: his outward appearance, self-control, composure, and the confident style of his play. It seemed that the Alekhine of San Remo and Bled had returned to the chess world. What could Euwe do against such a player, what could any of the grandmasters of that time have done?

In the 1935 match Alekhine had been made to pay for his poor opening preparation. He had, in effect, not prepared anything new for the match, and had not had any outside help. But Euwe had been assisted by the cream of the contemporary theorists: Flohr, Grünfeld, and Kmoch. Two years later Alekhine saw grandmaster R. Fine accept an invitation to join the Euwe camp from across the ocean.

Especially brilliant was Alekhine's innovation in the sixth game (see No. 61). Just imagine, in a variation of the Slav Defence, well known to Euwe, and analysed by him together with his seconds, Alekhine gives up a knight on the sixth move. Euwe is perplexed: should he take the knight or not? He sees clearly that, if he accepts the sacrifice, White will gain a very strong attack. Should he subject himself to Alekhine's attack, when the latter has specially prepared for it, studied many variations, and knows all the subtleties? Euwe does not take the knight, and immediately falls into a hopeless position. Alekhine's innovation was so complicated, and the variations associated with it so complex and confusing, that it was only in the following year that a refutation was found.

In other games as well, Alekhine demonstrated not only an excellent knowledge of opening problems, but also a subtle understanding of psychology. The correct choice of opening, such as the contemporary approach to the Catalan System, and certain variations of the Indian-Nimzo Defence, invariably enabled him to impose his will on his opponent. And this superiority in the openings increased Alekhine's confidence, and enabled him to gain some quick victories. In one match there had never been so many short games decided in the very opening, and this is to Alekhine's credit as one of the greatest of opening theorists.

But chess is capricious, and good form and excellent preparation by no means bring their rewards immediately. Alekhine lost the first game, and one would have expected him to have been upset by this. But here is the statement which Alekhine made to correspondents after his defeat on the first day:

'So, the first game has gone against me! I am writing these lines immediately after my defeat. The result is unfortunate, but not unexpected to me, since I expect to lose a few games in the match, especially as the result of opening surprises prepared by Dr. Euwe. I base my hopes in the match on the following factors: 1. I will under no circumstances underestimate my opponent. 2. I will guard my health and keep up my morale. There are a further twenty-nine games ahead. Tomorrow is another day'.

Everything in this interview breathes confidence – the tone, the respect for the opponent, and the final phrase (taken from Margaret Mitchell's novel *Gone With the Wind*.)

And the new day began. After levelling the scores in the second encounter and playing two draws, Alekhine, it is true, also lost the fifth game, but then took his revenge with three victories. And what victories! Euwe put up a stubborn resistance, and with the score in decided games standing at 6–4 against him, it seemed that he had reasonable chances of retaining his title. But Alekhine was now irresistible, and 4½ points from the last five games ensured that the revitalized Russian gained the 15½ points necessary for victory as early as the twenty-fifth game.

For the reasons behind such a spectacular victory we can do no better than to ask one of the participants of the return match.

'After examining the games of the match from the purely technical point of view, and after a particularly careful analysis of Alekhine's play, I came to the conclusion that he had been playing splendidly all the time. He not only introduced a series of opening innovations, but also conducted the games by those simple strategic methods which are so characteristic of his play. Alekhine's tactical mastery and combinational talent are so well known, and so typical of his style, that there is no need to dwell on them here. His endgame play was also on a high level. But what I especially admired was the mastery with which he played games after the adjournment, particularly since I had also analysed these positions and knew them thoroughly. When I think of the creative ideas that my opponent was able to discover in some of the adjourned positions, and of the unexpected moves he found, I am filled with the greatest admiration for Alekhine's mastery'.

Euwe also gave the following opinion immediately after the return match:

'Alekhine has re-established his reputation as the strongest living chess player, and has confirmed the belief that he is the greatest player of all time!'

On this occasion there were no festivities in Holland, only an anti-alcohol society made a symbolic presentation to Alekhine – a basket with a collection of dairy products: Dutch milk, cream and cheese.

Once again the delighted admirers of Alekhine's inimitable talent returned to his camp (it didn't matter that some of them had been on Euwe's side for two years). There was no end to the adulation, and once again they talked about the inimitable combinational talent of the Russian chess genius.

But he was tired, he was approaching the end of the fifth decade of his life. . . .

DEVOTED SERVICE TO CHESS

Yet even so Alekhine once again threw himself into the heat of tournament battles. Montevideo, Plymouth, Margate and the AVRO tournament – and all these in just one year, 1938. Once again a creditable series of first prizes, except in the AVRO tournament where he shared fourth to sixth places. But this was a tournament for the young. How can you play well, when every day you have to travel from town to town? It was not without reason that all the 'old men' finished in the lower half of the table.

And there was no respite from those wishing to battle for the chess crown. Capablanca had not yet abandoned his old hope of a return match, and in the last few years had found new strength, taking first place in such strong tournaments as those in Moscow and Nottingham in 1936 (in the latter he shared first prize with Botvinnik). Not long before, Salo Flohr had agreed to a match with Alekhine. 'I have nothing to lose,' joked the witty Czech, 'I will lose, but will go down in history as having played a match with Alekhine'. The Soviet champion, Mikhail Botvinnik, was making serious attempts to arrange a match. He was a dangerous opponent, but a desirable one – in the negotiations Alekhine had stipulated the condition that he should be able to arrive in Moscow two months before the start of the match.

Alekhine's colleagues were amazed by the clarity of his thinking, which seemed unaffected by the advancing years. 'I met Alekhine at the chess board many, many times', writes Paul Keres. 'Although at that time I also used to play against the other strongest players in the world, an encounter with Alekhine was always somehow more important, it was a special test. Why was this? It was because Alekhine's attitude to chess was different from that of all the other masters of his generation. When playing against Alekhine, one could always be sure that he would put into the game all his strength, all his knowledge, and, like a true artist, would create a great work of art. He would never underrate the merits of his opponent, never played superficially, and, what is most important, always chose a deep and interesting plan of play. Even in those cases when his tournament position did not demand it, he would strive for the initiative, play for a win, and put the maximum energy into the game'.

'I will also say this: everyone who knew Alekhine personally was amazed that a person could devote himself so entirely to the magic of chess', says Savilly Tartakower about the Russian champion, 'and at the same time gain so much from it. And if there is anyone who has not wasted his talent, but has used it fully for the enjoyment of others, then it is Alekhine'.

. . . Alekhine was happy and contented. At home things were relatively quiet, and he was at the height of chess fame. The future appeared to be bright and promising. Ahead were tournaments, appearances, his book – an annotated collection of the games from the Nottingham tournament – had been published. This was another 'revision', similar to the one which followed the London tournament of 1922. After suffering a failure, straight away seek out the cause. And this is best done by analysing one's own games, and the games of one's rivals. He had plans for a number of books, including a book of instruction – let later generations study chess 'à la Alekhine'.

Young players were full of the desire to overthrow the 'old man' from the throne – well, never mind, let them try! We will hold out for some time! The most dangerous is Botvinnik. See how at the AVRO tournament he exploited the slightest positional error by Alekhine! If it comes to playing with him, the most serious attention will have to be paid to opening preparation. A match in Moscow, I will once again see my place of birth. . . . What's happening there with chess! Not long ago there was a tournament for Trade-Union workers, and seven thousand took part. Seven thousand!

But now it was time to travel to Buenos Aires for the next Olympiad. It would be pleasant to visit the town where victory was gained over Capablanca. Alekhine loved chess Olympiads – he would meet friends and acquaintances from all corners of the world, he would make arrangements for new tournaments and displays. And everything was fully devoted to chess.

Only one thing spoiled Alekhine's humour in Buenos Aires: representing Cuba on board one, José-Raul made a significantly better score than Alekhine. And there was a special prize for the best result by the leaders (someone had presented a diamond brooch). It was not the matter of the brooch, of course, but to finish behind Capablanca! . . .

The peaceful course of the Olympiad was interrupted by terrible news – a report was received by telegraph that Nazi Germany had invaded France and that the Second World War had started. Forgetting about chess, many set off on the same day for Europe. When it came for the match between France and Germany to be played, the captain of the French team Alexander Alekhine informed the judges that he was withdrawing his team, and would not play against the Germans. The judges recorded the result as a draw – they had to complete the tournament table somehow!

The Olympiad finished, practically everyone had dispersed. Only the European masters remained. What to do? It was dangerous to go by boat: the war at sea had begun. Najdorf, Stahlberg and Eliskases decided to stay in Argentina. Alekhine set off for Europe with his wife.

This was, to say the least, an illogical decision. What drew the world champion towards Europe, towards the turmoil and the shooting? Why did he not prefer to wait together with his young colleagues?

No one can answer these questions. Only the facts remain. And these are that in December 1939 Alekhine set foot in Europe to meet his destiny.

GAMES FROM THE YEARS 1935–1939

53) **Winter-Alekhine,** Nottingham 1936

French Defence

1 P–Q4	P–K3
2 P–K4	P–Q4
3 P × P	P × P
4 B–Q3	N–QB3
5 N–K2	B–Q3
6 P–QB3	Q–R5!

This energetic queen move allows Alekhine to already seize the initiative at this early stage. This game once more illustrates the ineffectiveness of exchanging pawns on the 3rd move.

7 N–Q2	B–KN5

This move involves the sacrifice of a pawn, which the English master wisely declines. After 8 Q–N3 0–0–0 9 Q × QP N–B3 Black would have a marked lead in development, and would obtain a very strong attack from the very opening.

8 Q–B2	0–0–0
9 N–B1	P–KN3
10 B–K3	KN–K2

The aim of this move is to exchange off White's KB – his one actively placed piece.

11 0–0–0	B–KB4
12 N1–N3	B × B
13 Q × B	P–KR3
14 P–KB4?	(*117*)

It is difficult to say what plan

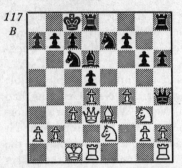

117
B

Alekhine would have adopted after some other move by White; now however, the correct plan, prompted by the characteristics of the changed situation, becomes completely obvious. Winter has incautiously weakened his K3 and K4 squares, provoking Black into action along the K-file. First of all Alekhine brings his queen back from her now pointless expedition to ... R5, and at the same time takes control of his KB4 square.

14 ...	Q–N5 !
15 P–KR3	Q–Q2
16 KR–B1	P–KR4 !

Now White will never be able to play P–KB5. If he plays 17 P–B5 immediately, there follows 17 ... P–R5 18 P–B6 N–KN1 19 N–R1 R–K1, and the presumptuous pawn will soon fall.

17 N–N1	P–R5
18 N3–K2	N–B4
19 N–B3	P–B3

The harmony of the arrangement of Alekhine's pieces and pawns on the K-side is admirable. White's K3 and K4 squares are weakened, whereas his K5 square is unavailable, being reliably guarded by Black's KBP.

20 N–R2	QR–K1
21 B–Q2	R–K3
22 N–N4	R1–K1
23 QR–K1	R1–K2 !

We have already seen this set-up in the Alekhine–Nimzowitsch game

(No. 49): the queen takes up a position behind the rooks, and they will feel her powerful support when they break through onto the seventh and eighth ranks.

24 K–Q1	Q–K1
25 Q–B3	N–R4 !

The cavalry goes into action. The flimsy cover which White hurriedly puts up proves to be no obstacle to the black knights.

26 P–QN3 (*118*)

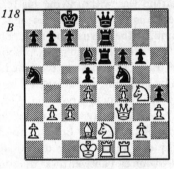

118
B

26 ...	N–B5 !

This natural sacrifice suggests itself. Since White's pieces are congested, he will find it difficult to defend his king. After 27 P×N Q–R5+ 28 K–B1 B–R6+ 29 K–N1 R–N3+ 30 K–R1 Q–B7, mate is unavoidable. But even refusing the sacrifice does not delay disaster for long.

27 B–B1 !	N5–K6+
28 B×N	N×B+
29 N×N	R×N
30 Q–B2	Q–N4 !

The end! The threat of 31 ... Q–Q6+ forces White to give up his QBP, after which further resistance is hopeless.

31 N–B1	R×BP
32 R×R	B×R
33 Q–K1	K–Q2
34 P–B5	

Or 34 Q×R Q×R+ and 35 ... Q×BP.

34 ...	R–K6
35 Q–B2	P–N4
36 R–K1	R–K5
37 R × R	P × R
38 K–Q2	B–Q3!

Preparing a pretty check – 39 ... P–K6+ !

39 K–B2	B–B5
0–1	

54) Alekhine–Tylor, Margate 1937
Ruy Lopez

1 P–K4	P–K4
2 N–KB3	N–QB3
3 B–N5	P–QR3
4 B–R4	N–B3
5 0–0	B–K2
6 Q–K2	

Alekhine often employed this move, but nowadays the queen is rarely developed on K2.

6 ...	0–0
7 P–B3?	

This is characteristic of Alekhine's form at that time. White could have simply won a pawn by 7 B × N QP × B 8 N × P Q–Q5 8 N × P Q–Q5 9 N–KB3, and Black cannot play 9 ... Q × KP because of 10 Q × Q N × Q 11 R–K1 winning a piece.

7 ...	P–Q3
8 P–Q4	B–Q2
9 P–Q5	N–N1
10 B–B2	N–K1
11 P–B4	P–KB4

A serious positional error, which gives White complete control of his important central K4 square. The advance of the KBP should have been prepared by 11 ... P–KN3, so as to be able to recapture on ... B4 with the pawn.

12 P × P	B × P
13 B × B	R × B
14 N–B3	N–Q2
15 N–K4	N–B1!

Well played. Realizing that he will not be able to drive the white

pieces off their K4 square, Tylor aims to place this knight on ... KB5.

16 B–K3	N–N3
17 P–KN3	P–R3
18 N3–Q2	K–R2
19 Q–Q3	Q–Q2
20 P–B4	

This is not so much an attacking move as a defensive one, directed against the unpleasant threat of 20 ... R–R4 and 21 ... Q–R6.

20 ...	K–R1
21 N–KB3!	

White must somehow release the tension in the centre, and with this aim he carries out an unusual tactical operation.

21 ...	P × P
22 N–Q4	R–B2
23 B × P?	

'A slight strategic mistake, as a result of which White is unable to fully exploit his positional advantage. There are two considerations which speak in favour of capturing with the pawn: 1) Since Black's position is cramped, White should avoid further exchanges. 2) In practice White's bishop would have been useful for defending the black squares' (Alekhine).

23 ...	N × B
24 P × N	Q–N5+
25 K–R1!	N–B3!

Once again the English master is equal to the occasion. After 25 ... R × P 26 R × R Q × R 27 R–KB1 ! White would win, for example; 27 ... Q–Q4 28 R–B5, or 27 ... Q–R5 28 N–B5, or 27 ... Q–N5 28 R–B7 Q–R5 29 N–KB3.

26 N–KB2

Alekhine once again, just as on his 7th and 23rd moves, fails to find the strongest continuation. White would have a very imposing position after 26 N–K6 or 26 QR–K1. Now there begins a complicated struggle of manoeuvre, from which however the ex-world champion still emerges with honour.

26 ...	**Q–R4**

Or 26 ... Q × P 27 N–K6 Q–R5 28 N–R3 with the threat of N–B4 and N–N6 +.

27 R–KN1	**N–Q2**
28 N–K6	**N–B4**
29 Q–K3	**N × N**
30 P × N	**R–B3**
31 QR–K1	**R1–KB1**
32 Q–KN3	**P–KN4?**

In the sequel Alekhine brilliantly exploits this mistake. After the correct 32 ... R–KN1, a hard struggle could still lie ahead.

33 N–R3	**R–B4**
34 Q–N2!	

This sort of manoeuvre is already well known to us. White transfers his other rook to the KN-file, after which the pressure of the battery of heavy pieces becomes irresistible.

34 ...	**P–B3**
35 R–K3!	**K–N2**
36 R–KN3	**P–Q4**
37 Q–Q2	**B–Q3** (*119*)

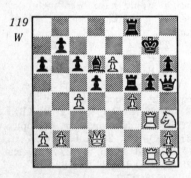

38 N × P !

This sacrifice is based on precise calculation. The formation of the white pieces in this concluding combination is most unusual.

38 ...	**B × P !**

Of course, capturing the knight would lose Black his queen.

39 Q–B3 + !

This is the point! The bishop can not be interposed because of 40 N–B3 +.

39 ...	**R1–B3**
40 N–K4+!	**B × R**
41 R × B+	**K–R1** (*120*)

Or 41 ... K–B1 42 Q–N4+ and mates in a few moves.

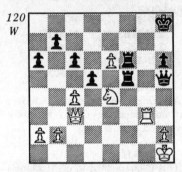

42 Q × R + !

The point of this very pretty combination is only revealed on the following move.

42 ...	**R × Q**
43 R–N8+!	**1–0**

After 43 ... K × R   44 N × R+ and 45 N × Q White remains with an extra knight.

A complicated struggle developed in the following well-known game. And in it one senses Alekhine's lack of self-confidence which, as we have already said, appeared after the loss of his title.

55) **Alekhine–Bogoljubow,** Nottingham 1936
Slav Defence

1 P–Q4	**P–Q4**
2 P–QB4	**P–QB3**
3 N–KB3	**N–B3**
4 N–B3	**P × P**
5 P–QR4	**P–K3?**

As we have already seen (game No. 46), this leads to a difficult position for Black. Correct is 5 . . . B–B4.

6 P–K4	**B–N5**
7 P–K5	**N–K5**

In game No. 46 Black played this knight to . . . Q4, but . . . N–K5 is no improvement.

8 Q–B2	**Q–Q4**
9 B–K2	**P–QB4!**

This is Black's best chance, enabling him to exchange off White's QP.

10 0–0	**N × N**
11 P × N	**P × P** (*121*)

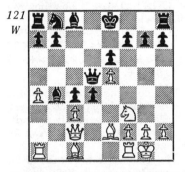

Now White has three possibilities. It is not difficult to establish that the first is bad – 12 P × B P–Q6 with an excellent position for Black. The second was chosen by Alekhine in the 19th game of his match with Euwe in 1935: 12 P × P P–B6 13 B–Q2 Q–R4 14 B × P B × B 15 R–R3 with an excellent game for White. The reason why Alekhine did not play this in the present game can be explained by the same state of uncertainty and lack of confidence in his own powers. Perhaps Bogoljubow had something prepared? When a grandmaster is in good spirits he fears nothing; when he is depressed he is afraid even of his own shadow.

The continuation chosen by Alekhine promises less, although he still keeps the advantage.

12 N × P	**B–B4**
13 N–B3 !	**N–Q2**
14 R–Q1	**Q–B3**
15 B × P	**0–0**

After 15 . . . B × P+ 16 Q × B Q × B 17 B–R3 Black's king is stuck in the centre and comes under a dangerous attack.

16 N–N5	**P–KN3**
17 B–N5	**Q–B2**
18 N–K4	**B–K2**
19 P–KB4	

A poor move, typical of Alekhine's play during his period of depression. The weakness of the black squares would be more marked after the natural 19 B–KR6 R–Q1 20 P–KB4 and 21 B–N5.

19 . . .	**N–B4**
20 N–B6 +	**B × N**
21 P × B	**B–Q2**
22 B–K3 ?	

And this move is simply a blunder. By continuing 22 B–R3 KR–Q1 23 R–Q4, White could have still kept the initiative. White has had to make a number of mistakes in order to lose the advantage presented to him by his opponent's poor 5th move.

22 . . .	**B × B**
23 P × B	**N–Q2!**

Winning a pawn. The game enters a new phase, in which Alekhine sets up strong pressure on the black squares and along the open K-file, which fully compensates for the pawn.

24 P–N3	**N × P**
25 B–Q4	**N–Q2**
26 Q–B2	**P–N3**
27 R–K1	**Q–B5**
28 QR–N1	**QR–B1**
29 Q–K3	**KR–K1**
30 Q–B3	**P–B3**

Black shows unwarranted self-confidence. By continuing 30 . . . Q–Q4 31 Q × Q P × Q 32 R × R+ R × R 33 R–R1 R–R1 he could have gained a draw, whereas now White has the chance to exploit this new weakening of the K-side.

31 R–N4	Q–B2
32 R–N2!	R–K2
33 R2–K2	K–B2
34 P–N4	R1–K1
35 P–N5!	

White's threats increase with every move. Alekhine threatens now 36 Q–R3, attacking the KRP and KP.

35 ...   **P × P** *(122)*

This boldness comes of necessity. After 35 ... Q–Q3 36 Q–R3 P–KR4 37 P × BP N × P 38 Q–R4 White's attack on the black squares would become most threatening.

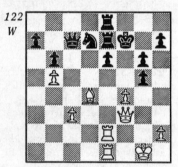

122
W

36 P–B5

Alekhine overestimates his position. By continuing 36 P × P+ K–N1 37 B–B6 N × B 38 P × N R–B2 39 R × P R × R 40 R × R Q–B4+ 41 K–N2 Q × NP 42 Q–K3 and 43 P–R4, he could have kept the superior position.

Instead of this Alekhine goes in for a forced manoeuvre with sacrifices, and commits a serious oversight in a relatively simple variation.

36 ...   **Q–KB5?**

A mistake which loses the game. After the correct reply 36 ... P–K4 37 Q–Q5+ K–B1 38 Q–B6, as Alekhine intended to continue, Black is by no means forced to capture the queen, and could retreat his queen to ... Q1, or else play 38 ... R–B1.

In both cases Black could successfully defend his position.

37 P × KP+	R × P
38 Q–Q5	N–B3

Black is unable to simultaneously defend his rook on K3, and his knight as well as meet the threat of 39 R–KB2 winning his queen. The continuation played also leads to the loss of a piece.

39 B × N	Q–KN5+
40 R–KN2	Q–B4
41 B–K5!	

It was still not too late to lose after 41 Q–B4? Q–B4+! Now however Black could resign.

41 ... K–N1 42 R–KB2 Q–N5+ 43 K–R1 P–KR4 44 R–KN1 Q–KR5 45 R–B6 K–R2 46 R × R R × R 47 Q–Q7+ 1–0.

Even during this difficult period of depression Alekhine produced several splendid examples of his favourite strategy – the sacrifice of a pawn for the initiative.

The following game surprised the chess world at the time by its unusual opening, and then by the subtlety and mastery with which the defeated world champion drove home his advantage.

56) Alekhine–Flohr, Nottingham 1936, French Defence

1 P–K4	P–K3
2 P–Q4	P–Q4
3 N–QB3	B–N5
4 B–Q2	

A move which provoked heated discussions and arguments. Alekhine sacrifices two pawns, in return for which he obtains compensation which is, to say the least, problematic. While some were praising the sacrifice and others were criticizing it, the tournament book appeared. Alekhine wrote in it: 'I touched the wrong piece. I intended to play 4 P–K5 and later P–KB4, as occurred in my game against Nimzowitsch in the San Remo tournament, but instead made the bishop move too soon.'

The critics of the move 4 B–Q2 were delighted, while those who had been delighted by the move were shamed. But then a comment by Alekhine to this move was discovered in his book *My Best Games of Chess 1908–1923*: 'An interesting idea, by which, however, nothing in particular is gained. 4 P×P is usually played here'. And once again the chess world was left in doubt: had Alekhine really picked up the wrong piece, was it just absent-mindedness?

This, one can definitely state: the bishop move is very risky, and gives Black the chance to gain a considerable advantage. Nowadays this sacrifice of two pawns is never met in tournament practice.

4 ...	**P×P**
5 N×P?	

This is already a mistake. After 5 Q–N4 Q×P 6 N–B3 or 5 ... N–KB3 6 Q×NP play would still be sharp, whereas now White's chances of an attack are minimal.

5 ...	**Q×P**
6 B–Q3	**B×B+**
7 Q×B	**Q–Q1?** *(123)*

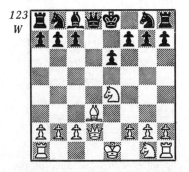

123
W

One can readily understand Flohr: he was always uncertain when playing against Alekhine, and so he simply did not 'dare' to take the second pawn. In fact, capturing the QNP would have given Black a good game. Alekhine makes the following appraisal of his opponent's indecisiveness: 'The refusal to capture the QNP is based on a completely incorrect understanding of the position: the queen's retreat gives White the chance to move his king to a safe place even with gain of tempo. White thus gains an advantage in development which fully compensates for the lost pawn.

'After 7 ... Q×NP 8 R–Q1 N–Q2 Black would have every hope – with careful play – of keeping his two extra pawns'.

8 0–0–0	**Q–K2**
9 N–KB3	**N–KB3**
10 KR–K1	

A 'typical' position has been reached, of the type often met in Alekhine's games. White is a pawn down, but on the other hand all his pieces are mobilized and occupy excellent positions, whereas Black still needs three or four moves to complete his development.

10 ...	**N×N**
11 R×N	**N–Q2**
12 R–KN4!	

A typical method of play in such positions. While the opponent is still occupied with developing his pieces, one must bother him with various concrete threats. The rook manoeuvre provokes Black into advancing one of his K-side pawns, so giving White an object of attack.

12 ...	**P–KB4**

Better was 12 ... 0–0 *(13 Q–R6? P–KB4)*.

13 R–KB4	**N–B3**
14 R–K1	**B–Q2?**

Flohr loses his head. For better or worse Black had to hang on to his extra pawn by playing 14 . . . P–KN3.

15 R × BP	0–0–0
16 R–QR5	K–N1
17 N–K5	B–K1
18 P–KN3	

This move is characteristic of Alekhine at that time. It would seem that White would have excellent chances if he kept a large number of pieces on the board, and continued to play for the attack. Instead of this Alekhine exchanges queens, taking play into a favourable ending. There is no doubt that this decision was influenced by his general lack of confidence in his powers, and also by the fear of committing an oversight in complications.

18 . . .	N–Q4
19 R–K4	N–N3
20 Q–K3	R–Q4
21 R–R3	Q–B4
22 Q × Q	R × Q (*124*)

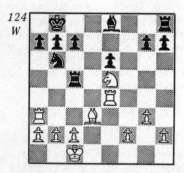

124
W

In the resulting ending Alekhine has, strictly speaking, only one significant advantage – the weakness of Black's KP. If this pawn stood on KB2, then the most probable outcome of the game would be a draw. The reader will find it interesting to follow the accuracy with which Alekhine realizes his advantage.

23 P–KB4	R–Q4

This makes it easier for White to win. However it is not at all easy for

Black to defend his KP. Thus, on 23 . . . N–Q2 24 N–B3 N–B1 there follows the simple 25 N–N5 B–Q2 26 B–B4 and 27 R3–K3 and the pawn falls.

24 N–B3 !	B–Q2
25 N–N5	R–K1
26 P–B4	R–KB4
27 R–Q4	R4–B1
28 P–QB5	

Weaker is 28 B × P P–K4, and Black can still resist.

28 . . .	N–Q4
29 B × P	B–B3
30 B–N6	R–K2
31 N–B3	

'Now White's plan is clear: he places his pieces on the best possible squares, so as to support the advance of his K-side pawns, which must sooner or later be decisive' (Alekhine).

31 . . .	N–B3
32 N–K5	B–Q4
33 R–K3	R–R1
34 P–KR4	P–B3
35 B–B2	R–Q1
36 B–N3	R–QB2
37 N–B3	R–K1
38 N–K5	R1–QB1
39 B–B4	K–R1
40 P–QN4	R–QN1 (*125*)

125
W

41 P–N4 !

The long-awaited advance of the K-side pawns, which at the same time involves a typical Alekhine combina-

tion: 41 ... B × B   42 N × B N × P
43 N–N6 + P × N   44 R–QR3 mate.

41 ...	P–QN3
42 P–KN5	P × P
43 P × P	N–Q2
44 N × N	R × N
45 P–R5	R–KB2
46 R × P !	

This is the simplest road to victory – the white pawns become irresistible.

46 ...	B × R
47 B × B	R2–N2
48 B–N3	R–K1
49 P–R6	P × P
50 P–N6	R–N2

Or 50 ... R–KB1   51 P–B5 R × P
52 R–Q8+ R–N1   53 R × R +
K × R 54 P–N7.

51 P–B5	R–KB1
52 B–B2	P–KR4
53 R–Q6	R–K2
54 P–B6	R–K8 +
55 K–Q2	R–KB8
56 P–B7	P–R5
57 R–Q7	1–0

The following game by Alekhine, which the reader can now play through, was received with delight by the chess world, for it is a model game in all its stages, beginning with a boldly played opening, and concluding with a brilliant final combination.

57) Alekhine-Reshevsky, Kemeri 1937
Alekhine's Defence

1 P–K4	N–KB3
2 P–K5	N–Q4
3 N–KB3	P–Q3
4 P–Q4	B–N5
5 P–B4	

This move involves the sacrifice of a pawn. A quiet game results after 5 P × P or 5 B–K2.

5 ...	N–N3
6 B–K2	P × P
7 N × P	B × B

| 8 Q × B | Q × P |
| 9 0–0 | |

An inaccuracy, which allows Black to exchange off the important and very active knight on K5. Stronger was 9 N–R3 N1–Q2 10 N–B3.

| 9 ... | N1–Q2 |
| 10 N × N | N × N? |

A serious error. After 10 ... Q × N !
11 P–QR4 Q–B3   12 N–R3 P–K3
13 P–R5 N–Q2 Black would be ready to meet his opponent's offensive. Now however, Alekhine's pieces rapidly take up threatening positions.

11 N–B3	P–QB3
12 B–K3	Q–K4
13 QR–Q1	P–K3
14 Q–B3 !	

A simple move, but it forces Black to give back his extra pawn. On 14 ... B–K2 very strong is 15 B–Q4 Q–KN4   16 N–K4. Also bad is 14 ... N–B3   15 N–N5 or 14 ... B–Q3 15 P–KN3.

| 14 ... | 0–0–0 ! |
| 15 B × P ! | |

But not 15 Q × KBP?? B–Q3   16 P–KN3 KR–B1, and Black wins.

15 ...	Q–QR4
16 B–Q4	Q–KB4
17 Q–N3 (126)	

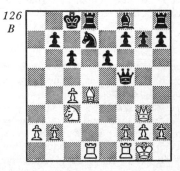

126
B

Here is what Alekhine has to say about this move: 'The decision of a former world champion ... Before

1935 and at the present time (i.e. after 1937, when Alekhine won back his title. This game was played when the world champion was Euwe. – Author's note) I would doubtless have chosen the simple 17 Q×Q, which would in effect give me an extra pawn on the Q-side, without the slightest shadow of danger. But during the whole period leading up to the return match I simply could not rely on my nerves and self-control, which would, of course, have been needed for the winning of this ending'.

An example of Alekhine's concrete thinking – after all, in the previous game the mistake was the decision to go into the ending!

17 ...	P–K4
18 B–K3	B–N5
19 N–R4	B–R4!
20 P–B4!	B–B2
21 P–N3	P–B3
22 P×P	Q–K3
23 P–KR3!	

Preventing the black queen from moving to ... KN5 in the case of 23 ... N×P   24 N–B5. Later this move turns out to be useful for the attack, since the queen is able to keep on the important diagonal KR2–QN8 by retreating to R2.

| 23 .... | KR–N1 |
| 24 B–Q4 | N×P |

This move looks good, but the sounder 24 ... P×P! would have given Black better chances for a successful defence.

| 25 Q–QB3! | N–Q2 |

Hoping to defend the approaches to the black king's position – his ... QN3 and ... QB4 squares. But White's army is ready for the decisive storm, and first the infantry goes into battle.

| 26 P–B5! | R/N1–K1 |
| 27 P–QN4! | N–N1 |

This allows the exchange of his bishop, after which disaster hits him on the black squares. However, Black had no reasonable defence against the white pawn offensive.

| 28 N–N6+ | B×N |
| 29 P×B | Q×QRP |

Only despair can explain why Black should open a file along which the white rooks can break through to the eighth rank. Evidently Reshevsky already considered his position to be hopeless.

30 Q–KN3!	R–Q2
31 B–B5	Q–B2
32 R–R1	Q–N3
33 Q–R2!	

Moving the pawn to KR3 has turned out to be very far-sighted!

| 33 ... | R–K4 |
| 34 R–R8 | R–Q7 (*127*) |

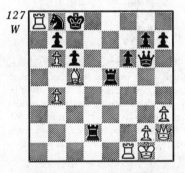

127
W

The best continuation 34 ... Q–K would not have prolonged Black's agony for long after 35 Q–N3 and 36 Q–R3.

35 R×N+!

A simple, but spectacular combination.

| 35 ... | K×R |

36 Q×R+! and mates.

In the following game the overthrown chess king wins a wonderful queen ending against the young Paul Keres.

58) **Keres-Alekhine,** Dresden 1936
Nimzo–Indian Defence

1 P–Q4	N–KB3
2 P–QB4	P–K3
3 N–QB3	B–N5
4 Q–B2	N–B3
5 P–K3	P–K4
6 P–Q5	N–K2
7 N–B3	

This allows Black to play ...
P–KB4 and establish a knight on
... K5. More possibilites were offered
by the following arrangement of his
forces: B–Q3 and KN–K2–N3.

7 ...	B × N+
8 Q × B	P–Q3
9 B–K2	0–0
10 0–0	N–K5!
11 Q–B2	P–KB4

The rapid advance of the KNP
to ... N5 will now give Black good
prospects of a K-side attack. To
prevent this dangerous possibility
Keres makes a series of simplifying
exchanges.

12 N–Q2	N × N
13 B × N	P–B5

Black shows that he has not
'forgotten' about the K-side, and
at the same time makes room to develop his bishop. This is why Keres
once again strives to simplify the
position.

14 P × P (*128*)

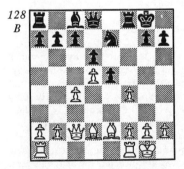

128
B

The turning point of the game.

By exchanging, White finally ends
up in an inferior queen ending, which
Alekhine is able to win, despite the
desperate resistance of the young
Estonian champion.

For this reason a more energetic
plan suggests itself, involving the
immediate opening of the QB-file,
and an attack on the Q-side. An
analysis of the possible variations
shows that, in the resulting sharp
struggle, White would not just have
equal chances, but would even have
an advantage in time.

After 14 P–K4 P–KN4 15 P–B3
P–KR4 16 P–B5 P–N5 17 KR–B1!
White's attack would develop very
smoothly, and he would soon have
forced his powerful opponent onto
the defensive.

14 ...	P × P
15 B–Q3	B–B4
16 P–B3	B × B
17 Q × B	N–N3

The knight aims for the strong
square ... K4, where White will be
obliged to exchange it.

18 B–B3	Q–N4
19 QR–K1	QR–K1
20 R × R	R × R
21 R–K1	N–K4
22 B × N	R × B
23 R–K4?	

A serious positional mistake. White
not only gives the black king and
queen the 'eternal' square ... K4,
but also weakens significantly his
position in the centre – the resulting
white pawn on K4 will demand
constant defence, whereas Black's
'liberated' KBP will be an active
participant in all the coming battles.
Of course, White should have captured immediately on K5, after
which he would have had chances of
saving the game.

23 ...	Q–N3
24 Q–Q4	

Even worse was 24 R–Q4 Q×Q 25 R×Q R–K7, and White is defenceless.

24 ...	**R × R**
25 P × R	

It is easy to see that Black easily wins the pawn ending, by first bringing his king to the focal point ...K4.

25 ...	**P–N3** (*129*)

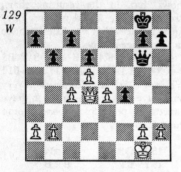

129
W

Why does Black have the advantage in this queen ending? The most important factor is the serious weakness of White's KP, which makes almost any pawn ending hopeless for him. Besides this, Black has the opportunity of creating threats against the white king, while in some cases he can attack White's Q-side pawns.

All these advantages enable Alekhine, by excellent play, to win.

26 P–QN3

A little should be said about the tactics in this position. If Keres had tried to rid himself of his weak KP and played 26 P–K5, he would have lost in the tactical complications after 26 P–K5 P–B6   27 P–KN3 Q–B7 28 Q–B2 Q–B8+   29 Q–B1 Q×Q+ 30 K×Q. Equally unsatisfactory was 27 Q–B2 Q–N8+   28 Q–B1 because of 28 ... P–B7+! 29 K×P Q×NP+ and 30 ... Q×KP.

26 ...	**Q–R4!**

This forces the opponent to guard

his K2 square, and so allows the black king to move towards the centre.

27 Q–Q3	**K–B2**
28 P–N3!	

Keres defends very stubbornly. The elimination of Black's KBP not only means the removal of a dangerous enemy, but also opens up the black king for all sorts of counterattacks by the white queen.

28 ...	**P × P**
29 P × P	**K–K2!**

Alekhine manoeuvres with great accuracy. After 29 ... Q–K4, White's queen would have the chance to break out – 30 Q–KB3+ K–K2 31 Q–N4!

30 K–N2

Stronger was 30 Q–B1, so as to transfer the queen to KB4. A possible variation would be 30 Q–B1 Q–K4 31 Q–B4, offering Black the choice between a drawn pawn ending and the complications resulting from 31 ... Q–R8+   32 K–N2 Q×P+ 33 K–R3. In the latter case the threats of 34 Q–N5+ and 34 Q–B5 would be most unpleasant.

30 ...	**Q–K4**
31 Q–KB3	**P–KR4!**

This is the subtle point. Now on 32 Q–B4 Black replies simply 32 ... Q–B3, and White does not have the move 33 Q–N4.

32 K–R3	**P–N3**
33 Q–B4	**Q–B3**
34 Q–R6! (*130*)	

After this strong move the black queen is unable to move far away, since White will have a perpetual check. So how can Black still play for a win? Alekhine finds a plan: first of all he has to drive the white queen away and occupy his KR3 square with his king. Black's next few moves are directed towards this aim.

34 ...	**K–B2!**

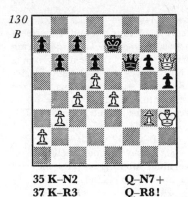

130
B

| 35 K–N2 | Q–N7+ |
| 37 K–R3 | Q–R8! |

An excellent move! Black threatens to mate on . . . KR8, and White dare not check on R7 because of 37 . . . Q–N2. White's king also has no move, and so he is forced to retreat his queen, which allows Black's king access to his KR3 square.

| 37 Q–B4+ | K–N2 |
| 38 Q–B3 | |

In the hope that Black will capture the QRP, after which White plays 39 Q–B3+ K–B2 40 P–K5! with a dangerous initiative. But Alekhine is accurate to the end.

38 . . .	Q–B3
39 Q–K2	K–R3
40 K–N2	P–KN4
41 P–QN4	Q–K4
42 Q–B3	K–N3
43 P–N4?	

A mistake, which hastens the end. After 43 P–R3 Alekhine would still have a lot of work to do, whereas now he simply wins a pawn.

43 . . .	P×P
44 Q×P	Q–N7+
45 K–B3	Q–R6+
46 K–K2	Q×RP+
47 K–Q3	Q–N6+
48 K–Q4	Q–N7+
49 K–Q3	Q–B3

Everything is just as it was, except that now Black is a pawn to the good. True, Keres is able to block the Q-side

with his next move, but even so, all White's calculations must take into account the fact that Black's QRP is an extra pawn.

50 P–N5	Q–B5
51 Q–K6+	K–R4
52 Q–R3+	Q–R5
53 Q–B3+	Q–N5
54 Q–B7+	K–R5
55 Q×P	Q–B6+
56 K–Q4	Q–B3+
57 K–Q3	P–N5! (*131*)

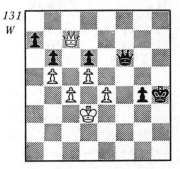

131
W

Alekhine's winning method is simple. The far-advanced KNP will soon be on the point of queening, and all White's attempts to exploit his own pawns are too late.

58 Q–R7+	K–N4
59 Q–N8+	K–B5
60 Q–K6	K–N4
61 P–K5	

White pins his hopes on his QP. But Alekhine calculates the variations move by move, and beats his young opponent in the sharp race to queen.

61 . . .	Q×P
62 Q×Q+	P×Q
63 K–K4	K–B3
64 K–K3	K–B4
65 K–B2	P–K5
66 K–K2	P–N6
67 K–K3	K–N5

There was also a longer path to victory: to play the king to . . . QN2, play . . . P–R4 and force

White to capture en passant, then
return the king to . . . Q3 and decide
matters by the undermining move
. . . P–N4.

68 P–Q6	P–N7
69 K–B2	K–R6
70 P–Q7	P–K6+
71 K–B3	

White seeks salvation in an ending
with a new pair of queens. Other
moves by the white king would lose
more quickly.

71 . . .	P–N8 = Q
72 P–Q8–Q	Q–B7+
73 K–K4	P–K7
74 Q–Q7+	K–N7
75 Q–N4+	K–B8
0–1	

Another excellent ending which
Alekhine played during this period
was against a special opponent –
Max Euwe.

59) Alekhine–Euwe, Nottingham
1936
French Defence

1 P–K4	P–K3
2 P–Q4	P–Q4
3 P–K5	P–QB4
4 N–KB3	N–QB3
5 B–Q3	P×P
6 0–0	P–B3

Thus Black eliminates completely
his opponent's pawn centre. Practice
has shown that the method of play
chosen by White gives him no advantage.

7 B–QN5	B–Q2
8 B×N	P×B
9 Q×P+	P×P
10 Q×KP	N–B3
11 B–B4	B–B4
12 N–B3	0–0

The pieces of both sides have been
developed, and both have castled.
How should the position be appraised? Black has a powerful pawn
centre, while White has no central

pawns. However Black's pawns are
securely blockaded, and at present
there is no question of them advancing
further. During the next few moves
White strives to exchange Black's
KB, which will render this advance
even more difficult. Therefore White
prepares the manoeuvre N–QR4.

13 B–N3	Q–K2
14 P–QR3?	

This delay is uncharacteristic of
Alekhine. After 14 N–QR4 the goal
is achieved immediately.

14 . . .	P–QR4
15 KR–K1	R–R2?

Now it is Euwe who errs, once
again allowing White's knight to
attack his KB. Stronger was 15 . . .
B–N3.

16 N–QR4	R–N2
17 Q–B3	

This is once again unnecessary. He
should have captured the bishop
straight away.

17 . . .	B–R2
18 Q×RP	N–K5
19 Q–R6!	

Black threatened the terrible 19 . . .
R–R1 followed by 20 . . . B×P+
winning the queen. The queen can
now escape along the white diagonal.

19 . . .	B–K1
20 P–N4	P–N4?

A further mistake by the champion,
and this time decisive. However
Black's position was already difficult.
Thus on 20 . . . P–K4, White's ex-
cellent position would enable him to
sacrifice the exchange: 21 R×N!
P×R 22 Q–B4+ B–B2 23 Q×KP
B–Q4 24 Q×KP B×N 25 Q×Q
R×Q 26 P×B R×P 27 K–N2
R–B1 28 P–QB4. Alekhine con-
sidered that 20 . . . B–R4 was the
strongest continuation, after which
Black would have chances of a suc-
cessful defence.

21 N–B5	B×N

At last this bishop is exchanged. Black could not capture with the knight – 21 . . . N × N 22 P × N B × P 23 R × P!

22 P × B	N × QBP
23 Q–K2	N–K5
24 Q–K3	B–N3
25 N–K5!	P–B4
26 N × B	P × N
27 P–KB3	N × B
28 P × N	K–B2 (*132*)

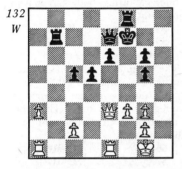

132
W

Who stands better in this battle of heavy pieces? Two factors determine that the advantage is with White. Firstly, his king is better protected by pawns, and it is difficult for Black to set up threats against it. Secondly – and this is the more important factor, and this makes White's position preferable – there is the outside passed QRP, which in many cases paralyses Black. It is the strength of this pawn that Alekhine exploits in the following struggle.

| 29 P–R4! | R–QR1 |
| 30 K–B2! | |

And now Alekhine exploits the open position of the black king. He plans to play 31 R–R1 and 32 Q–K5, which may give him a decisive attack.

| 30 . . . | R–N7 |
| 31 R–K2 | P–B5 |

Alekhine makes the following comment to this move: 'It is impossible to defend simultaneously: 1) the

QR-file, 2) the KR-file, 3) the QBP, 4) the KP, 5) the pawn on KN4, 6) the K4 square. This really is a little too much !'

| 32 R–R1 | K–N1 |

This move finally determines the direction of the struggle. Euwe had at his disposal the continuation 32 . . . Q–B3, after which White would win by the combined attack of all his pieces by 33 R–R7+ K–N1 34 R–QB7 R–K1 35 Q–B5, and the advance of the QRP, combined with threats to the black king, would soon decide the game. Euwe chooses a different path – he agrees to an inferior queen ending, hoping to 'snatch' a perpetual check.

33 Q–K5!	Q–QR2+
34 K–B1	R–N8+
35 R–K1	R × R+
36 K × R	Q–KN2!

The only defence against mate by 37 Q–R8+ and 38 R–R7. True, it costs Black two pawns.

| 37 Q × KP+ | K–B1 |
| 38 Q × QP! | Q–B6+ |

Or 38 . . . Q–R8+ 39 K–B2 Q × P 40 Q–Q6+ with a quick mate. 38 . . . R–K1+ 39 K–Q2 Q–B3 does not save the game in view of 40 R–R7 R–Q1 41 R–R8+.

| 39 K–B2! | R–K1 (*133*) |

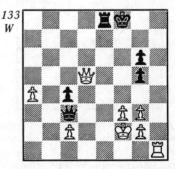

133
W

Very bad is 39 . . . Q × QBP+ 40 K–N1 Q–N8+ 41 K–R2 Q–N1

42 Q × BP.

40 P–N4

Every tempo is vital at this point. The white king is also in an uncomfortable position, and much depends on the precise calculation of variations. Alekhine carries this out brilliantly.

40 ...	Q–K6+
41 K–N3	Q–B5+

Or 41 ... K–N2   42 Q–Q7+ R–K2 43 Q–Q6 R–K3 44 Q–B7+ R–K2 45 Q × P, and Black's attack gets nowhere.

| 42 K–R3 | R–K2 |

The white king is on the point of being mated. But it becomes clear that Alekhine has seen his way through all the possible complications.

| 43 Q–QB5 | Q–B3 |
| 44 P–N3! | |

Only not 44 R–QN1?? Q–R1+ 45 K–N3 Q–R5 mate.

44 ...	Q–R1+
45 K–N2	Q–B6
46 R–R7	Q × QBP+
47 K–R3	Q–K7
48 R × R	Q × R
49 Q × P (*134*)	

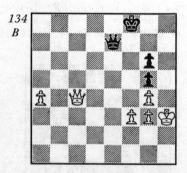

134
B

A new transformation of the position has resulted in a queen ending. White's two extra pawns should promise him victory, although accurate play is required in order to avoid perpetual check.

49 ...	Q–K8
50 Q–B5+	K–B2
51 K–N2	Q–QR8
52 Q–QB2	K–B3
53 Q–N3	K–K4?
54 K–B2?	

Both sides make mistakes in time trouble. The advance of the king to ... K4 could have been refuted by 54 Q–QN8+ K–K3 55 Q–K8+ or 54 ... K–Q4 55 Q–N8+, and White, capturing both KN pawns, wins easily.

54 ...	K–B3
55 Q–N6+	K–N2
56 Q–N4!	

The beginning of the accurate concluding plan. So that Black should not have the chance of playing for stalemate, Alekhine first of all carries out the important pawn advance P–B4.

56 ...	Q–R8
57 Q–K1	Q–R7+
58 K–K3	K–R2
59 P–R5	Q–R7
60 Q–Q2	Q–R8
61 K–K2	K–R3
62 P–B4!	

At last. Now White will have two 'healthy' pawns, while the threat of stalemate is removed. The end is near.

62 ...	P × P
63 P × P	Q–R5
64 K–B2!	

The final finesse. Alekhine wishes to play P–N5, but without the black king being able to go to ... R4.

64 ...	K–R2
65 P–N5	Q–R6
66 Q–Q7+	K–R1
67 Q–B8+	K–R2
68 Q–B7+	K–R1
69 K–K2	Q–R7+
70 K–K3	Q–N6+
71 K–Q4	Q–N5+
72 K–Q5	Q–N4+
73 K–Q4	Q–R3

74 Q–N6	Q–B1
75 Q–Q6!	

All the pawns are defended, and the king moves in to support the final attack.

75 ...	Q–B7
76 P–R6	Q–Q7+
77 K–K5	Q–B6+
78 K–K6	Q–B1+
79 K–K7	K–R2
80 Q–Q7!	Q–B6
81 K–K6+	1–0

In the following game Alekhine conducts a complex, many-piece ending with great mastery.

60) Alekhine-Fine, Kemeri 1937
Queen's Gambit Accepted

1 P–Q4	P–Q4
2 P–QB4	P × P
3 N–KB3	N–KB3
4 Q–R4+	

It has long been known that this move promises White no advantage. The opponent can exchange queens, as in the present game, while 4 ... N–B3 also gives Black a good game. If White wishes to play for a win, then more chances are offered by the usual continuation 4 P–K3.

4	Q–Q2
5 Q × BP	Q–B3
6 N–R3	Q × Q
7 N × Q	P–K3
8 P–QR3	P–B4?

A move which Alekhine describes as 'dogmatic'. Black weakens his Q3 square, and also falls seriously behind in development. Playing energetically, Alekhine obtains an appreciable advantage within a few moves.

Black should have continued the development of his pieces.

9 B–B4	N–B3
10 P × P	B × P
11 P–QN4	B–K2
12 P–N5	N–QN1
13 N–Q6+	B × N

14 B × B	N–K5
15 B–B7	(135)

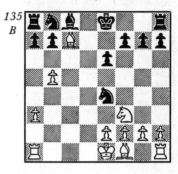

135
B

White has a marked advantage: he has the two bishops, and most of Black's pieces are still on their original squares. With the following subtle manoeuvres Alekhine further emphasizes the superiority of White's position, and soon forces his opponent to go over completely to passive defence.

15 ...	N–Q2
16 N–Q4!	N–N3
17 P–B3	N–Q4
18 B–R5	N5–B3

Or 18 ... N–Q3 19 P–K4 N–K6 20 B–N4 P–K4 21 B × N P × N 22 B–Q3! N × P+ 23 K–B2 N–K6 24 B–K5 with advantage to White.

19 N–B2!
But now Alekhine guards his K3 square, and both black knights are forced into passive positions.

19 ...	B–Q2
20 P–K4	R–QB1
21 K–Q2	N–N3
22 N–K3	0–0

23 P–QR4! (136)
This prevents the knight's advance to ... QR5, and leaves his opponent's pieces completely cramped. White dominates the centre, while the position of his king on the open central file is not at all dangerous, since the black pieces are so passive

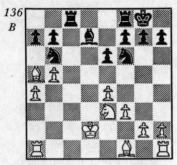

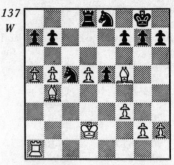

that they are unable to exploit this circumstance.

| 23 ... | KR–Q1 |
| 24 B–Q3 | P–K4 |

This is a case where activity is only harmful to the defender. By setting up defensive lines along the back ranks by 24 ... B–K1 and 25 ... N/B3–Q2, Black could have prolonged the game considerably. Now, however, his weaknesses become more vulnerable.

25 KR–QB1	B–K3
26 R × R	R × R
27 B–N4	

Preparing the advance of the QRP, and, incidentally, preventing the black king from reaching the centre.

27 ...	N–K1
28 P–R5	N–Q2
29 N–Q5!	

This initiates some deep and accurately calculated complications. In view of the simple threat of 30 N–K7+, Black is forced to capture the knight.

| 29 ... | B × N |
| 30 P × B | N–B4 |

Just one more move (31 ... N–Q3), and Black would have an excellent position, but he is not allowed to make it.

| 31 B–B5! | R–Q1 (*137*) |

Black relies on tactics: 32 B × N R × P+. He would lose immediately after 31 ... N–N6+   32 K–Q3

N–B8+   33 K–K3 R–B5   34 P–Q6.

32 K–B3!

Alekhine had foreseen this cunning move. If now 32 ... R × P   33 K–B4 and Black can resign.

32 ...	P–QN3
33 P × P	P × P
34 B × N!	

An accurate appraisal of the situation. The QNP becomes irresistible.

34 ...	P × B
35 P–N6	N–Q3
36 B–Q7	R × B
37 R–R8+	1–0

61) Alekhine–Euwe, 6th match game, 1937
Slav Defence

1 P–Q4	P–Q4
2 P–QB4	P–QB3
3 N–QB3	

Usually 3 N–KB3 is played, since 'after the early development of the QN Black gets a good game by capturing the QBP'. This is what theory stated, and it was well known to Euwe.

The innovation prepared by Alekhine, and adopted in the present game, stunned the chess world, and forced the move 3 N–QB3 to be considered anew.

| 3 ... | P × P |
| 4 P–K4 | P–K4 |

It is this counter-blow in the centre which caused the system with the early development of White's

QN to be considered unfavourable. After 4 . . . P–QN4 White could choose a sharp line of play; 5 P–QR4 P–K4 6 RP × P KP × P 7 B × P B–QN5 8 R–R4 P–QR4 9 P × Pep and White stands better.

5 B × P   **P × P** (*138*)

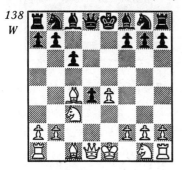

138
W

Now it appears that Black has seized the initiative, but there follows a stunning move.

6 N–B3

This is the innovation that Alekhine had prepared. The variations associated with it are so complicated and obscure that the theorists were able to come to a definite conclusion regarding it only a year after the game was played.

What should Black's reply be? The move chosen by Euwe was very poor, and was easily refuted by Alekhine. For several months theorists analysed this position, but only succeeded in convincing themselves that the position is complex and obscure, and were unable to give preference to either of the two sides.

Here are some of Black's defensive possibilities which were considered in this analysis: 6 . . . P × N 7 B × P+ K–K2 8 Q–N3 N–B3 9 P–K5 N–K5 10 0–0 ! – no one doubted that these moves were the best. The further moves 10 . . . N–R3 and 10 . . . Q–N3 were considered.

a) 10 . . . N–R3 11 Q–B4 ! N3–B4 12 B–N5 + ! N × B 13 N × N, with a very strong attack for White.

b) 10 . . . Q–N3 11 Q–B4 P × P 12 B × P Q × B 13 Q × N K × B 14 N–N5 + K–K1 15 Q–KB4 B–K2 16 Q–B7 + K–Q1 17 QR–Q1 + B–Q2 18 N–K6 + K–B1 19 Q × B Q × KP 20 KR–K1 Q–B3 21 R × B N × R 22 Q–Q6, and White wins.

After coming to this conclusion, the theorists relaxed, especially since their opinion coincided with the opinion of Alekhine himself. But the numerous chess enthusiasts from all corners of the globe do not even think of relaxing, and in 1938 the amateur I. Goncharov, in the magazine *64*, indicated a defence, which, in effect, refuted Alekhine's entire plan.

This was Goncharov's defence: 6 . . . P × N 7 B × P+ K–K2 8 Q–N3 P × P !! – and he demonstrated that White's attack is insufficient compensation for the piece. His variations, the publication of which caused the sacrifice of the knight to disappear from tournament play, were the following:

a) 9 B × P Q–N3 10 B–R3 + P–B4 11 B × N R × B 12 B × P + (*12 Q × R Q–R4 +*) 12 . . . Q × B 13 0–0 (with the threats of *14 Q × R* and *14 QR–B1* followed by *15 R × B*).

It appears now that Black is defenceless, but he can defend everything by 13 . . . Q–KR4 !!, for instance 14 Q × R? B–K3 15 Q–R8 N–B3, and the white queen is trapped.

b) 9 B × P Q–N3 10 B × N R × B 11 Q × R Q–N5 + 12 N–Q2 Q × B 13 R–QN1 Q–B7, and White's attack fizzles out.

How should we appraise Alekhine's innovation? Of course, it has been discarded, after all, who would adopt a variation that has been refuted ! But the discovery of such a possibility as early as the 6th move is proof of Alekhine's boundless imagination. The refutation was found only a year later, and, of course, to find it during the game was out of the question. After all, for his forty moves a player is only allowed two and a half hours!

6...   **P–QN4?**

Euwe cannot find a refutation, and makes one of the worst possible moves. Besides the capture of the knight, Black had another defensive possibility – 6 ... B–QB4   7 0–0! N–B3 8 N–QR4 B–K2, with a perfectly satisfactory position.

7 N × NP

Simple and convincing – the knight cannot be taken because of 8 B–Q5.

7...   **B–R3**

8 Q–N3

This move has three aims: to defend the bishop on QB4, to attack Black's KB2, and to deny the black bishop its QN5 square.

8...   **Q–K2**

Or 8 ... B × N   9 B × P+   K–Q2 10 N × P! with a winning attack.

9 0–0   **B × N**

10 B × B   **N–B3**

11 B–QB4   **QN–Q2**

12 N × P

Weaker is 12 P–K5 N × P   13 N × N Q × N.

12...   **R–QN1**

13 Q–B2   **Q–B4**

14 N–B5   **N–K4**

15 B–B4

Alekhine is accurate to the end. After the hasty 15 N × P+ K–Q1 16 R–Q1+ K–B2 both White's knight and his bishop would be en prise, and the question of his winning would be in doubt.

15...   **N–R4** (*139*)

16 B × P+!

The shortest way. White's two extra pawns in the ending will ensure him an easy win.

139
W

16...   **K × B**

17 Q × Q   **B × Q**

18 B × N   **R–N4**

Or 18 ... R/N1–K1   19 B–Q6, also maintaining his extra pawns.

19 B–Q6   **B–N3**

20 P–QN4   **R–Q1**

21 QR–Q1   **P–B4**

22 P × P   **B × P**

23 R–Q5   **1–0**

Great mastery of opening preparation was demonstrated by Alekhine in the following important game, the winning of which enabled him to regain his lost world championship title.

62) **Euwe–Alekhine,** 25th match game, 1937
Nimzo-Indian Defence

1 P–Q4   **N–KB3**

2 P–QB4   **P–K3**

3 N–QB3   **B–N5**

4 P–K3   **0–0**

5 KN–K2

This move was devised about fifty years ago, and is still to be found in the arsenal of today's strongest grandmasters. It is of interest to hear Alekhine's opinion of the move:

'One of the less successful inventions of the openings artist Rubinstein. Its weakness lies in the following: the knight has no great future either on KB4, or on KN3, while, with a few simple moves, Black can obtain a small lead in development.

Preferable was therefore 5 B–Q3, and if Black replies 5 . . . P–QN3, then 6 KN–K2 (or even 6 Q–B3); while if 5 . . . P–Q4, then 6 N–B3 with good prospects' (Alekhine).

It has to be said that the world champion's appraisal of this elastic knight move is not completely accurate. Well, even the opinions of the great can turn out to be inaccurate when examined several decades later.

5 . . . .   **P–Q4**
6 P–QR3   **B–K2**
7 P × P

Alekhine considers that 7 N–N3 is stronger, although the pawn exchange is the usual continuation in tournament games today.

7 . . .   **P × P**
8 N–N3   **P–B4**
9 P × P

The beginning of an unsuccessful plan. Euwe, who at the end of the match was in a depressed state due to a number of defeats, simply overlooks an elementary tactical blow. By continuing 9 B–K2, White would have a satisfactory game with prospects of soon setting up pressure on Black's QP, or, in the case of . . . . P–B5 by Black, of carrying out the energetic undermining thrust P–K4. Also good enough was 9 B–Q3 N–B3 10 P × P B × P 11 0–0.

9 . . .   **B × P**
10 P–QN4   **P–Q5!** (*140*)

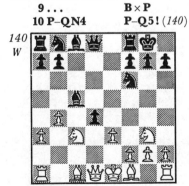

140
W

This is the tactical stroke that White had overlooked. It is bad now to capture on Q4, since White's king becomes too exposed. 11 N–R4 also loses to 11 . . . P × P!   12 Q × Q (*12 N × B P × P+   13 K–K2 B–N5+*) 12 . . . P × P+   13 K–K2 B–N5+ and 14 . . . R × Q+. There remains only one possible reply.

11 P × B   **P × N**
12 Q–B2

Euwe still does not sense the imminent danger, otherwise he would have exchanged queens and settled for a slightly inferior ending after 12 Q × Q R × Q   13 N–K2 N–K5 14 P–B3 N × P   15 N × P. Now the pawn on B6 gives Black a number of tactical possibilities.

12 . . .   **Q–R4**
13 R–QN1

And here better was 13 N–K2 N–Q4   14 P–K4 N–N5   15 Q–N1 N5–R3. Euwe hopes to remove the black pawn 'at his leisure', but has not seen an interesting combinational manoeuvre.

13 . . .   **B–Q2!**

It becomes clear that White is unable to meet the threat of 14 . . . B–R5. If he plays the direct 14 R–N4, then after 14 . . . N–R3   15 B × N Q × B the white king cannot castle, and is trapped in the centre. The same would result after 14 B–B4 B–R5 15 B–N3 B–N4.

14 R–N3   **B–R5**
15 Q × BP (*141*)

Now it appears that the QBP has been lost, while White has everything under control. But . . .

15 . . .   **Q–Q1!**

This elastic retreat wins the exchange for Black.

16 B–B4   **N–R3**

Alekhine conducts this deciding game of the match very skilfully. He aims to exchange off White's KB,

141
B

after which the white squares in the enemy camp become hopelessly weakened.

17 B × N	P × B
18 0–0	B × R
19 Q × B	R–N1

There begins the technical phase of realizing the advantage, which Alekhine carries out consistently and accurately.

20 Q–B2	Q–Q4
21 P–K4	Q–N6
22 Q–K2	

After the exchange of queens White's pawns on QR3 and QB5 would become hopelessly weak.

22 ...	Q–N4
23 Q–B3?	

He should not have given up his important QBP without a fight. After 23 Q–K3 N–Q2 24 N–B5 it is not easy for Black to win due to the threats to his KN2 square. Thus 24 ... N × P is bad because of 25 N × P!, while only a little better is 24 ... Q × P 25 Q–KN3 P–N3 26 B–K3 Q–B5 27 B–Q4, and the white pieces have taken up menacing positions.

With the fall of the QBP Black's task is made easier.

23 ...	Q × P
24 N–B5	R–N8
25 Q–B4	N × P
26 P–KR4	R–K1
27 R–K1	Q–B6

The black pieces are fully mobi-

lized, and his KN2 square is securely defended. White could have terminated his resistance here, but 'by inertia' Euwe continues playing.

28 R–Q1	N–Q7!

By this means Alekhine forces exchanges and a simplification of the position.

29 R × N	R × B+
30 K–R2	Q–B2
31 R–Q6	R–B4
32 P–N3! *(142)*	

142
B

The tactician Euwe sets a cunning trap. If now Black incautiously captures the knight 32 ... R × N? then he loses all his advantage after 33 R–K6 !

32 ...	R–KB1!
33 P–N4	P–B3
34 K–R3	P–KR4
35 Q–Q2	P × P+
36 K × P	Q–B2
37 P–R5	R × N!

The simplest way. The white king comes under a mating attack.

38 K × R	Q × P+
39 K–B4	Q–R5+
40 K–B3	Q–R6+
41 K–K4	R–K1+
42 K–Q5	Q–QN6+
43 K–Q4	Q × P
0–1	

63) Alekhine-Euwe, 8th match game, 1937
Nimzo–Indian Defence

1 P–Q4	N–KB3

2 P–QB4	P–K3
3 N–QB3	B–N5
4 Q–B2	

Alekhine considers this move to be the most logical of all the possibilities in this position. It is perfectly possible to agree with him, although allowance should be made for improvements which have been made with time. It has long been decided that the reply 4 ... P–B4 gives Black a comfortable game by arranging his pieces (in the case of 5 P×P) according to the scheme: ... N–R3, ... B×P–K2, ... N–B4, ... P–QN3, ... B–N2 and ... P–Q4.

4 ...	P–Q4

But this move, in my opinion, allows White to maintain the tension in the position.

5 P×P	Q×P
6 P–K3	P–B4
7 P–QR3	B×N+
8 P×B	QN–Q2

In the twelfth game Euwe found a 'certain' way to achieve equality by 8 ... P×P 9 BP×P P–QN3, and then, at the appropriate moment, ... B–R3.

9 P–B3

An inaccuracy. More precise was 9 N–K2, so as after 9 ... P×P 10 P×P N–N3, as occurs in the game, to be able to place the knight on QB3.

9 ...	P×P
10 BP×P	N–N3
11 N–K2	B–Q2
12 N–B4	

It now becomes clear that 12 N–B3 fails to the simple 12 ... Q–B3. Even so White still has the better position, however Black replies. After 12 ... Q–B3, the exchange of queens gives White the better ending, while after the queen retreats to ... Q3, the transference of the QB to QN4 via Q2 is strong.

12 ...	Q–Q3
13 B–Q2	R–QB1
14 Q–N2	NB3–Q4
15 N×N	P×N
16 B–N4	Q–K3
17 K–B2	N–R5?

White has an undisputable advantage. Black's king is unable to castle, and White is master of the black squares. Even so, White's chances of victory would still be problematic, were it not for this serious mistake, which quickly loses the game. The correct plan was to transfer the king to KB2, beginning with 17 ... P–B4 !

18 Q–Q2	P–QN3

And here 18 ... P–B4 was better, although White would have time to make a central break-through by 19 B–Q3 followed by KR–K1 and P–K4.

19 B–R6	R–QN1
20 P–K4!	P–QN4

It appears that the bishop on R6 is lost, but Alekhine has accurately worked everything out, and, with a series of tactical blows, obtains a decisive advantage.

21 Q–B4	R–N3
22 P×P	Q×P
23 KR–K1+	B–K3
24 QR–B1 (*143*)	

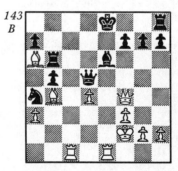

143
B

A quiet move. White occupies the open file, and threatens both to check on B8, and also to simply penetrate to the seventh rank. Black is unable to meet the second threat, and his king, which has not been able to save himself by castling, perishes.

24 ...	P–B3
25 R–B7	K–Q1
26 R × RP	1–0

In the return match Alekhine's tactical talent sparkled especially brilliantly, and he used his unexpected moves and traps in defence as well as in attack. See with what elegance and mastery he saves the following game, which at one moment looked very dubious for him.

64) Alekhine-Euwe, 18th match game, 1937
Queen's Gambit Declined

1 N–KB3	P–Q4
2 P–B4	P–K3
3 P–Q4	N–KB3
4 N–B3	P–B4
5 BP × P	N × P
6 P–K4	N × N
7 P × N	P × P
8 P × P	B–N5+
9 B–Q2	B × B+
10 Q × B	0–0

A variation which displays exceptional vitality. It was adopted at the very start of this century, and is still to be found in the repertoires of tournaments today. The reason is simple – the resulting position is full of problems, the solving of which is to the taste of modern masters. Black arranges his pieces according to the scheme: ... P–QN3, ... B–N2, ... N–B3–R4, ... Q–B3, ... KR–Q1; against this White supports his two central pawns with his rooks, so as to be ready to advance them.

11 B–B4	N–B3
12 0–0	P–QN3
13 KR–Q1	B–N2
14 Q–B4	R–B1

In a number of games Black successfully carried out the simplifying manoeuvre 14 ... Q–B3 15 Q–K3 Q–R3. It is clear that it is to Black's advantage to take play into an ending, since his king is no longer threatened, and can even be used in the battle against the enemy pawn centre.

15 P–Q5	P × P
16 B × P	Q–K2 (*144*)

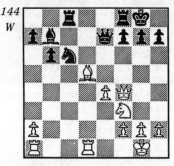

144
W

17 N–N5 !
An interesting position. White threatens to capture three times on KB7 and then check with his rook on Q7. Euwe parries this unpleasant threat with a clever tactical stroke.

17 ...	N–K4 !
18 B × B ?	

Alekhine simply overlooks his opponent's 20th move. Stronger was 18 P–KR4, keeping his pieces in their active positions.

18 ...	N–N3
19 Q–B5	Q × B
20 R–Q7	Q–R3 !

A brilliant concept ! On the natural 21 R × BP there follows 21 ... Q × P !! 22 R × NP+ K × R 23 Q–Q7+ R–B2 24 Q–Q4+ K–N1 25 N × R Q × N or 22 R × R+ N × R, and White's attack dies out, while Black's Q-side pawns are very dangerous. White has to make an immediate escape square for his king.

21 P–KR4   R–B4
22 R–Q5   R × R?

Euwe in his turn makes a mistake. Why give his opponent a dangerous passed pawn in the centre? He should have maintained equality by 22 ... Q–B1 !, for example 23 R × R Q × R 24 Q × Q P × Q   25 R–QB1 R–B1.

23 P × R   Q–B1
24 Q–K4   R–K1
25 Q–R4 !

This manoeuvre with attacks on Black's rook and QRP enables White to further advance his menacing passed pawn, which leaves the initiative in his hands. By combining threats to the black king with the advance of his QP and KRP, Alekhine does not allow his opponent a moment's peace.

25 ...   R–K2
26 P–Q6   R–Q2
27 R–Q1

And now White threatens to throw forward his KRP to R5 and R6.

27 ...   N–B1
28 Q–KB4

Alekhine has just made a series of such strong moves, that one doesn't feel inclined to criticize him for this error. After the quiet 28 P–N3 it would be easier for White to keep all three black pieces tied down.

28 ...   Q–B3
29 N–K4   Q–B7
30 R–QB1 (*145*)

This pawn sacrifice gives White a dangerous initiative, which should have been sufficient to bring Alekhine victory. The other, more prudent idea, was to take no risks and play 30 R–Q2, keeping material equality and setting the opponent a difficult question: how long can the black pieces stand inactive?

30 ...   Q × RP
31 P–R5?

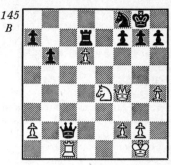

145
B

A serious mistake, which hands the initiative over to Black. By playing 31 R–B8 ! Q–K3 32 R–N8 ! P–B4 33 N–N5 Q × P 34 Q–B4 + Q–Q4 35 Q × Q + (not *35 N–K6? Q–Q8 + 36 K–R2 Q–Q3 + !* and *37 ... Q × R*) 35 ... R × Q 36 N–K6 K–B2 37 N × N P–KR3 38 P–R5 P–B5 39 N–N6, White would have every chance of realizing his advantage.

31 ...   P–KR3
32 N–N3

32 R–B8 was still the strongest move.

32 ...   N–K3
33 Q–K5   Q–R3
34 N–B5   Q–Q6
35 K–R2

Curious complications could follow after 35 R–B8 + K–R2 36 N × RP !? N–Q1 37 N–B5, although even then after 37 ... Q–Q8 + 38 K–R2 Q × RP + 39 K–N1 the question remains: does White's initiative compensate for the sacrificed pawn?

35 ...   K–R2
36 R–B3   Q–Q8
37 P–B3   Q–Q7
38 R–B4   Q–N4
39 R–KR4?

Having reached a drawn position, Alekhine attempts to play for a win, and, as so often happens, finds himself on the edge of defeat. After 39 R–KN4 ! Q × P + 40 R–KR4 Q–N3

41 R–KN4 Black would be forced to repeat moves, since 41 . . . Q–B3? loses to 42 R × P +, and 41 . . . N–N4? is met by 42 P–B4 P–B3 43 Q–N5.

39 . . .	**Q–B3!**
40 Q–K4	**N–B4**
41 Q–B2	

Here the game was adjourned, and home analysis convinced Alekhine that he should be able to draw. The way in which he saves the game is interesting for its curious tactical subtleties.

41 . . .	**P–R4**
42 P–N3!	

The first preparatory measure for the coming skirmish. The white king must be covered against possible checks.

42 . . .	**P–R5**

Alekhine thought that strongest for Black was 42 . . . K–R1   43 R–KN4 P–R5   44 R × NP P–R6 45 R–N4 R–Q1   46 R–KB4, with two alternatives here: 46 . . . N–Q6 47 Q × N P–R7   48 R–QR4, or 46 . . . P–R7   47 Q × P N–Q6   48 Q–B4 N × R   49 Q × N and 50 P–N4. In all cases White's strongly-placed knight ensures that his defence will be successful.

43 R–KN4

The first move of a spectacular saving combination.

43 . . .	**P–N3**
44 N–R4!	**Q × QP**

Or 44 . . . P–R6   45 P × P+ P × P 46 N × P Q–N7   47 N–B8 + + K–R1 48 N–N6+ K–N2   49 N–K5 + !, and the black king can move to neither B3, nor B1, since the rook is then captured with check.

45 P × P+	**P × P** (*146*)
46 R–Q4!!	

A splendid move! The rook cannot be captured: 46 . . . Q × R   47 Q × NP+ K–R1   48 Q–K8+ with a draw by perpetual check, since the

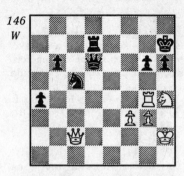

146
W

king cannot move to N2 because of check by the knight on B5.

46 . . .	**Q–K3**
47 R × R+	**N × R**
48 Q × RP	

And now Black is unable to realize his extra pawn due to the exposed nature of his king.

48 . . .	**P–R4**
49 Q–B2	**N–K4**
50 K–N2	**N–B5** (*147*)

This allows a further tactical stroke. Stronger was 50 . . . Q–B5! though even then white has good chances of a draw after 51 Q–Q2 Q–B4   52 P–B4 Q–B3+   53 K–N1 N–B6+ 54 N × N Q × N   55 Q–K1.

147
W

51 N × P!	**½–½**

After 51 . . . N–K6+   52 K–B2 N × Q, White is a queen down for a moment, but wins it back by 53 N–B8+.

In this last game we have seen how

well Alekhine was able to analyse adjourned positions, and the following game is a further example of this.

65) Alekhine-Euwe, 22nd match game, 1937
Reti Opening

1 N–KB3	P–Q4
2 P–B4	P–Q5
3 P–K3 -	N–QB3
4 P × P	N × P
5 N × N	Q × N
6 N–B3	N–B3

A variation which was met equally rarely during Alekhine's time as it is nowadays. Black has the chance to maintain equality, and so most of the games which commence with this variation are of a quiet, manoeuvring, character.

7 P–Q3	P–B3
8 B–K3	Q–Q2
9 P–Q4	P–KN3
10 B–K2	B–N2
11 P–KR3	0–0
12 0–0	P–N3
13 B–B3	B–N2

As expected, the game is completely level. With his next swift pawn advance Alekhine weakens Black's QNP, but this makes little significant difference to the course of the struggle.

14 P–QR4	QR–Q1
15 P–R5	Q–B2
16 Q–N3	N–Q2
17 P × P	P × P
18 R–R7	R–R1
19 R1–R1	P–K3
20 R × R	B × R (*148*)

Black is ready for anything, and waits to see what his opponent will do. Alekhine decides to break through in the centre, but even so this does not bring him any noticeable advantage.

21 P–Q5!	BP × P
22 P × P	N–B4

An inaccuracy. True, Black could

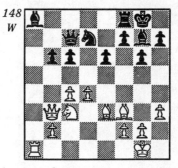

148
W

have made an even worse move: 22 ... B × N? 23 P–Q6!! Q × P 24 Q × B B × B 25 B–R6! winning the exchange, but there was also a better move. By continuing 22 ... P × P!, Euwe would be fully justified in counting on equality.

23 Q–B4
Weaker was 23 B × N Q × B 24 P × P B × B 25 P × P+ R × P 26 P × B B × N 27 R–R7 Q–KN4+ with perpetual check.

23 ...	P × P
24 B × P	B × B
25 N × B	Q–K4
26 R–N1	N–R5
27 P–QN3	N–N7
28 Q–B6	P–QN4
29 B–B4	

The QNP cannot be captured because of 29 ... R–Q1.

29 ...	Q–K3

29 ... Q–K7 was stronger.

30 Q × P	Q–K5
31 R–QB1	N–Q6
32 Q–B4!	

The only way to maintain his advantage.

32 ...	Q–K7
33 R–B1	N × B
34 Q × N	Q–N4
35 Q–B3!	R–N1
36 R–N1	Q–R3
37 R–Q1	

Of course, 37 P–QN4 was stronger, but time trouble was evidently having its effect.

37 ...	Q–R6
38 R–N1	Q–R7
39 Q–Q3	B–Q5
40 R–KB1	Q–N7 (*149*)

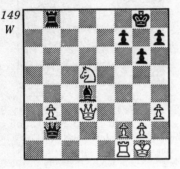

149
W

Here the game was adjourned. See what an amazing path to victory Alekhine found, and how precisely he worked out the complicated variations, not missing even the most hidden possibility! The astonishing manoeuvres of the white knight are truly delightful.

41 N–K7+	K–B1

Other king moves lose immediately:
a) 41 ... K–N2 42 N–B5+ P×N 43 Q–N3+ and 44 Q×R.
b) 41 ... K–R1 42 N–B6 B×P+ 43 R×B Q–B8+ 44 K–R2 Q×N 45 R×P, and Black is defenceless.

42 N–B6	B×P+
43 K–R2!	

Just so. The reason why becomes clear later. Weaker was 43 R×B Q–B8+ 44 Q–B1 Q×N 45 R×P+ K–N1 46 R–B3, and the realization of the extra pawn in the heavy-piece ending is not a simple matter.

43 ...	R–K1
44 Q–KB3	R–K7

This is the point. With the white king on R1 Black would be able to exchange rooks by 44 ... R–K8, after which a win for White would be out of the question.

45 N–Q4!	R–Q7
46 N–K6+	K–K2
47 N–B4!	

What a wonderful knight! Having already been on a number of important squares, it now aims for the most important—Q3. Black can only meet this threat by moving his queen off the seventh rank.

47 ...	Q–Q5
48 K–R1	R–R7 (*150*)

Black has no defence against 49 N–K2, and he decides to sacrifice his queen. On 48 ... B–R5 Alekhine intended 49 Q–N7+ Q–Q2 (*49 ... K–Q3 50 Q–N8+*) 50 Q–N4+ K–K1 51 N–K6! B–K2 52 Q–N8+ B–Q1 53 N×B Q×N 54 Q–K5+ Q–K2 55 Q–R8+ K–Q2 56 Q×P R–KB7 57 R–Q1+ K–B2 58 Q–R8 with an extra pawn plus an enduring attack.

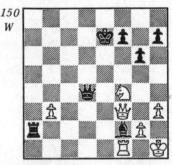

150
W

49 N–K2	R–R8
50 Q–N7+	

A very important move – the queen moves off the KB-file so as not to be lost to a discovered check by the bishop.

50 ...	K–B3
51 N×Q	R×R+
52 K–R2	B–N8+
53 K–N3	B–B7+
54 K–B3	B×N+
55 K–K4	R–Q8
56 Q–Q5	

Simpler was 56 Q–B6+ and 57 Q–B2, but it makes no essential difference.

56 ...	K–K2
57 P–KN4	P–R4
58 P × P	P–B4+
59 K–B3	R–Q6+
60 K–K2	R–K6+
61 K–Q2	R–K5
62 P × P	1–0

Several games of the return match with Euwe were decided in the endgame. Especially delightful are Alekhine's manoeuvres in the following game, in which he convincingly exploits the advantage, at first sight imperceptible, of bishop against knight.

66) Alekhine–Euwe, 2nd match game, 1937
Slav Defence

1 P–Q4	P–Q4
2 P–QB4	P–QB3
3 N–KB3	N–B3
4 N–B3	P × P
5 P–QR4	B–B4
6 N–K5	P–K3
7 B–N5	B–QN5
8 N × P/B4	

One of the sharp variations of the Slav Defence, which was very popular in the 1930s, but which is rarely adopted nowadays. Why should such an interesting opening system sink into oblivion? It is most probably a question of fashion. It is not beyond the bounds of possibility that some grandmaster will suddenly take up this opening, win a brilliant game with it, and the variation, covered by the dust of time, will once again become a frequent guest in tournaments.

Alekhine's last move is not the strongest – he allows Euwe to equalize without difficulty. 8 P–B3 followed by 9 P–K4 leads to a sharp struggle.

8 ...	Q–Q4

A strong move which threatens both 9 ... Q × N and 9 ... N–K5.

9 B × N	Q × N
10 Q–Q2!	

This tactical finesse enables White to spoil his opponent's pawn structure.

10 ...	P × B
11 P–K4	Q–N6
12 P × B	N–Q2
13 P × P	P × P
14 B–K2	0–0–0
15 0–0	P–K4!

Euwe had won the first game of the return match, and so here on the following day he plays with great spirit. To some extent the Dutch grandmaster improves the placing of his central pawns, though he cannot completely escape from his difficulties.

16 P × P	N × P
17 Q–B1	B × N

Over-hasty. Euwe does not realize that in the ending White's bishop will be significantly stronger than the black knight. For this reason he should have refrained from capturing the knight, and should have attempted to set up threats along the open KN-file with 17 ... KR–N1.

18 P × B	KR–N1
19 Q–K3	K–N1
20 P–N3	R–Q2
21 QR–N1	Q–B7
22 KR–K1	Q–Q7!

Black himself aims for the ending, since the position of his king opposite the white rook can be a motif for various tactical threats.

23 Q × Q	R × Q
24 P–KB4	N–N3
25 B–B4	R1–Q1
26 R–K6	R1–Q3
27 R1–K1	K–B2
28 R × R	R × R (151)

151
W

152
B

Now follow, dear reader, how accurately Alekhine exploits the power of his bishop in the subsequent play. Although at present its strength is not apparent, the white bishop soon becomes the principal actor.

29 P–R4!

An excellent move. The black knight is thrown back, while the pawn threatens to advance further and then await (after the fall of Black's KRP) the chance to become a new queen.

29 . . .	**K–Q2**
30 K–B2	**N–K2**
31 K–B3	**N–Q4?**

A mistake which allows White to transfer his bishop to the strong square KB5, where it will support his K-side pawn mass.

32 B–Q3!   **P–KR3**

All other moves are totally bad. Black must hinder as long as possible the dangerous KRP.

33 B–B5+	**K–Q1**
34 K–N4	**N–K2**

So as to defend his K-side pawns. In this situation the capture of White's two Q-side pawns would be equivalent to suicide.

35 B–N1	**K–K1**
36 K–R5	**K–B2**

37 B–R2+ (*152*)

This demonstrates the strength of the bishop. From its own camp this long-range piece is able to spread confusion in the enemy ranks. The KRP falls, after which the immediate advance of the white pawns forces capitulation.

37 . . .	**K–B1**
38 K × P	**R–Q7**

A belated counter-attack. However, no better for Black was 38 . . . N–B4+ 39 K–N6 N × NP 40 P–R5. The possibility of a united offensive by the white pieces was foreseen long before by Alekhine.

39 B–K6	**R–Q6**
40 P–N4	**R × P**
41 P–N5	**1–0**

Alekhine sealed this move, and then informed Euwe of it, whereupon the latter resigned immediately.

Out of the twenty-five games of the return match, six have been given above, and they show that Alekhine had once again become Alekhine, although, if we judge strictly, the effects of age were bound to tell on his play. After the return match, Alekhine, once again chess king, played a number of excellent games, admired to this day for their depth of concept. Particularly outstanding are the following two games, played by Alekhine against his historic rivals.

67) Alekhine-Euwe, AVRO 1938
Slav Defence

1 P–Q4   **P–Q4**

2 P–QB4	**P–QB3**
3 N–KB3	**N–B3**
4 P × P	

Alekhine simplifies the position. Does this indicate a desire to draw the game as quickly as possible? Nothing of the sort! He simply sets up a sound centre, so as to then draw the opponent into a tactical struggle.

4 . . .	**P × P**
5 N–B3	**N–B3**
6 B–B4	**B–B4**

This active move and Black's subsequent inaccurate play give Alekhine the chance to gradually assume the initiative. The other usual continuation is 6 . . . P–K3.

7 P–K3	**P–QR3**

An inaccuracy. Better is 7 . . . Q–N3.

8 N–K5	**R–B1**
9 P–KN4!	

The idea of such a thrust cannot be called an invention of Alekhine. A similar manoeuvre had often been met, for instance, in the Caro-Kann Defence, and in previous games with the Slav Defence. The idea of the move is to force Black after 9 . . . B–N3 10 P–KR4 to play 10 . . . P–R3, after which the exchange on N6 fundamentally ruins Black's pawn structure. For this reason Euwe prefers to retreat the bishop to Q2, which leaves him with a cramped, but sound position. Unsatisfactory is 9 . . . N × N 10 P × B N–B5 11 Q–N3, and Black has a dubious position.

9 . . .	**B–Q2**
10 B–N2	**P–K3**
11 0–0	

White has a promising position. On the K-side he stands actively, and the weakening of his castled position by the move P–KN4 is immaterial, since his QB is able to hold things together from N3.

11 . . .	**P–R3**

12 B–N3	**P–KR4?**

This pawn sacrifice is difficult to understand. It is probable that Euwe wished to display some sort of activity. It has to be taken into account that it will be difficult now for Black to find a safe spot for his king.

13 N × B!	**N × N**

Black agrees to the loss of a pawn, since 13 . . . Q × N 14 P–N5 leads to a completely cramped position for him. Alekhine now hangs on to his extra pawn until such time as he is able to strengthen the position of his pieces to a maximum.

14 P × P	**N–B3**
15 B–B3	**B–N5**
16 R–B1	**K–B1**

It soon becomes clear that on . . . B1 also the black king will not find peace. And of course, castling would be equivalent to suicide.

17 P–QR3	**B × N**
18 R × B	**N–K2**
19 Q–N3	**R × R**
20 P × R	**Q–Q2**
21 Q–N6! (153)	

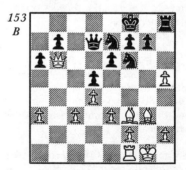

153
B

Up to this point White's operations have been of a preparatory nature, but now Alekhine embarks on the decisive offensive. The simple 22 R–N1 is threatened, winning the QNP. Black has to take urgent measures to defend this pawn, and so has no time to even think of capturing the KRP.

21 ...	N–B1
22 Q–B5+	K–N1
23 R–N1	P–QN4

It would appear that all Black's difficulties are behind him: on the Q-side everything is defended, and White's KRP must soon fall. However Alekhine has for a long time been preparing a tactical blow, which creates fresh weaknesses in his opponent's position, and instills new energy into the white pieces.

24 P–R6!

This is the point! The pawn was doomed in any case, but by sacrificing it White inflicts decisive damage on the enemy position. If Black now captures the pawn with his rook, then the undermining 25 P–QR4! takes on new force, since Black cannot capture the QRP because of 26 R–N8, while the defence 25 ... N–QR2 leads after 26 Q–N6 to the loss of the Q-side pawns.

24 ...   P×P

But after this the white bishops literally tie up the black knights hand and foot.

25 B–K5	K–N2
26 P–QR4!	P×P
27 P–B4!	

These three undermining pawn moves create a great impression. Diagonals are opened for the bishops, and they soon become masters of the whole board.

27 ...   N–K2

Capturing the QBP leads to the loss of his rook: 27 ... P×P 28 B×N+ K×B 29 Q–K5+.

28 P×P   N×P

While here 28 ... P×P loses to 29 R–N6.

29 K–R1!

Alekhine conducts the attack, as usual, very strongly. He now threatens

30 B3×N followed by 31 R–N1+.

29 ...	R–QB1
30 R–N1+	K–R2
31 Q–R3	R–KN1 (154)

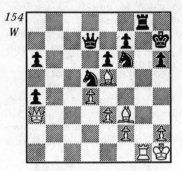

154 W

This loses a piece, but Black could no longer meet all the threats. There threatens not only 32 P–K4, but also 32 Q–Q3+ K–R1 33 P–K4 R–B6 34 P×N! R×Q 35 B×N+ K–R2 36 B–K4 mate. If Black's rook moves off the back rank, then 32 Q–B8 wins.

32 P–K4!

This modest move wins one of the knights. The outcome of the game is settled, and White only has to endure a few checks.

32 ... R×R+ 33 K×R Q–N4 34 P×N Q–N8+ 35 K–N2 Q–KN3+ 36 K–B1 Q–QN8+ 37 K–N2 Q–KN3+ 38 B–N3 N×P 39 B×N P×B 40 Q×P P–KR4 41 P–R4 1–0.

The following game is an authentic work of art. It is the last of a large number of encounters over the board between two chess genii. It, as it were, summed up their great battle, which had lasted for a quarter of a century. The game was a worthy culmination of that battle, and made the score between Alekhine and Capablanca equal – seven wins each.

68) Alekhine-Capablanca,
AVRO 1938, French Defence
1 P–K4 P–K3   2 P–Q4 P–Q4
3 N–Q2 N–KB3

An interesting moment. The most usual move here is 3 . . . P–QB4, but this leads to Black having an isolated QP, which was foreign to Capablanca's positional views. He would gladly play against an isolated QP, but did not like to have one himself, and would certainly not wish to incur one voluntarily.

4 P–K5	N3–Q2
5 B–Q3	P–QB4
6 P–QB3	N–QB3
7 N–K2	Q–N3
8 N–B3	P × P
9 P × P	B–N5+
10 K–B1	

A variation which has long been known to theory. White has two ways of answering the check by the bishop: to move the king, or to block with the bishop. The way chosen by Alekhine leads to the sharper struggle.

10 . . .   **B–K2**

After the active 10 . . . P–B3, the play would be of a double-edged nature, whereas now White gradually 'squeezes' his opponent.

11 P–QR3   **N–B1**

Again this is very passive. Better was 11 . . . P–B3 or even 11 . . . P–B4.

12 P–QN4   **B–Q2**
13 B–K3   **N–Q1?**

It is probable that it is difficult to play an important game on the day of your fiftieth birthday. Capablanca manoeuvres his pieces without conviction. Now he hopes to exchange the white-squared bishops, but Alekhine, of course, prevents this. Although time had already been wasted, even here he should have considered the energetic 13 . . . P–B4.

14 N–B3   **P–QR4**

It is already difficult to recommend a good plan for Black. White could answer 14 . . . N–N3 with 15 P–KR4! and then 16 P–R5.

15 N–R4   **Q–R2**

This is very bad. Some chance was still offered by 15 . . . B × N 16 Q × B+ N–B3 17 K–K2 R–QB1 followed by 18 . . . N–Q2 and 19 . . . 0–0. Now Alekhine constricts the black pieces to an extremely limited part of the board.

16 P–N5   **P–QN3** (*155*)

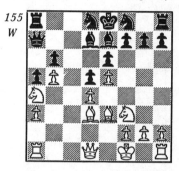

155
W

17 P–N3

Having 'put things in order' on the Q-side, Alekhine turns his attention to the king's wing. Here his plans include, first of all, finding a safe place for his king, and then the advance of his KRP, which will act as a reconnaissance before the massed offensive of the white army.

17 . . .   **P–B4**
18 K–N2   **N–B2**
19 Q–Q2!

When attacking, never forget about defence! Alekhine radically prevents . . . P–N4, which, combined with . . . N–N3 and . . . P–R4 could have given Capablanca fair chances.

19 . . .   **P–R3**
20 P–R4   **N–R2**
21 P–R5!

Alekhine blocks the K-side, and plans to transfer his knight to KN6. He is not afraid of the answering sorties by the black knights to . . . N4 and . . . K5, since he will always have the possibility of driving them away.

21 . . .	N/B2–N4
22 N–R4	N–K5
23 Q–N2	K–B2

Capablanca decides to give up castling, which finally ruins his position. 23 . . . B × N would be a blunder, since the reply 24 P × B! takes away the black knight's last retreat square, and white can win it by 25 P–B3.

24 P–B3 (*156*)

156
B

The beginning of the deciding attack on the K-side. White's first task is to drive away the knight, and open the important QN1–KR7 diagonal.

24 . . .	N5–N4
25 P–N4	P × P
26 B–N6+ !	

It was here, no doubt, that Capablanca regretted that he had not castled. From now on the black king has no peace.

26 . . .   **K–N1**

Who likes to make such a move, shutting in one's own rook? But here it is forced, since after 26 . . . K–B1, 27 KR–KB1! decides. For example:

a) 27 . . . P–N6 28 P–B4 N–K5 (*28 . . . N–B2 29 P–B5!*) 29 P–B5 B × N 30 P × P+.

b) 27 . . . P × P+   28 N × BP

K–N1   29 N × N N × N   30 B × N B × B   31 N × P Q × N   32 Q–KB2, and there is no defence to the threatened mate.

27 P–B4   **N–B6?**

But this is an oversight, which costs a piece. Capablanca has simply not seen the original way by which Alekhine can win this knight. It is only fair to point out that even the best defence 27 . . . N–B2 would not hold out for long. White would simply retreat his bishop to Q3, and then make a decisive intrusion with his knight on KN6.

28 B × N+ !

This forces the black rook to take up an extremely poor position. Black cannot capture with his king: 28 . . . K × B   29 Q–N1+ K–N1 30 N–N6.

28 . . .	R × B
29 N–N6	B–Q1
30 QR–QB1	

A wise precaution. Since the black knight has nowhere to run away to, Alekhine first ensures himself control of the open file on the Q-side.

30 . . .   **B–K1** (*157*)

157
W

31 K–N3 !

This is, no doubt, what Capablanca overlooked when he played his knight to B6. The enemy steed is dealt with by His Majesty the King himself!

31 ...	Q–KB2
32 K × P	N–R5

Or 32 ... N–N4 33 P × N Q–B4+ 34 K–N3 threatening 35 R–KB1.

33 N × N	Q × RP+
34 K–N3	Q–B2
35 N–KB3	P–R4
1–0	

As Capablanca was making this move, his flag fell, but this made no difference – Black's position is hopeless.

69) Alekhine-Fine,

Hastings 1937, Ruy Lopez

1 P–K4	P–K4
2 N–KB3	N–QB3
3 B–N5	P–QR3
4 B–R4	N–B3
5 0–0	B–K2
6 R–K1	P–QN4
7 B–N3	P–Q3
8 P–B3	N–QR4
9 B–B2	P–B4
10 P–Q4	Q–B2
11 QN–Q2	

Experts on the Ruy Lopez are constantly discussing the question: should Black play ... B–KN5, or not? At that time the bishop move was not feared, whereas nowadays White usually prefers P–KR3.

11 ...	0–0
12 N–B1	B–N5 *(158)*

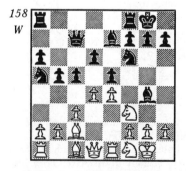

158
W

Alekhine considers this move to be ineffective because of the following pawn sacrifice, and recommends quiet development: 12 ... B–Q2, 13 ... KR–QB1 and 14 ... B–B1.

13 N–K3!

Typical of Alekhine – he sacrifices a pawn for the initiative.

13 ...	B × N
14 Q × B	

Also possible was 14 P × B with subsequent play along the KN-file, but Alekhine prefers to carry out his intended plan.

14 ...	BP × P
15 N–B5	P × P
16 Q × P!	KR–B1!

A tactical defence – after 17 N × B+ Q × N 18 Q × N White loses his bishop.

17 Q–KN3	B–B1
18 B–Q3	N–B3
19 B–N5	N–K1 *(159)*

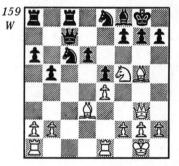

159
W

Let us examine the resulting position. Black has an extra, backward, pawn on Q3, but on the other hand, how many positional advantages has Alekhine gained! The white pieces are actively placed, his rooks are ready for play along the open central files, while Black's pieces are cramped onto the back ranks, and his whole army is passive.

20 QR–B1?

An inaccuracy, which wastes time. Correct was 20 QR–Q1 followed by

21 P–QR3 and the transfer of his KB to QR2. Alekhine returns to this plan a little later.

| 20 ... | Q–N2 |
| 21 P–QR3 | P–N3 |

Fine decides to weaken himself on the black squares, if only so as to gain some counter-play through the advance of his knight to ... Q5.

22 N–R6+	B×N
23 B×B	N–Q5
24 R/B1–Q1	P–N5
25 P–B4!	

White's plan is to open the KB-file and begin a seige of Black's KB2 square. Black must capture this pawn, since otherwise P–B5 will create dangerous threats on the K-side.

25 ...	KP×P
26 Q×BP	P×P
27 P×P	R–B6!

Intending to answer 28 P–K5 with 28 ... R×B   29 R×R N–K7+ 30 R×N Q–N8+   31 K–B2 Q×R and if 32 P–K6, then 32 ... Q–B4 33 Q×Q P×Q   34 P–K7 P–B3, when a draw is the most likely outcome.

This does not satisfy Alekhine, and he regroups his whole army for a new offensive.

| 28 Q–B2 | N–K3? |

This makes his defensive task considerably more difficult. By transferring the knight via ... QB3 to ... K4 Black would have been able to use this versatile piece both for counter-attack, and for the defence of the key square KB2.

29 P–QR4	R1–B1
30 R–KB1!	R6–B2
31 R–N1	Q–B3
32 P–R5!	

Alekhine skilfully combines his attack on the K-side with threats on the Q-side. 33 R–N6 is the threat.

| 32 ... | N–B4? |

This loses immediately, though Black's position was already difficult. In answer to the best defence – 32 ... R–R1, White would play 33 R/N1–B1 and 34 B–QB4, with control of all the important lines of communication.

| 33 B–QB4 | Q–Q2 *(160)* |

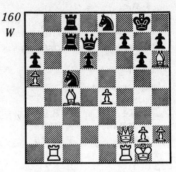

160
W

| 34 Q–R2! | |

Catastrophe on Black's KB2 is now inevitable, and with the disappearance of this pawn his king becomes completely defenceless.

34 ...	N×P
35 R×P	Q×R
36 B×Q+	R×B
37 Q–K6!	1–0

In the following game Alekhine displays his great skill in the playing of heavy-piece endings.

70) Alekhine-Eliskases,
Buenos-Aires 1939
Caro-Kann Defence

1 P–K4	P–QB3
2 P–Q4	P–Q4
3 P×P	P×P
4 P–QB4	N–KB3
5 N–QB3	P–K3
6 N–B3	B–K2
7 P×P	

White has chosen the well-known Panov variation, which has been popular already for almost half a century. Usually in this variation White plays for the attack, but, perhaps from psychological considerations, Alekhine prefers to stabilize the pawn position in the centre, and simplify the game.

7...	**N × P**
8 B–QN5+	**B–Q2**
9 B × B+	**N × B**

Alekhine considers that the following line offered Black better chances: 9 ... Q × B   10 N–K5 N × N   11 P × N Q–N4   12 P–QB4 Q–R4+   13 B–Q2 B–N5. Now Black submits completely to the will of his opponent.

10 N × N	**P × N**
11 Q–N3	**N–N3**
12 0–0	**0–0**
13 B–B4	**B–Q3**
14 B × B	**Q × B** (*161*)

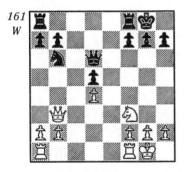

161 W

Apparently Alekhine was aiming for this kind of position; in any case he didn't try to avoid it. Although the position appears to be absolutely level, a closer examination reveals the advantages of White's game. His queen and knight are more actively placed, and his opponent is already tied to the defence of his QP. Although it is very difficult to realize such small advantages, one has to take into account Alekhine's mastery in such positions.

15 KR–K1	**QR–B1**
16 QR–B1	**P–KR3?**

The white knight should not have

been allowed to move to K5, and therefore 16 ... P–B3 should have been played.

17 N–K5

Now there is no question of Black playing ... P–B3 – it would weaken his KN3 square too much. White's superiority becomes still more marked, although, of course, it is early as yet to talk about him winning.

17...	**R–B2**
18 P–N3!	**R1–B1**
19 R × R	**R × R**
20 Q–N5	**N–Q2**

An incorrect decision, since the heavy-piece ending is significantly in White's favour. Chances of a draw were offered by 20 ... R–K2 followed by driving the knight away by 21 ... P–B3, since, with the small number of pieces remaining, it would be difficult for White to exploit the weakening of the ... KN3 square.

21 N × N	**R × N** (*162*)

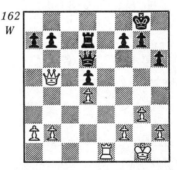

162 W

In what ways are White's position superior? He is master of the open K-file, and can use it to break through into the enemy camp. Also the black king is badly placed, and comes under the fire of the white pieces.

Alekhine gives a classical demonstration of how to exploit these two slight positional advantages.

22 R–K8+	**K–R2**
23 P–KR4!	

Intending P–R5, which will make the black king's position even more unhappy.

23 ...   **P–R3**

Or 23 ... P–KR4   24 R–QR8 P–R3 25 Q–K2, attacking the KRP and threatening to intrude on the eighth rank.

24 Q–K2	R–Q1
25 R–K7	R–Q2
26 R–K5	P–KN3

Black agrees to a weakening of his K-side. The dangers facing the black king are shown by the following variation: 26 ... Q–KN3 27 P–R5 Q–N8+ 28 K–N2 Q×RP 29 Q–B2+ P–KN3 30 Q–B8 Q–R5 31 P×P+ K×P 32 Q–KN8+ K–B3 33 P–KN4 Q×P 34 Q–KR8+ K–N3 35 R–N5+ winning the queen.

27 P–R5	Q–KB3
28 Q–K3	R–Q3
29 Q–QN3	R–N3
30 P×P+	Q×NP

He cannot capture with the pawn: 30 ... P×P 31 Q×P R×P 32 Q–Q7+ with a quick mate.

| 31 Q×P | R×P |
| 32 R–B5 | R–N4? (*163*) |

163
W

Black's position was very difficult, but this oversight brings the end nearer. 32 ... K–N1 would have held out longer.

33 R×P+ !

This is immediately decisive, since

it leads to a rook ending in which the win for White is simply a question of time. Black probably underestimated this move, expecting White to capture with the queen, when he would have had good chances of a draw.

33 ...	K–N1
34 R–B6+	K–R2
35 R×Q	R×Q
36 R–N6	R×P
37 R×NP+	

An extra pawn, and an active rook – here this is sufficient to win.

37 ... K–N1 38 R–N6 R–QR5 39 R×KRP R×P 40 K–N2 P–R4 41 R–R6 P–R5 42 R–R7 P–R6 43 P–N4 K–B1 44 P–N5 K–N1 45 K–N3 R–R8 46 K–N4 R–KN8+ 47 K–B5 R–N7 48 P–B4 P–R7 49 K–B6 1–0.

In the following game Alekhine elegantly exploits the well-known motif of smothered mate.

71) Alekhine - Golombek,
Margate 1938
Nimzo-Indian Defence

1 P–Q4	N–KB3
2 P–QB4	P–K3
3 N–QB3	B–N5
4 P–KN3	

In an effort to refute the Nimzo–Indian Defence even this move has been tried, since it is to some extent useful in the struggle for the important squares K4 and Q5. The present conclusion, however, is that the fiancetto gives Black no difficulties, and it has ceased to be adopted.

4 ...	P–Q4
5 B–N2	0–0
6 N–B3	P–B4

Sounder was 6 ... P–B3, since now he falls behind in development.

7 BP×P	N×P
8 B–Q2	N–QB3
9 P–QR3	N×N

10 P×N	B–R4
11 0–0	

Black now experiences certain difficulties over the development of his queen's bishop. Although he now carries out simplifying exchanges, the main defect in his position – his undeveloped bishop – remains.

11 ...	P×P
12 P×P	B×B
13 Q×B	Q–K2
14 Q–N2!	R–Q1?

A decisive loss of time. The move 14 ... R–N1 was indicated, with hopes of obtaining an equal game by ... P–QN3 and ... B–N2. Alekhine would have probably carried out a pawn attack in the centre—P–K4 and P–Q5—but this plan would have demanded much time without being terribly promising. Now the world champion's pieces become very active.

15 KR–B1	Q–Q3
16 P–K3	R–N1

The necessary move is made at last, though Black has lost a lot of time. Alekhine begins a series of excellent manoeuvres, the aim of which is to force weaknesses in the opponent's position.

17 N–N5!	B–Q2
18 Q–B2!	P–B4 (*164*)

Golombek overlooks White's elegant combination. Better, of course, was 18 ... P–KN3 19 N–K4 Q–K2,

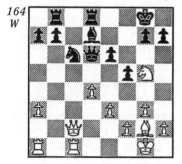

164
W

although even then 20 Q–N2! (with the threat of 21 P–Q5 and 22 N–B6+) would leave White with the better game. Even so, Black could have put up a lengthy resistance, whereas now the issue is settled literally within a few moves.

19 P–Q5!

Only here did the English master perceive White's intention. On 19 ... P×P there follows 20 B×P+! Q×B 21 R–Q1, and the black queen is lost, since it dare not abandon the QR7–KN1 diagonal because of the smothered mate (22 Q–R2+ K–R1 23 N–B7+ K–N1 24 N–R6++ K–R1 25 Q–N8+ R×Q 26 N–B7 mate).

Retreating the knight costs Black a pawn.

19 ...	N–K2
20 P×P	B×P
21 R–Q1	Q–K4

Black loses a piece after 21 ... N–Q4 22 N×B Q×N 23 Q–B4, while other moves allow White to win a pawn by the same way as in the game.

22 B×P

The bishop can be captured neither immediately, nor after the exchange of rooks, because of mate by the rook on Q8.

22 ...	P–KR3
23 N×B	Q×N
24 Q–B7	

Besides his extra pawn, White also has a great positional advantage. It is not surprising that the game finishes within a few moves.

24 ... R×R+ 25 R×R R–K1 26 B–B3 P–R3 27 R–Q6 Q–K4 28 Q–B4+ K–R2 29 R×QRP R–QB1 30 Q–KB7 R–B8+ 31 K–N2 1–0. Black is unable to meet the threats of 32 R–K6 and also mate in two moves by 32 R×P+ and 33 Q–R5.

5 The War and Chess

Slowly and carefully did the boat from distant Buenos Aires thread its way through to Europe; at that time anything could happen on the open sea.

'In January 1940 we were told that, for the first time in history, the world champion and his wife were coming to Portugal', writes the Portuguese champion Lupi, who witnessed Alekhine's last days. 'We were very excited. The best rooms were booked in the luxury hotel of Estoril, and an eight-cylinder car was put at the disposal of the guests.

'On a misty February morning we arrived at the port to meet the boat from Buenos Aires. Even before the boat had docked we saw on the upper deck a very white-haired man, smiling, and holding two kittens in his hands.

'Later we saw him often enough during simultaneous displays, always in evening dress made from the best English material. His manners were, perhaps, a little theatrical, and he was rather on the stout side.

'Alekhine delighted the Portuguese chess enthusiasts by the brilliance of his play, by his benevolence, by his constant readiness to help young players and by his work for charity . . .'

Alekhine spent two weeks in Portugal, and then left for Paris, from where he informed Lupi that he was a lieutenant in the French army. He served in the forces under General de Gaulle as an interpreter – once again his knowledge of several languages came in useful. This second occasion on which he had joined the battle against the Germans, both times voluntarily, could not fail to subsequently arouse the displeasure of certain influential members of the Fascist Reich.

Nevertheless, when Alekhine the interpreter, in the uniform of an officer of the French army, was taken prisoner, things were not too unpleasant for him. This is, no doubt, because the directors of fascist propaganda immediately understood that they would be able to exploit the fact that the world champion was taking part in tournaments in occupied Europe. Alas, they were not mistaken. Alekhine was later to pay dearly for this. . . .

Commencing in 1941, Alekhine took part in nearly all the tournaments which were held during the next two years in various European countries.

The crisis, which he had experienced prior to his match with Euwe and immediately after it, had long since passed, and Alekhine took part in strong tournaments with invariable success. He would soon be fifty years old, but from his play you would never guess that he had behind him three and a half decades of tournament appearances – there was still the same freshness of thought, the same fervour of youth, the same boldness and energy.

True, at the tournament in Munich in 1941 the world champion shared second and third places, but following this throughout all the war years his name practically always heads the tournament tables. In Cracow in the same year he scored six wins and five draws, in Salzburg 1942, seven wins gave him clear first prize, despite two defeats. Alekhine suffered one defeat in each of the tournaments at Munich and Cracow in 1942, but, playing sharply and boldly, a series of brilliant victories each time brought him first prize.

After this there began a two-year period (1942–1944) during which Alekhine did not lose a single tournament game. And yet among the competitors were grandmasters such as Keres, Bogoljubow, and Sämisch, and others of the strongest players in Europe. It is curious that Keres, who played Alekhine on a number of occasions during the war years, was not able to beat him once, while he suffered several defeats.

After winning the tournament at Salzburg in 1942, the world champion had twice come first in tournaments in Prague (in 1942 and 1943), when once again fate struck him a cruel blow. At the age of 51 Alekhine suddenly became ill with scarlet fever. By a strange coincidence he was admitted to the same Prague hospital where Alekhine's chess friend, the outstanding theorist Richard Reti, had died of scarlet fever fourteen years previously. Alekhine managed to overcome the disease, so dangerous at his age, but his health was seriously undermined.

This serious illness marked a turning point in Alekhine's chess career; if before it his tournament appearances had carried the stamp of a grandmaster of extra class, and had resembled San Remo and

Bled, after it the world champion changed sharply. True, he still took first places in tournaments, but these were tournaments of second or third class, and the character of Alekhine's victories was not at all the same as previously.

Alekhine's attempts to break out of the regions occupied by the Nazis, which he had long been undertaking, finally met success. The German Reich had already begun to collapse, and there was no time for chess, while the Fascist leaders were tired of seeing how this indomitable Russian could crush all the strongest German players. And there were also the simultaneous displays – here Alekhine's victories over several dozen officers of the army of the Reich seemed improper to the Fascists.

Soon after leaving hospital Alekhine left Prague first for Spain, and then for Portugal. But on this occasion he travelled alone; Grace insisted on staying in Paris to look after the things that had been saved from their house near Dieppe, which, as Alekhine expressed it, had been 'scientifically ransacked by the Germans'.

'In 1943 I went to a tournament in Gijon', writes Lupi. 'At the station I saw a tall, thin man, who was waiting for me: his gestures were those of an automaton. It was Alekhine. I winced on seeing him, he had changed so much. In place of the proud, portly man, with gestures which appeared to have been learned in front of a mirror, before me stood a ghost, who spoke nervously, and whose hands, when he spoke, sought for your hands, as if saying in his weakness: "But you do understand? You do understand what I mean?"

Loneliness, poverty, poor health. Lupi continues his description of Alekhine's last days: 'I received a letter from Dr. Martinezza Morano. In it the well-known Spanish heart surgeon wrote that Alekhine's blood pressure was up to 280, that he was still taking too much sympathin, and that he had already suffered a stroke. . . .'

Spanish chess players did all they could to somehow encourage the dying world champion and support him materially. Several relatively weak tournaments were arranged, in which Alekhine received cash prizes. Simultaneous displays became less frequent; it was difficult for Alekhine to give them. Other ideas had to be tried: they arranged for Alekhine to give a special series of lessons to the young Spanish player A. Pomar, who was later to become a grandmaster. Alekhine's chess books, which were by no means sold out in Spain, were re-issued with a Spanish writer as co-author.

But even so, to support for more than a year a man who was living in a hotel, and who spent every spare peseta at the bar counter, soon became intolerable.

Alekhine himself understood this, and asked his Lisbon friends to invite him to Portugal. In the Portuguese capital special tournaments with prizes were again organized specially for Alekhine, and even simultaneous displays, though not popular in those days, were held. But all this was of little help – every day the world champion became weaker.

But then came some good news – the war had ended. Alekhine made preparations to go to France, though he had received no news from there. More important, he could not obtain a visa. One of the Portuguese wrote Grace a despairing letter. 'Since his arrival here' – ran the letter of entreaty, – 'your husband has been in an impossible situation – sick, without material means, living in effect on charity, in furnished rooms. . . .' Days passed, and then weeks, but there was no news from his wife. . . .

As soon as the guns had been silenced, chess life began to return to normal. It was the English who decided to organize the first post-war international tournaments, which were in London in December 1945, and the traditional Christmas tournament at Hastings at the end of 1945 to the beginning of 1946.

The world champion was not forgotten – an official invitation to both tournaments for Alexander Alekhine arrived in Portugal.

The prospect of returning to the international chess scene encouraged Alekhine, and, together with Lupi, who had also been invited to England, he joyfully prepared for the journey. He was still weak and ill, but was this the time to think about his condition? Was not the future bright? Alekhine imagined before him new tournaments, his head was full of new chess ideas, while opening innovations were written in his notebooks. 'Wait till I get to London, they will see that I can still play!'

And then, suddenly, terrible news arrived by telegraph: the English, the strict, sporting, and conservative English, had withdrawn their invitation. At first Alekhine could not believe it. How was it possible? It was pitiless, inhuman. Couldn't they see?

JUDGEMENT OF THE INDIFFERENT

Yes, this was the judgement of the indifferent, and although the speeches were animated, the feelings of the speakers were excited by dislike for Alekhine. This was the judgement of people who were indifferent to the fate of the greatest living chess genius, indifferent to his life, his future, and to his participation in chess events. After all, the self-appointed judges knew that Alekhine was dying of illness, hunger and poverty. Instead of coming to his aid, they scorned him, and left him to die alone, helpless and unprotected.

Outwardly everything had been done decently. Not long before the start of the London tournament, the Chess Federation of the U.S.A. (more accurately, certain of its over-active members – R. Fine, A. Denker and others) sent an ultimatum to London: either you exclude Alekhine from the tournament, or we will withdraw from the tournament in England, and will completely break off dealings with you. The complaisant organizers who were in charge of chess in England in those days, decided not to spoil relations with the all-powerful 'Yankies' and it was the poor world champion who had to lose.

During the London tournament a meeting was unexpectedly called which took on the form of a trial of Alekhine. As Lupi later informed Alekhine, there was a great deal of noise – 'the meeting was lively, and certain firm convictions were expressed'. Although no one had given them any right, the self-appointed judges turned out to be 'more catholic than the Pope', and recommended to the chess world, in effect, that Alekhine (for a time, but if the state of his health was taken into account, for ever) should no longer be considered world champion. It was demanded that he should not be admitted to tournaments – the English had already done just this – or allowed to give lectures and simultaneous displays. Obstruction, the deprivation of all rights, a death from hunger. . . .

How could this happen? After all, there was in existence the International Chess Federation – FIDE. What right did the over-impatient participants of the meeting have to avoid the official paths in favour of their own interests? The chess world found out later, after Alekhine's death, by whom they had been influenced. When the proposition was suggested and even put to the vote (at the FIDE general assembly) that a match for the world championship should be played between Euwe and Reshevsky, everything became clear. While Max Euwe, as the only ex-champion still alive, had a lawful right, the pretensions of the American grandmaster betray the cause of the activity of certain representatives of the U.S.A.

Hopelessly ill, abandoned by all, and rejected by people, together with whom he had trodden a great path, and who now did not even wish to see him and question him personally, Alekhine was slowly dying in a small room of the hotel 'Park', half closed for the winter, in Estoril. He had no prospects, no means, and no friends to support him; he realized that Lupi alone was unable to do anything for him.

The days passed, but not even the slightest piece of consoling news arrived. Alekhine either spent the time in bed, or else paced about the room like a lion in a cage. 'One day he phoned me', writes Lupi. 'I have absolutely no money', said the fading world champion with difficulty. 'I need just a few escudos to buy a cigarette ... Lupi! This loneliness is killing me. I must live, I must feel life around me. I have already worn out the floor-boards in my room. Take me somewhere. ...

'DON'T SEW ME, MOTHER, A RED SARAFAN . . .'*

During the Alekhine Memorial tournament in 1956, I was told that the well-known Belgian tutor and violinist Neumen had come to Moscow as a judge at the Tchaikovsky International Competition for violinists. On the flight to Moscow, Neumen had told his travelling companion that in 1946 he had been living in the 'Park Hotel' in Estoril, and that next to him had lived the world champion Alexander Alekhine. His companion on the plane turned out to be the well-known Danish chess player From. Needless to say, on the first free day of the competition I visited the Belgian!

'It was a sad time', M. Neumen began his story. 'I used to give music lessons, would become very tired, and would hurry back to the "Park Hotel" to rest a little. Each time Alekhine would be waiting for me in the hotel. He was terribly lonely, all day he had literally no one to even exchange a word with. To understand the depths of Alekhine's despair in those days one only had to look at him. Twenty years have passed, but even now I shudder when I remember his condition. . . . On top of everything he had once again begun drinking a great deal.'

'With what?!' I exclaimed, 'he didn't have a penny to his name!'

'My dear fellow, when a man has nothing, and people around him have something, there is always the hope of receiving charity. Even such a trifle as a glass of cognac or wine. He was after all the king of chess!

* (An old Russian folk song – a sarafan is a Russian peasant woman's dress) – Translator's note.

'Sitting in my room, Alekhine would often ask me to play him something. . . . He was especially fond of one old song . . . "Don't sew me, mother, a red sarafan".'

'There would be two of us in the room, in semi-darkness. I would play my violin. Never did I have such a listener! He would sit quietly, immobile, his fine head hanging down over his chest, his eyes closed, his eyelashes moist. Alekhine was extremely sensitive, and there was something incredibly delicate about him, which was especially apparent when he was listening to music. . . . What did he see, what was painted in his imagination? His birthplace, his own people, his mother?'

"Don't sew me, mother, a red sarafan" . . .

A GLIMMER OF LIGHT IN THE DARKNESS

The happy evenings, when M. Neumen would return to the hotel, were rare, and more often than not it was loneliness, the empty hotel, deserted for the winter, the whistling of the wind. . . . Three steps forward, three steps back – that was the room measured out. One-two-three, one-two-three. . . . No hope at all. . . .

And suddenly an unexpected gleam of light. A letter! 'I am sorry that the war interfered with our match in 1939. I once again challenge you to a match for the world championship. If you are agreeable, I will await your reply, in which I would ask you to state your opinion on the time and venue of the match. 4th February 1946. Mikhail Botvinnik'.

Through his tears, Alekhine stared vacantly at these lines, which meant life itself to him. . . . Salvation! A new life! He was still recognized, he was still considered to be the world champion. What was this question about 'the venue of the match?! I said in 1939: Moscow, only Moscow. And let them give me the chance to arrive a few months before the start of the match. I want to see my homeland, so near to my heart, I want to visit Leningrad. . . .

The 'English Judges' were now in a most unenviable position, and they answered the Soviet champion's telegram with a series of strongly-worded articles. 'Disgraceful! The Russians wish to play with Alekhine', wrote those who were displeased with the decision of the Soviet champion. 'We have taken away Alekhine's title, and now Botvinnik has put him back on the chess throne. The International Chess Federation should prohibit this match'.

Those who really loved chess for its own sake, and not for the titles involved, were delighted by the news of the forthcoming match between the two strongest contemporary chess players. 'Like a loving mother, Russia has supported her prodigal son at the most difficult moment of his life', wrote one of the Czech newspapers.

The news from his homeland transformed Alekhine instantly. He gave up drinking, and began studying openings. 'I asked him', writes Lupi, 'what opening he was going to play against Botvinnik. And he answered with a playful sparkle in his eyes that he was going to play a little trick on Botvinnik. 'I am thinking of playing open games, I hope to persuade him to let me play the Ruy Lopez'. Then he added: 'Who would think of such a secret weapon?'

The last hours of the dying Russian chess genius were cheerful ones. . . .

'I woke late', said M. Neumen, concluding his story, 'and waited in my room for breakfast to be brought. There was a knock on the door, and the waiter came in. From the look of him I sensed that there was something wrong.

'Are you ill?' I asked.

'N-no, I am all right', whispered the waiter, although his lips had turned blue, and the tray in his hand was shaking.

'What's happened?'

'Alekhine . . . is dead'.

'Alekhine?!' I exclaimed, utterly stunned. 'When? How?'

'Senor Professor, it was terrible! I was taking him breakfast. . . . He was sitting at the table. . . . Yesterday's supper had not been touched, although his serviette was already tucked in. . . . He was dead!'

I rushed off to Alekhine's room.

'You can't go in there,' said a policeman, barring my way. We are waiting for a forensic specialist. We have to establish that death was from natural causes. What? Yes, you may have a look through the door. . . .'

I opened the door of the room. The curtains were still drawn, and the light was on, although outside it was sunny. On the table were plates, while to the side, on a support for suitcases, was a chess board with the pieces set out. My friend was sitting in an armchair; one arm was hanging down helplessly, while his fine head had sunk down onto his chest. He was sitting there as though alive, as though he was still listening intently to my violin:

'Don't sew me, mother, a red sarafan' . . .

HIS BIOGRAPHY CONTINUES

Alekhine had died, but his 'biography' continued. Restless in life, contradictory and guilty of mistakes, Alekhine caused problems to those around him even after his death. The Portuguese chess players, who wished to bury the chess genius with due respect, met with unforeseen difficulties.

Heated arguments raged about the apparently fairly simple question of how to bury Alekhine. The Portuguese chess players had to wait twenty-three days for permission to commit to the earth the body of the world champion. Various important organizations took part in the arguments: the French Legation in Lisbon, the Ministry of Foreign Affairs and the religious rulers of destinies of men's souls. To whom was the world champion and the memory of him important? What was important was to get one's own way, to carry out the burial according to one's own laws.

On 16th April 1946 a solution was at last reached: a grave for Alekhine's body was provided in the tomb of the chess player Manuel Estev in the cemetery of St. Joan near Estoril. What if this ordinary chess player had known that one day he would be sharing a grave with the greatest genius of chess?

Alekhine had died, but his heritage remained. First of all, there was his title of world champion. 'I want to die undefeated' he had told his colleagues many times; this sad wish of his had been fulfilled. Violent arguments broke out on the question of his successor. 'The title must be given to the only rightful inheritor – ex-world champion Euwe' suggested some. 'No, American grandmasters are also rightful pretenders to the inheritance' came from across the ocean, though without any good reason. The majority of objective chess players were for the method which is most appropriate in matters of sport: to assemble the best grandmasters in the world, and let them fight it out for the right to occupy the throne.

This last suggestion was accepted by the FIDE congress in 1947. The five best players were admitted to this tournament by invitation: Mikhail Botvinnik, Paul Keres and Vasily Smyslov of the Soviet Union, Max Euwe of Holland, and Samuel Reshevsky of the United States. Mikhail Botvinnik became the new world champion, while the following places were taken by Smyslov and Keres, (in fact, Reshevsky finished level with Keres – Translator's note) demonstrating the justification of the pretensions of the grandmasters from Alekhine's homeland to be considered the best in the world.

Masters of the sixty-four squares – representatives of the enormous army of chess enthusiasts – have always rated very highly the principles of strategy and tactics which were worked out by Alexander Alekhine. He successfully demonstrated their correctness in his most important chess battles. The best Soviet theorists have mastered and developed further everything that the late champion introduced into the theory of his beloved art. The games of Alekhine, with his deep annotations, have been printed in the USSR in enormous numbers; even more important, all that was stated by him in articles and books has been assembled together into books from which new masters are able to learn.

Only after death was Alexander Alekhine able to return to his homeland – to return in his deep and interesting works. There he was understood, and his memory revered. On the tenth anniversay of his death, it was decided to ask for his ashes, half-forgotten in the 'chess backwater' of distant Portugal, to be transferred to his homeland, to Moscow. It was suggested that this should be the finale to a great festival dedicated to his memory. The programme included a series of lectures on the life and games of Alekhine, to be held over the whole country, and Alekhine memorial tournaments, among them an important international tournament which would be held in the capital of the Soviet Union.

And so a delegation of Soviet chess players travelled to Paris for discussions. An agreement was reached for Alekhine's remains to be transferred from Lisbon to Moscow. The stately President, Folke Rogard and his Vice-Presidents were present. Alekhine's remains to Moscow? We have no objections. We ask only that the Soviet Union should bear the cost.

It seemed that the question was settled – the poor wanderer would finally find peace in his homeland after death. But for some, fate is cruel even after death. At the very conclusion of the discussions, an old woman, though still with her head held high, came into the hall.

'Grace Wishaar, the widow of the late world champion' – the gallant French Vice-President Berman introduced her.

'I want my poor husband to be laid alongside my window, so that I can shed tears over his grave'.

The officials of the FIDE did their best to persuade the stubborn widow, but to no avail. They offered to arrange for her to go to Moscow, to be present at the memorial tournament for her husband, to attend the meetings and discussions dedicated to the works of Alekhine, but Grace was implacable.

The law was on the side of the widow, and two months later a small box brought from Portugal was buried in the Montparnasse cemetery in Paris. But Grace was not able to be present there: she had died two weeks before the date of the anniversary.

Ten years later I visited the Montparnasse cemetery together with a group of tourists. The warden showed us a modest gravestone with the inscription: 'Alexander Alekhine. 1892–1946. Chess genius of Russia and France'. And beside it was another inscription: 'Grace Wishaar'. On the grave there lay some flowers which had not yet completely faded. We placed a bouquet of roses beside them.

'Who looks after the grave?' I asked the warden.

'People come . . . ' said the Frenchman, in the gloomy fashion of all cemetery wardens.

'Do his or Grace's relations visit the place?'

'No . . . The flowers are from chess followers . . . They arrive from various countries . . . '

GAMES FROM HIS FINAL YEARS

Below we give a game which was played by Alekhine at the age of fifty. Just as in his first days of chess, the Russian champion displays a youthful ardour, a bold imagination, and a great mastery in the calculation of the most complicated combinational variations.

72) **Alekhine–Podgorny,**
Prague 1942, Sicilian Defence

	White	Black
1	P–K4	P–QB4
2	P–QB3	

One way of avoiding well-known theoretical variations. The move 2 P–QB3 does not give White any particular advantage, though Black must play carefully.

2 ...	P–Q4

It is just this reply which would suit Alekhine, who was usually striving for open piece play. Theory recommends the elastic move 2 ... N–KB3.

	White	Black
3	P×P	Q×P
4	P–Q4	N–QB3
5	N–B3	B–N5
6	B–K2	P×P
7	P×P	P–K3
8	N–B3	B–N5
9	0–0	Q–QR4

Both sides have made logical moves, though imperceptibly White has gained a certain advantage in development, which is especially significant in view of the possibility of tactical thrusts such as P–Q5. Retreating the queen to ... QR4 gives Alekhine the chance to carry out yet another tactical idea: the sacrifice of a pawn for the sake of weakening the opponent's black squares.

10 P–QR3!   N–B3 (*165*)

This gives Alekhine the opportunity to carry out an interesting and far-sighted combination. However, the acceptance of the sacrifice was no better: after 10 ... B/QN5 × N 11 P × B Q × BP White has two ways of continuing the attack.

a) 12 R–N1, after which the QNP

cannot be defended: 12 . . . R–QN1 13 B–KB4 or 12 . . . P–QN3 13 Q–R4.

b) 12 B–Q2 Q–N7 13 Q–R4! B × N 14 B × B KN–K2 15 B–QN4 Q × QP (*15 . . . 0–0 16 B3 × N*) 16 QR–Q1, and White will be able to punish his opponent for his lack of development.

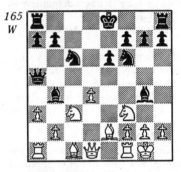

165
W

11 P–Q5!

Before making this most complicated combination, Alekhine had to work out a large number of variations. The black king stuck in the centre, the tension on the Q-side (Black's KB is en prise), the fact that the whole white army is ready for battle – all this gives Alekhine the basis for starting an immediate attack.

11 . . .   **P × P**

Black's other defences are no better:

a) 11 . . . N × P   12 N × N   P × N (*12 . . . B × N   13 RP × B   B × B   14 P × Q   B × Q   15 N–B7+* leaves White the exchange ahead) 13 N–Q4! (also possible is *13 P × B Q × R 14 Q–N3 B × N 15 B–KN5*) 13 . . . N × N (*14 N–N3* and *15 P × B* is threatened, and on *13 . . . B × B* there follows *14 Q × B+ B–K2 15 R–K1 Q–B2 16 N–B5* with a very strong attack) 14 B × B.

Alekhine, apparently, must have made an accurate appraisal of this position when he started the combination. Can Black save the game? If the knight retreats to . . . K3, then 15 B × N P × B   16 Q–R5+ P–KN3 17 Q–K5 0–0 18 B–R6 and 19 P × B decides. On the other hand, if the knight moves back to . . . B3, then there follows 15 P × B   Q × R 16 Q–K2+ K–B1 17 P–N5! Now the black knight has four moves, but they all lose: 17 . . . N–Q1   18 B–B4 and 19 B–Q6+; 17 . . . N–Q5 18 Q–K5 N × P 19 B–R6!; 17 . . N–R4 or 17 . . . N–N5 18 R–K1! P–KR4 19 B–B5 and Black is mated or loses his queen.

b) 11 . . . B/KN5 × N   12 P × N B × B (*12 . . . B × BP 13 P × B Q × R 14 Q–B2 P–QN4 15 N × P!*) 13 P × P! R–QN1   14 P × B! Q × R 15 Q × B, and the black queen can not escape.

12 P × B!   **Q × R**
13 N–Q2!

This is the point of Alekhine's play. The threat of having his queen trapped by 14 N–N3 forces Black to exchange bishops.

13 . . .   **B × B**
14 Q × B+   **N–K2** (*166*)

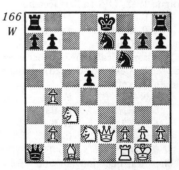

166
W

A fine variation could occur after 14 . . . K–B1 15 N–N3 Q–R3 16 P–N5 Q–N3 17 N–R4! N–Q5! 18 Q–Q1 Q × P   19 N × N, and the white queen manages to defend both knights!

15 R–K1!

The concluding subtlety. It appears now that Black can calmly castle, since White cannot capture the knight in view of 16 . . . R–K1. But . . .

15 . . .   **0–0**

16 N–N3!

This move completes an excellent combination. Black is now forced to exchange queens, after which White's rook can capture the knight without fear.

  16 . . .   **Q–R3**
  17 Q × Q   **P × Q**
  18 R × N

With knight and bishop for a rook, White has a significant material advantage. Alekhine gains the win without difficulty.

  18 . . . QR–N1 19 P–N5 P × P 20 R × RP P–N5 21 N–K2 KR–B1 22 P–B3 R–R1 23 R × R R × R 24 K–B2 N–Q2 25 N–B4 N–N3 26 K–K3 R–QB1 27 K–Q3 P–N4 28 N–KR5 1–0.

The following game is yet another example of Alekhine's inventiveness.

73) Opocensky-Alekhine,
Prague 1942, Old Indian Defence

  1 P–Q4   **N–KB3**
  2 P–QB4   **P–Q3**
  3 N–QB3   **QN–Q2**

This is practically the only occasion on which Alekhine adopted a King's Indian type of set-up.

  4 N–B3   **P–K4**
  5 P–KN3   **P–B3**
  6 B–N2   **B–K2**
  7 0–0   **0–0**
  8 Q–B2   **P × P**

The waiting moves and slow build-ups practised by modern experts on the King's Indian Defence were simply not to Alekhine's taste. In place of this early surrender of the

centre, 8 . . . R–K1 and 9 . . . B–B1, followed by . . . P–KN3 and . . . B–N2 would be played today.

  9 N × P   **N–N3**
  10 P–N3   **P–Q4**
  11 R–Q1   **Q–Q2**

A poor move, which shuts in his own bishop. This was definitely not the way to prevent the white knight from reaching KB5; adequate was 11 . . . Q–K1.

  12 P × P   **N/N3 × P**
  13 N × N   **P × N**

He has to recapture this way since after 13 . . . N × N 14 P–K4 N–N5 15 Q–K2 the white pieces would be very active, while the black forces, lacking any strong points, would be badly placed.

  14 B–N2   **R–K1**

Alekhine plays this part of the game poorly. 14 . . . B–Q1 followed by 15 . . . B–N3 was a better defence.

  15 QR–B1   **B–Q1**
  16 P–K3   **B–N3** (*167*)

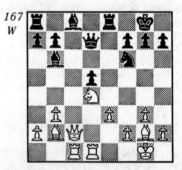

167
W

Now we see the results of playing an opening in which one is not at home. Black is forced to give up his QP and set his hopes on tactical complications. Opocensky obtains a marked positional advantage, but when tactical play begins he becomes a victim of Alekhine's inventiveness.

  17 N–K2   **N–K5**
  18 N–B4   **N × BP**

The QP is lost, and Alekhine's only hope lies in combinational complications.

19 Q × N?

In the very first skirmish the experienced master commits an oversight. However, we cannot really criticize him; the tactical stroke which he overlooks is so unexpected, and so stunning, that such a 'sin' can be easily forgiven.

19 . . .	**B × P**
20 Q × B	**R × Q**
21 N × P	

As yet White has only two minor pieces for the queen, but he is attacking both black rooks – one directly, and the other by the threat of 22 N–B7.

21 . . .   **R–K7!**

The rook takes up a menacing position. White had no doubts about his next move. 'I may not win, but the worst that can happen is a draw by perpetual check – 22 N–B7 Q–K2 23 N × R R × B/KN7+ and 24 . . . Q–K7+ – these were perhaps Opocensky's thoughts at this moment.

22 N–B7	**Q–K2**
23 N × R *(168)*	

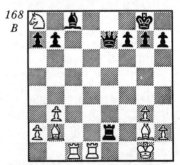

168
B

White's position seems excellent, and it appears that Black must settle for a draw. But this is a false impression. It turns out that Black has a sudden stroke which causes an instant transformation.

23 . . .   **B–R6!!**

A terrible move for White! The bishop moves out of danger to threaten White's KB, while at the same time keeping the QB1 square covered against possible intrusion by the white rook. The bishop may not be captured because of mate in four moves – 24 . . . Q–K6+ and then . . . Q–KB6–KB7 × RP.

This is an excellent example of Alekhine's inventiveness. I would dearly like to know at what moment the world champion noticed the decisive bishop move!

24 R–Q8+	**Q × R**
25 B × B	**Q × N**
0–1	

Alekhine also concluded the following game with some beautiful tactical blows.

74) **Alekhine–Richter,**
Munich 1942, Caro-Kann Defence

1 P–K4	**P–Q4**

From the Centre Counter Game play soon transposes into the Panov attack Variation of the Caro-Kann Defence.

2 P × P	**N–KB3**
3 P–QB4	**P–B3**
4 P–Q4	

Alekhine never used to capture 'dubious' pawns in the opening, and he would certainly not want to do this against Richter, who was a fine master of combinational attacks.

4 . . .	**P × P**
5 N–QB3	**N–B3**
6 B–N5	**P–K3**
7 N–B3	**B–K2**
8 B–Q3	**0–0**

A well-known position has been reached. After the inevitable capture of his QBP, White will have an isolated QP, which generally promises him attacking chances.

9 0–0	**P × P**

10 B × BP	P–QN3
11 P–QR3	B–N2
12 Q–Q3!	

A pawn 'sacrifice', which Black dare not accept, since after 12 . . . N–QR4 13 B–R2! B × N 14 Q × B Q × P 15 P–QN4 N–B5 16 QR–Q1 he loses immediately.

12 . . .	N–Q4
13 B × N	B × B

13 . . . P × B would have shut his QB out of play, and at the same time created a weakness on . . . Q4.

14 B–K4   P–B4

He has to go in for this weakening move, since 14 . . . P–N3 is dubious in view of 15 Q–N5 with a double attack on QB6 and KN5. For example: 15 . . . B–B3   16 B × N P–QR3! 17 Q–R4 P–QN4 18 B × P.

15 N × B   Q × N

Bad is 15 . . . P × B   16 N3 × P Q × P 17 N–B6+ R × N 18 Q × P+ K–B1 19 Q–R8+ K–K2 20 Q × P+ with a winning attack.

16 B–B3	K–R1
17 KR–K1	

A blunder would be 17 Q–B4? N–K4! 18 P × N B × B.

17 . . .   QR–Q1 (*169*)

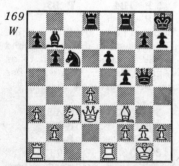

169
W

At first sight it appears that Black has an excellent position: he is attacking the QP, and has all sorts of tactical possibilities against White's KN2 square. However, Alekhine

deliberately went in for this position, since he had foreseen his next two, far from obvious, moves.

18 Q–B1!   R × P
19 Q–N5!

Beautiful – the queen moves to N5 only after Black has captured the QP with his rook, so that he does not have the reply 19 . . . N–Q5.

What should Black play now? Of course, the quiet 19 . . . N–Q1 20 B × B N × B would lead to a position where White has the better chances. He could continue his offensive both by 21 R × P N–B4 22 R–K8 R–Q1 23 R1–K1, and by 21 Q–K5 R–KN5 22 P–KN3 N–B4 23 QR–Q1, and White penetrates into the enemy camp.

Such a prosaic continuation does not suit Black.

19 . . .	R–Q3
20 N–K4!	Q–N3
21 N × R	

Alekhine is attracted by the possibility of reaching a position with an unusual balance of material. Meanwhile, there was another path he could have chosen to victory: 21 B–R5! Q × B 22 N × R N–Q5 23 Q–Q3, since the sacrifice on B6 does not work – 23 . . . N–B6+   24 P × N B × P 25 R–K3 Q–N5+   26 K–B1 Q–R6+ 27 K–K1, and Black's checks come to an end (the variation is given by Alekhine). Black can do better – 21 . . . R–Q4!, but even so after 22 Q × R P × Q   23 B × Q BP × N 24 B–R5 White has the advantage.

21 . . .	N–Q5
22 B × B	N × Q
23 N × N	Q–B3! (*170*)

White has rook, knight and bishop against queen and pawn – a sufficient advantage to win. All he has to do is to render harmless the activity of the black queen.

24 N–B3   P–K4

170
W

25 QR–Q1	**P–K5**
26 R–Q7!	

White not only establishes a rook on the seventh rank, but also sets a cunning trap. An attempt by Black to exchange rooks – 26 ... R–Q1 would lead to disaster after 27 N–Q5! Q–N4 28 R×R+ Q×R 29 R–QB1.

26 ...	**P–KR4**
27 P–R3	

Yet another tactical trap, which Alekhine sets in the process of carrying out his general strategic plan. Now 27 ... R–Q1 again gives White the chance to win quickly, this time by other means – 28 N–Q5 Q–N4 29 P–KR4! Q×RP 30 N–K7! R×R 31 N–N6+.

27 ...	**P–R5**
28 R1–Q1	**K–R2**
29 B–R6	**R–B2**
30 R7–Q6	**Q–N4**
31 R6–Q5	**Q–B5**
32 N–K2!	

The knight begins a lengthy manoeuvre, the aim of which is to comfortably establish itself on K3.

32 ...	**Q–N4**
33 N–Q4	**R–B3**
34 B–K2!	

Preparing, at a convenient moment, to force ... P–KN3 by B–N4, but Black soon makes the move anyway.

34 ...	**K–R3**

35 N–B2	**R–B2**
36 N–K3	**P–N3**
37 B–B4	**Q–B5**
38 R–Q6	**R–B2**
39 P–QN3	**K–R2**
40 P–R4	

These are necessary safety measures prior to the decisive offensive.

40 ...	**Q–K4**
41 R–K6	**Q–B6**
42 N–Q5	**Q–B7**
43 R–KB1	**R–KN2** (*171*)

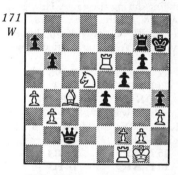

171
W

44 P–B3!	

This is the decisive blow. White's second rook becomes active, and soon all his pieces throw themselves on Black's unfortunate KNP.

44 ...	**P×P**
45 R×BP	**K–R3**

The king places himself under the blade of the guillotine. Against other defences White would win by playing N–B4 and B–N5–K8.

46 N–K3	**1–0**

The prospect of 46 ... Q–B8+ 47 R–B1 and 48 N×P+ does not suit him.

75) Alekhine-Keres,
Salzburg 1942, Ruy Lopez

1 P–K4	**P–K4**
2 N–KB3	**N–QB3**
3 B–N5	**P–QR3**
4 B–R4	**N–B3**
5 0–0	**B–K2**
6 Q–K2	

To the end of his life Alekhine remained true to his habits, one of which was his love for the move Q–K2 in the Ruy Lopez.

6 ...	P–QN4
7 B–N3	P–Q3
8 P–B3	0–0
9 R–Q1	N–QR4
10 B–B2	P–B4
11 P–Q4	Q–B2
12 B–N5	

This was probably thought up by Alekhine during the game. However, compared with the usual 12 QN–Q2–B1–K3 or N3 the bishop move gives White no particular advantage.

12 ...	B–N5
13 P×KP	P×P
14 QN–Q2	KR–Q1

Stronger was 14...N–R4! 15 P–KR3 B×N 16 N×B B×B 17 N×B N–KB5.

15 N–B1	N–R4
16 P–KR3	B–K3

This leaves White with a comfortable position, with chances of play against Black's Q4 and KB4 squares. 16...B×N 17 Q×B B×B 18 Q×N Q–K2 looks more convincing.

17 N–K3!	P–B3
18 N–R2	P–N3
19 B–R6	B–KB1
20 B×B	K×B

Keres is in no hurry to occupy his KB5 square, but he is wrong. With his next move, which involves the sacrifice of a pawn, Alekhine prevents the knight from reaching KB5.

21 P–KN3	R×R+

What would have happened if Black had captured the KRP? Let us examine the main variations:

a) 21...B×KRP 22 N–Q5 Q–R2 23 P–KN4! N–KB5 24 N×N P×N 25 Q–B3, and the bishop is lost.

b) 21...B×KRP 22 N–Q5 Q–KN2 23 P–KN4 N–KB5 24 Q–K3! (the idea in the previous line does not work, since Black can defend his bishop with his queen from ...KR3) 24...Q–R3 25 N×N P×N 26 Q×QBP+ K–N1 27 R×R+ R×R 28 Q–B7 R–Q7 29 Q×N R×B 30 R–Q1, and White has an irresistible attack. A possible conclusion could be: 30 ... Q–R5 31 Q–Q8+ K–N2 32 Q–K7+ K–R3 33 Q–B8+ K–N4 34 R–Q5+ P–B4 35 R×BP+! P×R 36 Q–N7 mate.

22 B×R	R–Q1
23 P–QR4	N–QB5
24 P×P	P×P
25 N–Q5! (172)	

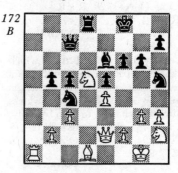

172
B

Alekhine's favourite sacrifice of a pawn for the initiative, which Keres prefers to decline. What if he had accepted it? 25...B×N 26 P×B R×P 27 Q–K4! R–Q1 28 B×N P×B 29 R–R6! White has significant threats, and it is hard to imagine that Black's passive pieces will be able to defend his king.

In other words, Keres was correct to decline the sacrifice.

25 ...	Q–QN2
26 P–N3	N–Q3
27 P–QB4	P×P
28 P×P	B×N

The knight on Q5 could not be

tolerated for long, but now diagonals are opened for White's bishop.

29 KP × B	N–N2
30 N–N4	Q–K2
31 B–B2	N2–K1
32 P–R4	

This is all with the same aim – to extend the range of his bishop. Keres is prompted to take urgent measures towards limiting the activity of this dangerous piece, but, following his modest 31 . . . N–K1, should have avoided the following pawn advance.

| 32 . . . | P–K5 |
| 33 N–K3! | |

Now this active knight has a new goal – N–N2–B4–K6.

| 33 . . . | Q–K4? |

And this is an inaccuracy – he should not have abandoned his second rank. Now Alekhine settles the outcome within a few moves.

| 34 R–R7 | K–N1 |
| 35 N–N4 | Q–Q5 (*173*) |

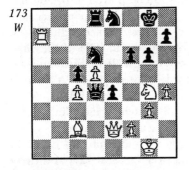

173
W

36 B × P!

An elegant combination. The bishop cannot be taken: after 36 . . . Q × B 37 Q × Q N × Q 38 N–R6+ Black either loses his rook or is mated.

| 36 . . . | P–B4 |
| 37 N–R6+ | |

There was a quicker path to victory: 37 B × P! N × B 38 Q–K6+ K–R1 39 N–K5 or 37 . . . P × B 38 Q–K6+ K–R1 39 Q–R6 N–KN2 40 N–B6.

37 . . .	K–R1
38 B–B2	Q–B3
39 Q–K6	Q × Q
40 P × Q	R–B1
41 N–B7+	N × N
42 P × N	N–Q3
43 B–Q3	K–N2

White's task would have been harder after 43 . . . R–B1, though after winning the QBP he should still have been able to win.

44 P–B8=Q+	K × Q
45 R × P	K–N1
46 R–Q7	N–K1
47 P–R5!	

Breaking up the black pawns, and further increasing the activity of his bishop.

47 . . .	P × P
48 B × P	R–R1
49 B–K6+	K–R1
50 R–Q5	

After the loss of this second pawn Black has absolutely no hope.

50 . . . N–B3 51 R × BP K–N2 52 K–N2 R–R7 53 B–B5 R–R6 54 R–B7+ K–R3 55 R–B7 R–R3 56 P–B4 P–R5 57 P–N4 1–0.

Epilogue: Live on into the Ages

As long as chess lives, the memory will remain of the great chess magician Alexander Alekhine. All his life, his strength, his thoughts, from his childhood years to his final breath in a hotel in Portugal, were given to this, his beloved art.

Alekhine and chess had a mutual love for each other, and they did not forgive each other for unfaithfulness and disloyalty. When the world champion insulted this love in 1935, chess jealously took its revenge on him; when he was devoted and true to chess, it opened to him all its innermost secrets.

It was this disinterested, whole-hearted love for chess which enabled Alekhine to produce results and creative achievements above those of any of his predecessors. He showed himself to be a rare fighter in both tournament and match play. During his life he played in 87 tournaments, in 62 of which he won first prize. It should be taken into account that in his life there were serious periods of chess 'silence' – during the two world wars, in the years 1935–1937, and also in 1908–1912, when he significantly spoiled his record of achievement. If we discount such periods of self-perfecting and enforced 'wasted time', Alekhine's success curve will hardly deviate from the level of first prize.

In addition Alekhine also played 23 matches, including 5 for the world championship (Capablanca, for example, played only two matches for the world title). Alekhine played a total of 1264 games in tournaments and matches, of which he won 735, lost 127, and drew 402 (these figures do not include Paris 1914, Madrid 1941 or the 1943 match against Bogoljubow, which swell the figures given in *Alekhine's Tournament and Match Record* to won 743, lost 128, drew 403 – editor's note). One often talks about Capablanca's faultlessness, but the Cuban had approximately the same percentage of losses as had Alekhine.

These numbers do not include the numerous games played by Alekhine during his demonstration appearances while on tour, nor the simultaneous displays against a small number of opponents with clocks. Even now, many years later, one can come across games of Alekhine which have never been published. Alekhine himself estimated that during his life he had played about three thousand serious games with clocks.

As a chess player who was brought up on the creative principles of Chigorin and the Russian chess school, Alekhine was an untiring popularizer of the game. For chess he travelled all over the world, carrying the word of chess to people everywhere, sharing with them his wisdom, and imparting to them his love for this intriguing game from the past.

Alekhine's numerous books, which have been published in various languages, have great propaganda value for the game of chess. The most popular of them are *New York International Chess Tournament 1924*, *My Best Games 1908–23*, *New York International Chess Tournament 1927*, *Nottingham 1936*, *My Best Games 1924–37* and others. In the games annotated in these books, chess enthusiasts have been amazed by the accuracy of Alekhine's appraisal of the strategic fundamentals of a position, as well as by the sharpness of his exceptional combinative vision.

Alekhine will remain for all time in the history of chess as a great artist who created unforgettable works of art. Over a period of almost four decades he gave the world games which were full of bold ideas, originality and breadth of fantasy – those qualities which have always characterized Russian chess thought.

Alekhine's contribution to chess theory is unmatched. There is not one opening in which Alekhine did not discover something new, did not suggest some original manoeuvre, or introduce some fresh idea. Alekhine's Defence – an opening which strictly conforms to the laws of chess – is even today a reliable weapon in the hands of many grandmasters and masters. And how many of Alekhine's systems of development are there in the Ruy Lopez, the French Defence, the Queen's Gambit. . . . This is without speaking of individual moves and bold pawn sacrifices for the sake of gaining the initiative – there are sacrifices of this type by Alekhine in almost every chess opening.

A player of such class could not fail to have an important say in the general understanding of chess principles, or to give his interpretation of a number of laws of strategy and tactics. In playing over the games, the reader will already have seen Alekhine's original approach to such problems as time in chess, usually measured in tempi, and sudden flank attacks. Worthy of special mention is Alekhine's method of sacrificing a pawn for the initiative. How many brilliant games did

Alekhine win, by surprising his opponent in the very opening with sudden pawn sacrifices!

An outstanding master of technique, Alekhine made a deep study into the secrets of many difficult endgames. In particular, he widened and put on a firm basis the technical methods of Chigorin, distinguished by their combination of subtle manoeuvres with numerous 'small combinations'. Alekhine made an unparalleled contribution to the theory of heavy piece endings – positions where the only participants are pawns, queens and rooks. Here we have dozens of examples of play which is at the same time both beautifully precise, and colourfully imaginative, in which the most insignificant, imperceptible advantages are realized. The Russian champion did much towards revealing the secrets of rook endings, and he wrote a special article on the struggle between a knight and three pawns against a rook and two pawns.

It remains to say that Alekhine worked out a number of questions on psychology in chess, which Emanuel Lasker had first drawn attention to. Alekhine taught himself to be strictly self-critical in appraising his own strong and weak points, and also to make a scrupulous study of the strengths and weaknesses of his opponents. And here he recalled that it is important to battle not only against the pieces on the board, but also against the character of the opponent.

Thus the great Russian chess player Alexander Alekhine presents himself to the reader as a versatile master of the game. Instruction can be found in his works regarding all fields of chess theory, and on any question of chess practice. This is why Soviet players, in their attempts to master the game, have always turned to Alekhine's teachings, and have found wisdom in his games and deep annotations.

Although they were separated from Alekhine by distance, nevertheless Soviet players never broke their connection with him. Our grandmasters and masters were always interested to play over and comment on every game played by Alekhine, while chess enthusiasts would read his annotations with fascination.

From his side, Alekhine would impatiently try to catch every new word from the chess experts living in his homeland. He understood perfectly well the leading importance of the Soviet chess school, and carefully followed the discoveries and achievements of Soviet theorists.

We have a high regard for the historical significance of Alekhine's chess creativity, and for his contribution to the theory and practice of the game. The characteristics of Alekhine's play, and his role in chess, have perhaps been best described by Alekhine's successor to the chess throne, the first Soviet world champion, Mikhail Botvinnik. In his review on Alekhine in 1956 he wrote: 'There is no doubt that Alekhine's strength was a successful combination of practical and creative elements, but Alekhine is dear to the chess world primarily as an artist. He possessed a brilliant technique – after all, without technique, mastery is not possible. Depth of planning, far-seeing calculation, and inexhaustible inventiveness were Alekhine's characteristics. However, his main strength, which developed from year to year, was his combinative vision: he saw combinations, and calculated forced variations with sacrifices, easily and accurately. Alekhine was aware of his combinative strength, and it seems to me that in his later years would sometimes even sacrifice the completeness of a game in order to imperceptibly create a combinative situation. Alekhine saw combinations where others would not even guess that they were possible; this is partly why Alekhine's combinations always possessed such shattering force, and would often crush the opponent's resistance. Yes, this truly was an amazing gift!

'Many of the chess creations of Alexander Alekhine, the greatest chess artist of the recent past, will live on into the ages; in playing through the Alekhine games, players of future generations will experience pure aesthetic delight, and will be amazed at the might of his chess genius'.

Index of Opponents

Alekhine's Tournament and Match Record

TOURNAMENTS

			+	=	−
1907	Moscow (*17 games*)		.	.	.
1908	Moscow	1	5	3	1
	Dusseldorf	4/5	8	2	3
1909	Moscow i	5	6	1	3
	Moscow ii	1	6	1	.
	St. Petersburg	1	12	2	2
1910	Hamburg	7/8	5	7	4
1911	Carlsbad	8/11	11	5	9
1912	Stockholm	1	8	1	1
	St. Petersburg	1	5	4	.
	Vilna, All Russian	6/7	7	3	8
1913	St. Petersburg, Quadrangular	1/2	2	0	1
	Scheveningen	1	11	1	1
	St. Petersburg, All Russian	1/2	13	1	3
1914	St. Petersburg	3	6	8	4
	Paris	−	2	1	.
	Mannheim	1	9	1	1
1916	Moscow	1	10	1	.
1918	Moscow, Triangular	1	3	3	.
1919	Moscow	1	11	.	.
1920	Moscow, All Russian	1	9	6	.
1921	Triberg	1	6	2	.
	Budapest	1	6	5	.
	The Hague	1	7	2	.
1922	Pistyan	2/3	12	5	1
	London	2	8	7	.
	Hastings	1	6	3	1
	Vienna	4/6	7	4	3
1923	Margate	2/5	3	3	1
	Carlsbad	1/3	9	5	3
	Portsmouth	1	10	1	.
1924	New York	3	6	12	2
1925	Paris	1	5	3	.
	Berne	1	3	2	1
	Baden-Baden	1	12	8	.
	Hastings	1/2	8	1	.
1926	Semmering	2	11	3	3
	Dresden	2	5	4	.
1926	Scarborough	1	7	1	.
	Birmingham	1	5	.	.
	Buenos Aires	1	10	.	.
1927	New York	2	5	13	2
	Kecskemet	1	8	8	.
1929	Venice	1	7	1	.
	Bradley Beach	1	8	1	.

216

1930	San Remo	1	13	2	.
	Hamburg Olympiad	–	9	.	.
1931	Nice	1	4	4	.
	Prague Olympiad	–	10	7	1
	Bled	1	15	11	.
1932	London	1	7	4	.
	Berne	1/3	2	.	1
	Berne	1	11	3	1
	Pasadena	1	7	3	1
1932	Mexico	1/2	8	1	.
1933	Paris	1	7	2	.
	Folkestone Olympiad	–	8	3	1
	Hastings	2/3	4	5	.
1934	Rotterdam, Quadrangular	1	3	.	.
	Zurich	1	12	2	1
1935	Orebro	1	8	1	.
	Warsaw Olympiad	–	7	10	.
1936	Bad Nauheim	1/2	4	5	.
	Dresden	1	5	3	1
	Podebrady	2	8	9	.
	Nottingham	6	6	6	2
	Amsterdam	3	3	3	1
	Amsterdam, Quadrangular	1/2	2	1	.
	Hastings	1	7	2	.
1937	Margate	3	6	.	3
	Kemeri	4/5	7	9	1
	Nauheim-Stuttgart	2/3	3	1	2
1938	Carrasco–Montevideo	1	11	4	.
	Margate	1	6	2	1
	Plymouth	1/2	5	2	.
	Avro	4/6	3	8	3
1939	Buenos Aires Olympiad	–	9	7	.
	Montevideo	1	7	.	.
	Caracas	1	10	.	.
1941	Munich	2/3	8	5	2
	Cracow	1/2	6	5	.
	Madrid	1	5	.	.
1942	Salzburg	1	7	1	2
	Munich	1	7	3	1
	Cracow	1	6	3	1
	Prague	1/2	6	5	.
1943	Salzburg	1/2	5	5	.
	Prague	1	15	4	.
1944	Gijon	1	7	1	.
1945	Madrid	1	8	1	.
	Gijon	2/3	6	1	2
	Sabadell	1	6	3	.
	Almeria	1/2	4	3	1

Melill	1	6	1	.
Cáceres	2	3	1	1
		665	**307**	**88**

MATCHES

1908	Blumenfeld (Moscow)	4	1	.
	v Bardeleben (Dusseldorf)	4	1	.
	Fahrni (Dusseldorf)	1	1	1
1909	Nenarokov (Moscow)	.	.	3
1913	Levitsky (Moscow)	7	.	3
	Ed Lasker (Paris–London)	3	.	.
	Nimzowitsch (St. Petersburg)	1	.	1
1921	Grigoriev (Moscow)	2	5	
	Teichmann (Berlin)	2	2	2
	Sämisch (Berlin)	2	.	.
1922	Dr. Bernstein (Paris)	1	1	.
	Golmayo (Madrid)	1	1	.
1923	Aurbach (Paris)	1	1	.
	Muffang (Paris)	2	.	.
1927	Euwe (Amsterdam)	3	5	2
	Capablanca	6	25	3
1929	Bogoljubow (Wiesbaden)	11	9	5
1933	Dr. Bernstein (Paris)	1	2	1
1935	Bogoljubow (Baden-Baden)	8	15	3
1935	Euwe (Amsterdam)	8	13	9
1937	Euwe (The Hague)	10	11	4
1937	Euwe (The Hague) Exhibition	1	2	2
1943	Bogoljubow (Warsaw)	1	.	1
1944	Rey Ardid (Zarragoza)	1	3	.
1945	Lupi (Lisbon-Estoril)	2	1	1
		83	**99**	**41**

Total: Played 1290   748+   406=   129−   (unknown 17)

Index of Openings

Numbers refer to games